KEY PAPERS IN LITERATURE AND PSYCHOANALYSIS

The Key Papers series brings together papers previously published in the *International Journal of Psychoanalysis*, each monograph featuring either influential papers of a particular decade, or those considered key to a particular subject.
   Previous titles in the series are:

Influential Papers from the 1920s
   R.D. Hinshelwood (editor)

Influential Papers from the 1940s
   R.D. Hinshelwood (editor)

Key Papers on Borderline Disorders
   Paul Williams (editor)

Key Papers on Countertransference
   Robert Michels (editor)

The Mind–Brain Relationship
   Regina Pally in collaboration with David Olds (editors)

Psychoanalysis and Film
   Glen O. Gabbard (editor)

Influential Papers from the 1950s
   Andrew C. Furman and Steven T. Levy (editors)

Is It Too Late? Key Papers on Psychoanalysis and Ageing
   Gabriele Junkers (editor)

KEY PAPERS IN LITERATURE AND PSYCHOANALYSIS

PAPERS IN
INTERNATIONAL JOURNAL OF PSYCHOANALYSIS
KEY PAPERS SERIES

Edited by

Paul Williams and Glen O. Gabbard

International Journal of Psychoanalysis Key Papers Series
Series Editors: Paul Williams and Glen O. Gabbard

KARNAC

First published in 2007 by
Karnac Books
118 Finchley Road
London NW3 5HT

British Library Cataloguing in Publication Data
A C.I.P. for this book is available from the British Library

ISBN-13: 978-1-85575-958-9

Edited, designed, and produced by Florence Production Ltd
www.florenceproduction.co.uk

Printed in Great Britain

www.karnacbooks.com

CONTENTS

The International Journal of Psychoanalysis Key Papers Series

This series brings together the most important psychoanalytic papers in *IJP*'s 80-year history, in a series of accessible monographs. The idea behind the series is to approach the *IJP*'s intellectual resource from a variety of perspectives in order to highlight important domains of psychoanalytic enquiry. It is hoped that these volumes will be of interest to psychoanalysts, students of the discipline, and, in particular, to those who work and write from an interdisciplinary standpoint. The ways in which the papers in the monographs are grouped will vary: for example, a number of "themed" monographs will take as their subject important psychoanalytic topics, while others will stress interdisciplinary links (between neuroscience, anthropology, literature, philosophy, etc., and psychoanalysis). Still others will contain review essays on, for example, film and psychoanalysis. The aim of all the monographs is to provide the reader with a substantive contribution of the highest quality that reflects the principal concerns of contemporary psychoanalysis and those with whom they are in dialogue. We hope you will find the monographs rewarding and pleasurable to read.

Paul Williams and Glen O. Gabbard
Joint Editors-in-Chief, 2001–2007
International Journal of Psychoanalysis
London, 2007

Paul Williams, PhD, is a Training and Supervising Analyst of the British Psychoanalytic Society, a Member of the Royal Anthropological Institute and a Consultant Psychotherapist in the British National Health Service in Belfast. From 2001 to 2007 he was Joint Editor-in-Chief of the *International Journal of Psychotherapists*. He was a professor at Queens University Belfast and Visiting Professor of Psychoanalysis at Anglia Ruskin University, UK. He has written widely on the subject of personality disorder and psychosis.

Glen O. Gabbard, MD, is Brown Foundation Chair of Psychoanalysis and Professor in the Department of Psychiatry and Behavioural Sciences, and Director of the Baylor Psychiatry Clinic, at Baylor College of Medicine in Houston, Texas. He is also Training and Supervising Analyst at the Houston-Galveston Psychoanalytic Institute in Houston. Dr Gabbard was also Joint Editor-In-Chief of the *International Journal of Psychoanalysis* between 2001 and 2007.

Paul Schwaber

Since Freud invoked the Oedipus story to exemplify and verify his findings with patients and in analysing his own dreams, psychoanalysis and literature have had a fruitful if often distrusting relationship. Through the years psychoanalytic claims to truth often condescended to imaginative literature by commenting imperiously on it; literature in turn could dismiss analytic formulations as reductive and predictable, as neither aesthetic nor historically based. But the example Freud set proved a better standard. His remarks on Sophocles's *Oedipus Rex*, first in his letters to Fliess (see Masson, 1985) and then among the "typical dreams" in his breakthrough book, *The Interpretation of Dreams* (1900), helped to focus his pursuit of unconscious processes and dream work and point the way, before he actually said so, to his recognition of infantile sexuality (1905–1915). Sexuality could no longer be thought to begin with puberty, and definitive revelations of the human soul were to follow. At the same time, Freud offered new, motivational, if to many upsetting, insights into Oedipus and Hamlet, which stimulated intense critical discussion pro and con, and still do. Psychoanalysis and imaginative literature proved of use to one another there, and each could contribute to the other's fund of knowledge, though not without raising hackles too.

Obviously much has changed, and much horrific world history has been gone through, since Freud's time. Psychoanalysis has amplified, become, inevitably with friction, more inclusive of points of view—ego psychological, Kleinian, object-relational, self-psychological, relational, Lacanian—more open to seeing itself as heuristic rather than solely scientific. Literature and theory have increased enormously in range. Education no longer insists upon classics of Western literature as building blocks for understanding. Yet the tie between psychoanalysis and imaginative literature remains vital, and the two disciplines can interact vibrantly, as these selected essays of recent years from the *International Journal of Psychoanalysis* handsomely show.

Aaron Esman's, for one, aims to inform the psychoanalytic community of the first novel to use psychoanalysis as a central plot device, *The Confessions of Zeno* (published in Italian in 1923). He provides a lively biographical account of Triestino Jewish business-man Ettore Schmitz, whose pen name was Italo Svevo, and whose career as a writer was revived by his admiring friend James Joyce. *Confessions* is a very funny book and is now recognized as a modernist classic. Svevo read Freud and was very curious about psychoanalysis, but he was never analysed; and Esman enjoys the double irony of the depicted analyst being more a vengeful bully than a therapist, while the narrator's sparkling, witty stream of consciousness, manner, and eccentric behaviours do invite analytic attention.

Several of the essays eschew a biographical approach to examine what I will call an aesthetics and ethics of knowing. In strikingly different ways they manage to overlap—but not equate—clinical process with experiences of reading, and thereby illuminate the phenomenology of understanding, for both analyst and analysand. James Fisher's piece on *King Lear* and generational transmission contemplates Lear's great rages at his daughters and his struggle not to go mad as bearing crucially on—and to an extent perversely illustrating—the passionate, delicately balanced, often unbearable combination of love, hate, and a desire to realize and accept a grown child's separateness. The balance topples easily, as it does tragically for Lear and Gloucester, to deep, often hidden wishes to control or to destroy. Fisher uses Bion's formulation of a continuum of loving, hating, and knowing, finally to give new meaning to blinded

Gloucester's heart-stopping reply to Lear's caustic "You see how the world goes." He says: "I see it feelingly." Lear himself may fall just short of such knowledge, Fisher suggests, but the audience does not.

"Seeing feelingly" may be said to continue as a preoccupying theme in Thomas Ogden's essay, and in Julia Kristeva's. Both describe an experienced fullness of knowing that characterizes psychoanalytic insight at its most meaningful. Ogden juxtaposes a paced, nuanced, and evocative reading of Robert Frost's "Acquainted with the night" to an account of an analytic session in which the patient's perceptiveness and his own drift of reveries—memories, associations, apparent distractions—prove noteworthy. He draws a parallel between the poem's resonances, rhythms, symbols, and surprises and the qualitative "music of what happens" between analyst and analysand, both of whom, at the right moment, with the right readiness, contribute to their awakening to a wider range of what can be known of "forms of human aliveness" when unconscious simplifications are overcome. They both experienced the session to have been especially moving, indeed as adumbrating termination. Amply and clearly expounded, the essay communicates "what happens" to analysand and analyst in their rich, joint experience of knowing.

In her own distinctive and powerfully allusive voice, Julia Kristeva radically interrogates psychoanalyic narratives and free association by way, mostly, of Proust's *Remembrance of Things Past*. She tracks the struggle to represent and communicate, from body and pre-psyche through necessary cruelties of separation, mourning, and sublimation—and the inevitability of sadomasochistic identification with an analysand's unconscious and intervention with it—to reach a delicacy of statement that helps to liberate understanding. Kristeva perceives a polyphony of psychosexual registers in effective statement. Beginning with an analysand's observation and ending with her own, she too winds through analytic and literary processes, to account for "what happens" in a clinical situation, when one sees feelingly and speaks aptly.

If the balance of interactions leans from literary experience to psychoanalytic in the essays already mentioned, it leans counter-vailingly in others. Sasha Brookes traces the remarkable growth in understanding and moral sense in the child protagonist of *What Maisie Knew*, explaining how she emerges to knowing selfhood in her world of manipulative parents and other grown-ups, most of whom use her as a go-between. Brookes brings Bion's notions cogently to bear. K.I. Arvanitakis probes the "essence" of the tragic using psychoanalytic light. Commenting on *The Bacchae*, Euripides's play about Dionysus and the dismembering of Pentheus, who resisted the god's appeal, he carefully—respecting the play and the traditionally cited origins of tragedy—suggests the primordial formative violence of differentiation we all go through informing tragedy's special power and encompassing civilized achievement.

Psychoanalytic attunement to primordial violence and its vicissitudes of liveliness and death figure in two final explorations of literary art, on the aesthetics and ethics of knowing. Beatriz Priel's explication of Borges's uncanny little story of the Shoah, understood as negating, in its representation, the unbearable actuality invoked in order both to defend against it and, by involved indirection, to allow it recognition, is a very perceptive study of literary form, of that which is unspeakable and the psychodynamics of negation. It is an admirable essay into violence at once inconceivable and realizable. Rozsika Parker's piece in turn reminds us of redemptive, relational, and creative energies of destructiveness. She reflects fascinatingly on creativity and creative block in artists, transforming and augmenting the tradition of feminine Muse to complement Virginia Woolf's coming to know that only by killing off the "Angel in the house" could she write sharply and honestly, as the works under review deserved.

These essays explore overlaps of literary experience and psycho-analytic process, both of which activate our capacity to "see feelingly"—which is to say, provide occasion for a structured richness of knowing with a felt tie to truth. Both enhance consciousness, expand the emotions, undermine unconscious closures, and provoke thought; and it is those very qualities that inform their illustra-tive and explanatory usefulness to one another. Both literary and analytic processes allow one to suspend disbelief and to ponder experientially. Both, however, require sufficient detachment to observe while giving oneself over to deep involvement. A reader thus, to get absorbed in a book, must be sitting comfortably. Similarly, an analyst sits to listen; and an analysand, lying on the couch, foregoes facial and social cues to speak whatever comes to mind and to reflect upon what he or the analyst says. The postures help to ensure that all responsiveness will lead in the moment only to mental action in silent or spoken words. In those safely bounded circumstances, and with that assurance, the imagination can roam adventurously—and the ego observe and reflect.

I have merely touched on the diversity and consistently high quality of these essays to whet your appetite to read them. They take on an enormous range of experience, from comedy to moments of distinct insight and issues of representation to struggles to create to historical horrors perpetrated by humans on other humans, and show psychoanalysis bearing on them all—and learning from them all.

References

Freud, S. (1900). The interpretation of dreams. *Standard Edition 4–5*.
Masson, J.M. (Ed.) (1985). *The Complete Letters of Sigmund Freud to Wilhelm Fliess, 1887–1904*. Cambridge, MA: Belknap.

CHAPTER ONE

Italo Svevo and the first psychoanalytic novel

Aaron Esman

The first fictional work that used psychoanalysis as a central plot device was La coscienza di Zeno [Confessions of Zeno], *published in 1923 by Ettore Schmitz, a Triestino Jewish businessman who wrote under the pseudonym of "Italo Svevo". This paper describes Svevo's background, his relations with such important literary figures as James Joyce and with such central figures in Italian psychoanalysis as Dr Edoardo Weiss. It seeks to demonstrate to the anglophone reader the particular psychoanalytic elements in the novel and to relate them to Svevo's personal experience (including his indirect contacts with Freud) and to the intellectual currents of the period in a city which had, until the aftermath of the First World War, been a crossroads of European culture.*

Some time in 1914, a feckless middle-aged, upper-middle-class Jewish idler named Zeno Cosini consults a psychoanalyst in Trieste, his home town, seeking a cure for a variety of neurotic and psychosomatic symptoms and, in particular, his unshakeable addiction to

Reproduced, with permission, from *International Journal of Psychoanalysis, 82*: 1225–33 (2001). © Institute of Psychoanalysis, London.

cigarettes. The analyst, Dr S, suggests to him that, in addition to his daily sessions, he write an autobiography as "a good preparation for the treatment." Zeno, in his characteristic passive–aggressive way, complies, and in a series of often hilarious chapters describes in intimate detail the history of his addiction, his reactions to the illness and death of his father, his marriage and his taking a mistress, and his dazzlingly unsuccessful attempts at a business partnership. His self-descriptions oscillate between penetrating self-observation and massive self-deception, the latter founded on copious use of such defences as denial, projection, and rationalization. Finally, in angry response to Dr S's insistent interpretation of Oedipal conflicts, he abruptly breaks off the analysis. In revenge, Dr S arranges for the publication of Zeno's memoirs, and thus is born the first psychoanalytic novel, *La coscienza di Zeno*, published in 1923 and issued in English translation in 1930 with the somewhat inaccurate title of *Confessions of Zeno*.

Or, at least, this is how it is told by the novel's actual author, the man who called himself Italo Svevo (which means "Italian–German"). Who was Italo Svevo? What were his connections with the Italian and European literary worlds of the time? And what was his place in the history of psychoanalysis? These questions have been extensively reviewed in Italian literature (e.g. Accerboni, 1992; Lavagetto, 1975; Palmieri, 1994).[1] The anglophone literature is, however, sparse; apart from the literary biographies by Furbank (1966) and Gatt-Rutter (1988), I have found only a perceptive 1931 review by Burrill Freedman and a 1970 paper by Paula Robison that touch on them in any significant way.

"Italo Svevo" was the pseudonym of a middle-aged, upper-middle-class Jewish Triestino businessman named Ettore Schmitz. He was born in 1861, the fifth of eight children and the oldest of four sons by Francesco and Allegra Schmitz. Francesco had come to Trieste from Transylvania and had worked his way up the commercial ladder to become a successful and moderately prosperous businessman. Allegra was of a middle-class Triestine Jewish family that had resisted her marriage to an immigrant. Like most of the small but thriving Jewish community in Trieste, the family was moderately observant but not orthodox. Ettore was educated in Jewish schools, but he identified most strongly with the Italian majority that formed the cultural and linguistic identity of the city, an Italian island in the sea of the Austro-Hungarian empire. Like most of his compatriots, he spoke the local dialect, a variant of the Venetian, and had difficulty all his life with literary Italian. As an Austrian citizen, and educated in a German boarding school, he was fluent in German and had at least a good reading knowledge of French as well.

Francesco Schmitz was determined that his sons should follow him into the business world and saw to it that they obtained business educations. Thus, despite his strong literary bent, upon his graduation Ettore Schmitz went to work as a clerk in the local branch of a Viennese bank, and there he remained for twenty years. All the while, he read voraciously in three languages and wrote continually, mostly in the form of critical essays for a local newspaper, theatre reviews, one-act plays, and occasional short stories, some published, most not. He remained a businessman *malgré lui* for the rest of his life.

In the years before *Zeno*, he wrote (as Italo Svevo) and published at his own expense two novels, *Una vita* [A life] in 1893 and *Senilità* in 1898, which when later translated into English bore the title *As a Man Grows Older*, suggested by no less a person than James Joyce (of whom more later). Both novels fell like stones in the sea of Italian literature of the period, and their neglect by both the public and the critics led Schmitz/Svevo to withdraw from the literary world for years. Instead, he concentrated on his business affairs which—following his marriage in 1896 (aged 35) to his beautiful and much younger Catholic cousin Livia Veneziani—consisted of serving as the manager of a successful marine paint factory owned by his wife's family. He was profoundly devoted to Livia; at the same time he was often wildly jealous of her, particularly when they were separated for any length of time, although she never gave him the slightest cause. Meanwhile, he wrote incessantly, essentially for his own amusement, plays and stories that went unpublished until much later, some only after his death. He had little use for poetry; "he said it seemed a pity to use a part of the paper when you have paid for the whole of it" (Furbank, 1966, p. 140).

It was not until after he met James Joyce in 1907 that he began, cautiously at first, then more actively, to resume a literary career while still attending to his business duties. Joyce, having left Dublin to forge in the smithy of his soul the uncreated conscience of his race, had come to Trieste in 1904 to work for Berlitz as an English instructor. He soon quit that position and left for Rome, only to return in 1907 to set up as an independent tutor, and it was thus that he met with Schmitz, who wanted to improve his English largely for business reasons. Despite the considerable difference in age, they soon became friends, and Schmitz began to show Joyce his early writings. It was Joyce's praise and encouragement that led him once again, despite his earlier failure, to think of himself seriously as a writer. In his turn, Joyce pumped Schmitz, who despite his adult atheism had had a traditional Jewish education, for information about Judaism that he used in developing the character of Leopold Bloom, the un-Jewish Jewish protagonist of *Ulysses* who appears to have been at least in part modelled on Schmitz. He also, as Gatt-Rutter (1988) tells it, borrowed from Schmitz's wife her name and her long blonde hair for the character of Anna Livia Plurabelle in *Finnegan's Wake*.

Joyce spent the war years in Zürich, but returned briefly to Trieste in 1919, when the relationship resumed. It was then, in the aftermath of the war, that Svevo began working on *Zeno*. The initial Italian response to its publication in 1923 (again at Svevo's expense) was disappointing, but Joyce vigorously promoted the critical acclaim and recognition that *Zeno* ultimately received, particularly among French critics to whom Joyce, by then in Paris and world-famous, had ready access. By 1927 Svevo was in demand as a literary personality in Italy as well as in Paris, and delivered in Milan a much-quoted lecture on Joyce, in which he spelt out his version of the controversial relationship between the Joyce of *Ulysses* and psychoanalysis:

> I can prove that Sigmund Freud's theories did not reach Joyce in time to guide him when he was planning his work. This statement will astonish those who discover in Stephen Dedalus so many traits that seem beyond doubt to have been suggested by the science of psychoanalysis: his narcissism which will probably be attributed not to his being an artist but to his being a firstborn son, the adored mother who turns into a haunting spectre, the father despised and shunned, the brother forgotten in a corner like an umbrella, and finally the eternal struggle within him between his conscience and his subconscious.
>
> There is something more. Might Joyce not have borrowed from psychoanalysis the idea of communicating the thoughts of his characters at the very moment in which they are formed in the disorder of a mind free from all control? On this head the contribution

of psychoanalysis can be ruled out for Joyce himself has told us from whom he learned this technique. In fact, his words were enough to confer celebrity on the venerable Edmond Dujardin, who had used this technique in his "We'll to the Woods No More".

For the rest I can bear good witness. In 1915 when Joyce left us he knew nothing about psychoanalysis. Moreover his knowledge of current German was too weak. He could read some poets, not scientists. Yet at that time all his works, including *Ulysses*, had already been conceived.

From Trieste he went to Zurich, the second capital of psychoanalysis. Undoubtedly he became acquainted there with the new science, and there is reason to think that for a while he more or less believed in it. But I never had the satisfaction of knowing him to be a psychoanalyst. I left him ignorant of psychoanalysis. I found him again in 1919 in open revolt against it—one of those scornful rebellions of his by which he shook himself free of everything that hampered his thought. "Psychoanalysis?" said he to me. "Well, if we need it let us keep to confession." I was dumbfounded. It was the rebellion of the Catholic in him, enhanced with greater harshness by the unbeliever.

Joyce's works, therefore, cannot be considered a triumph of psychoanalysis, but I am convinced that they can be the subject of its study. They are nothing but a piece of life, of great importance just because it has been brought to light not deformed by any pedantic science but vigorously hewn with quickening inspiration. And it is my hope that some thoroughly competent psychoanalyst may arise to give us a study of his books which are life itself—a life rich and heartfelt, and recorded with the naturalness of one who has lived and suffered what he writes. They are as worthy of study as that poor Gradiva of Jensen's, which Freud himself honoured with his comments. (1927)

In fact, it appears that Svevo was wrong in his assertion that in 1915 Joyce was completely ignorant of psychoanalysis. In his celebrated biography of Joyce, Richard Ellmann (1982) points out that Joyce had in his library in Trieste several books about psychoanalysis, including Freud's "Leonardo" essay, Jones's study of *Hamlet*, and at least one work of Jung, all published between 1909 and 1911 and presumably purchased during that period. Indeed, Ellmann speculates that Joyce learned about psychoanalysis from Ettore Schmitz, who was, as we shall see, quite caught up with Freudianism at that time. So although

Freud's works were virtually unknown to the general Triestine public of the pre-war period (C. Weiss, personal communication), Joyce appears to have been less innocent of them than Svevo contended.[2] In Gatt-Rutter's words:

> It was from the end of the war that Freudianism became part of Triestine culture, especially among Jews, as Georgio Voghera, Socialist schoolteacher and writer, and himself Jewish, relates with gusto: "The fanatical adherents of psychoanalysis in Trieste were constantly swapping stories and interpretations of dreams and telltale slips, carrying out amateur diagnoses of their own and other people's neuroses, attempting to fit them into one or another of Freud's three 'phases' (oral, anal, genital, as we then used to say), continually finding other people's 'id'—but really their ego as well—guilty of the nastiest intentions and the foulest sentiments." (1988, p. 306)

Svevo's daughter Letizia (n.d., p. 90) also noted the diffusion of psychoanalysis in Trieste, "above all in the Jewish intellectual circles of the city" during the second decade of the century.

But what of Svevo himself? What was his involvement with psychoanalysis? Where and how did he learn what he used to such fictional advantage in *Confessions of Zeno*? The evidence is clear, confirmed by all biographers including his widow Livia, that Schmitz/Svevo was never analysed nor did he ever consult with an analyst professionally for any reason. He did, however, have three principal sources of information about psychoanalysis. The first, of course, was reading. According to his own statement and echoed by all his biographers (Furbank, 1966; Svevo, 1990; Gatt-Rutter, 1988), he was introduced to Freud's writings as early as 1908 by Edoardo Weiss, a school friend of his wife's youngest brother, Bruno Veneziani. He disliked Freud's literary style—"I read something of Freud, with effort and antipathy" —but he was—and remained—fascinated by his ideas. It is not clear precisely what he read, but by 1918 he was venturing to translate Freud's essay "On dreams" (1901a) into Italian, with the hope of introducing Freud's writings to the Italian public. And, as Svevo himself said, "As a treatment it was of no importance to me. I was healthy, or, at least, I liked all my maladies" (Lavagetto, 1975, p. 40). Consequently, he noted, "I shall only say that after reading the works, I undertook treatment in solitude without a doctor" (Gatt-Rutter, 1988, p. 247); that is, by some effort at self-analysis.

Despite his fascination with the words, however, Svevo was less impressed with the practice. In 1910 his youngest brother-in-law, Livia's brother Bruno—a severely neurotic and, according to Edoardo Weiss (1970), actively and exclusively homosexual young man—was sent off to Vienna to be analysed, and referred by Weiss first to Viktor Tausk, then to Freud. The outcome was unsatisfactory. Bruno was, therefore, Svevo's second source. As Livia Svevo put it:

> He had himself psychoanalysed and returned from the cure destroyed, as lacking in will power as before, but with his feebleness aggravated by the conviction that, being as he was, he could not behave otherwise. It was he who convinced me how dangerous it was to explain to a man how he is made . . . (1990, pp. 74–5)

It seems that, in fact, both Tausk and Freud gave up on Bruno, considering him too rigid and narcissistic to be analysable. He appears to have had no interest in his family's expectation that he change his sexual orientation. Remarkably, in 1919 Weiss proposed to Freud that Bruno serve as his collaborator in the translation into Italian of the *Introductory Lectures in Psychoanalysis* (Freud, 1916–1917). Weiss wrote:

> I soon realized that Dr. A. [Weiss's disguise for Bruno] was too disturbed to be of any help in this work. He suffered from some addictions and led a very disturbed life. With his permission I complied with his mother's wish and wrote to Freud asking if he would be willing to take him back into treatment .... . Freud answered (3 October 1920):
> Dear Doctor: I was indeed surprised when you announced Dr. A. as your co-worker for the translation, considering all I knew about him. Since you are asking me today for a professional report on him, I shall not hesitate to give my opinion. I believe it is a bad case, one particularly not suitable for free analysis. Two things are missing in him: first, a certain conflict of suffering between his ego and what his drives demand, for he is essentially very well satisfied with himself and suffers only from the antagonism of external conditions. Second, he is lacking a halfway normal character of the ego which could cooperate with the analyst. On the contrary, he will always strive to mislead the analyst, to trick him and push him aside. Both

defects amount actually to one and the same, namely, the development of a fantastically narcissistic, self-satisfied ego which is
inaccessible to any influence. . . . It is also my opinion that nothing
would be gained by having him come into treatment with me or
anybody else. His future may be to perish in his excesses. . . . I do
not even consider the fact that he is a homosexual. He could remain
that and still live normally and rationally.

I also understand that his mother will not give him up without
further efforts. . . . I therefore recommend that he be sent to an
overwhelming, therapeutically effective person in an institution. I
know such a man in the person of Dr. Groddeck in Baden-Baden.
(Weiss, 1970, pp. 26–8)

Bruno was duly sent off to Dr Georg Groddeck. That treatment also
failed after four months.

Weiss continued his efforts to help his friend through various
crises in his life (including his opiate addiction). Finally, just before
leaving Italy for the USA in 1939, he referred him to a Jungian analyst
in Rome, Ernst Bernhard; years later, in 1952, he learned from
Bernhard that Bruno had died of a heart attack, "brought on by
various types of excesses and the kind of life he led" (Accerboni, 1992,
p. 60).

Svevo's third source was Edoardo Weiss himself. His role was a
complex one. As noted, he was a generation younger than Svevo,
but was highly influential in directing him to the Freudian canon.
Of the same Triestino Jewish background as Svevo (note the mixed
Italian–German name), the families were closely allied; Svevo's niece
Ortensia married Weiss's brother Ottocaro (who was also a friend
of Joyce). Edoardo Weiss went to medical school in Vienna with the
explicit intent to become a psychoanalyst. He grew to become one
of the pioneering figures in Italian psychoanalysis, a pupil and later
a devoted friend of Freud and an analysand and dedicated follower
of Paul Federn. He was the founder of the Italian Psychoanalytic
Society and the translator of Freud's works into Italian. Unable
to build a psychoanalytic practice in provincial Trieste, he settled in
Rome in 1931, until in 1939, fleeing Fascism, he went to the USA,
first to the Menninger Foundation, thence to Chicago where he
practised and taught psychoanalysis until his death in 1970.

When *Zeno* was published in 1923, Weiss was concerned that he
might have been the model for the hapless Dr S. Svevo succeeded

in convincing him that this was not the case; both Gatt-Rutter and Accerboni suggest that it may have been Wilhelm Stekel, whom Svevo had met in 1911, who was the actual model. Stekel was well known for badgering his patients as Dr S does in the novel. Palmieri (1994) proposes the Jungian analyst Charles Baudouin as a possibility. In any event, Svevo gave Weiss a copy of the novel and asked him to review the book for one of the psychoanalytic journals. (He also sent a copy to Freud, who did not respond.) After reading the novel, however, Weiss returned it and refused to review it because, he said, "it had nothing whatever to do with psychoanalysis" (Furbank, 1966, p. 178; Svevo, 1990, p. 98). As Lavagetto points out, Zeno's psychoanalyst observed none of the rules of technique: he dismissed his patient abruptly; talked too much; showed off his interpretations complacently; didn't concern himself with his patient's reactions; confused his own knowledge with that of Zeno; proceeded without caution and, at the same time, without the slightest diffidence (1975, p. 53). Svevo was, nonetheless, crushed by Weiss's refusal, since he seriously believed that the novel represented a significant contribution to the literature of psychoanalysis.

What, then, was psychoanalytic about *Confessions of Zeno*? Apart from using psychoanalysis as a structuring plot device, Svevo ingeniously incorporated psychoanalytic concepts and practices into the storyline itself. The style is at times a witty parody of free association, replete with seeming digressions, self-contradictions, and self-justifications. Zeno's reminiscences about the origins of his tobacco habit all revolved around conflicts with his father. In one case, he describes a blatant Oedipal situation, complete with conflict, self-punishment, and ultimate triumph:

> My father used to leave half-smoked Virginia cigars lying about on the edge of a table or a chest of drawers. I thought it was his way of getting rid of them and I really believe that our old servant Catina used to throw them away. I began smoking them in secret. The very fact of hiding them sent a kind of shudder through me, for I knew how sick they would make me. Then I would smoke them till cold drops of perspiration stood on my forehead and I felt horribly bad inside. No one could say that as a child I lacked determination. I remember perfectly how my father cured me of that habit too. I had come back one summer's day from a school excursion, tired and very hot. My mother helped me to undress and then made me lie down

in a dressing gown and try to go to sleep on the sofa where she was sitting sewing. I was very nearly asleep, but my eyes were still full of sunlight and I couldn't quite get off. The delicious sensation one has at that age, when one is able to rest after being very tired, is so real to me now that I feel as if I were still lying there close to her dear body.

My brother plays no part in the scene, which surprises me because he must have been on that excursion too and would surely have been resting with me. . . . All I see is myself resting there so happily, my mother, and then my father, whose words still echo in my ears. He had come in without noticing I was there, for he called out aloud: . . . "Maria!"

My mother made a soft hushing sound and pointed to me, lying, as she thought, drowned in sleep, but in reality wide awake, and merely afloat on the ocean of sleep. I was so pleased at my father having to treat me with such consideration that I kept perfectly still. My father began complaining in a low voice: "I really think I must be going mad. I am almost sure I left a half a cigar lying on that chest half an hour ago, and now I can't find it. I must be ill. I can't remember anything". Only my mother's fear of waking me prevented her from laughing. She answered in the same low voice: "But no one has been into this room since luncheon". My father muttered: "I know that. And that is why I think I am going mad."

He turned on his heel and walked out.

I half opened my eyes and looked at my mother. She had settled down again to her work and she still had a smile on her face. She would surely not have smiled like that at my father's fears if she believed he was really going mad. Her smile made such a deep impression on me that I immediately recognized it when I saw it one day long afterwards on my wife's lips (Svevo I, 1930, pp. 6–7).

The later chapter describing Zeno's response to his father's illness and death could be used as a prototype for the explication of the concept of ambivalence. All of this certainly provided Dr S with ample data for the Oedipal interpretations that Zeno so angrily rejected and projected back on to Dr S. (This theme is developed in detail by Robison, 1970.) In fact, Zeno's attitude towards the analysis and towards Dr S clearly exemplifies the concepts of resistance and negative transference, while Dr S's vengeful retaliation is a case of countertransference acting-out writ large. And, as noted earlier, Zeno's self-deceptions rest on graphically represented use of such defences as denial, projection, and rationalization, most evident in his endless ineffectual efforts to stop smoking. Every event in his life becomes the occasion for a "last cigarette", ultimately abbreviated to "L.C.". When Dr S suggests to him that maybe his smoking isn't such a big deal, that he's only using it as a stick to beat himself with because of his unconscious sense of guilt, he promptly goes home and "smokes like a Turk" to prove him wrong. (Needless to say, Svevo was engaged in precisely such a struggle with smoking, including innumerable "last cigarettes", until his dying day. At the very end, when his doctor forbade him to smoke, he said, "That would really have been the last cigarette" (Svevo, 1990, p. 128).)

Zeno enters into a business partnership with Guido, the husband of his wife's beautiful sister Ada with whom he himself had once been smitten and had, in fact, wanted to marry. The relationship is for Zeno a farrago of ambivalence, jealousy, sibling rivalry and reaction formation; at one point, as he struggles with murderous fantasies towards Guido, he is suddenly stricken with unbearable leg cramps. When Guido dies—a suicide—Zeno manages to get into the wrong mourning procession and misses the funeral. Svevo indicated on a number of occasions that he was particularly proud of this episode in the novel, and was well aware of its "Freudianism". It seems pretty clear that Svevo had read *The Psychopathology of Everyday Life* (Freud, 1901b). As Furbank puts it:

> It is as though the Freudian Id had been able to cheat the Ego, or as if the pleasure-principle had invented a novel means of outwitting the reality-principle. Not . . . that the Superego has ceased to function. . . . It punishes Zeno by inflicting the most painful cramps and other psychosomatic disorders on him. (1966, p. 187)

In the end, long after he breaks with Dr S, Zeno is "cured"—but, he insists, not by psychoanalysis, but by self-persuasion and above all by *business*. By dint of wartime speculation (it is 1916) the former idler makes a small fortune, and it is this "victory" that leads to his cure, to his newfound state of "perfect health". He takes pains to let Dr S know about this, and it is with this final "confession" and an apocalyptic coda that the book closes.

Schmitz/Svevo became a literary lion in the years that followed the ultimate success of *Zeno*. He did not have long to enjoy his triumph. In 1928, returning with his family to Trieste from a health resort, his car skidded off the road in a rainstorm, and he died two days later of complications from the injuries he sustained in the accident. Livia recounts how, when at the very end she asked him if he wanted to pray, he said, "When you haven't prayed all your life, there's no point at the last minute" (Svevo, 1990, p. 128). He was 67 years old. Livia survived until 1952, and her memoir of Svevo, written during the Second World War, when she was in flight from the Nazi persecution of the Jews (though a Catholic, she had a Jewish grandfather and had been married to a Jew), remains a major source of information about his life. There she quotes a previously unpublished note of Svevo's in which he sought to clarify his thoughts about psychoanalysis:

> But there is a science which helps us to study ourselves. Let me say at once what it is: psychoanalysis. Don't be afraid that I shall talk too much about it. I tell you merely to warn you that I have nothing to do with psychoanalysis and I'll give you proof of it. I read some books by Freud in, if I'm not mistaken, 1908. It is now said that *Senilità* and *La Coscienza di Zeno* were written under his influence. As far as *Senilità* is concerned, it is easy for me to reply. I published it in 1899 and psychoanalysis did not exist then, or insofar as it did exist, it was called Charcot.[3] As for *Coscienza*, for a long time I thought I owed it to Freud, but it appears that I was wrong.[4] Wait: there are two or three ideas in the novel which are actually taken entirely from Freud. The man who, not to attend the funeral of someone he called his friend who was really his enemy, followed the wrong funeral procession, is Freudian, and has a boldness I am proud of. The other man, who dreams of distant events, and in his dreams remoulds them as he would have liked them to be, is Freudian in style, as anyone who knows Freud will realize. It is a paragraph I would be proud of even if it didn't contain another little idea I'm pleased with. However, for a long time I thought I'd written a work of psychoanalysis. Now I have to say that when I published the book and looked forward to its success, as anyone who publishes anything does, there was a deathly silence. Today I can laugh in speaking of it, and I should have been able to laugh at it then if I had been a younger man. Instead, I suffered so much that I invented an axiom: literature is not good for the old . . . it would have been a great thing if Freud had sent me a telegram saying, "Thanks for having introduced psychoanalysis into Italian aesthetics". Now I am no longer upset.

... Novelists play games with the great philosophies without really being equipped to expound them. We falsify them, but we also humanize them. (pp. 97–8)

Italo Svevo was no psychoanalyst, and his attitudes towards psychoanalysis were, like those he held about virtually everything, including his Jewishness, ambivalent, conflictual, and profoundly sceptical. He believed, in the end, that it was their neuroses that defined individuals, and that they were better left alone with them. What sustained him throughout his double life as businessman and artist, as functioning capitalist and tepid Socialist, as devoted husband and closet sensualist, as Jewish atheist and baptized Catholic (at Livia's insistence) was his unswerving commitment to writing, his relentless search for truth, both about himself and others, and his unfailing sense of the fundamental irony of human existence. For Svevo, as Gatt-Rutter puts it, "writing is self-indictment and self-castigation on the fictive plane for guilt on the behavioural plane" (1988, p. 293). In psychoanalysis Svevo found a rationale, a "scientific" way of accounting for the internal conflicts with which he constantly struggled. Almost alone in his native town he grasped, without completely committing himself to, the possibility psycho-analysis offered for making sense of his complicated and essentially tragic, Schopenhauerian view of life, and it was his triumph to have succeeded in turning that tragedy into high comedy. It was this achievement that earned him a lasting place in the higher ranks of twentieth-century writers, and the distinction of having earned the plaudit he hoped for, but did not receive, from Freud—of having introduced psychoanalysis into, not only Italian, but the world's imaginative literature.

Notes

1. All translations cited here from this literature are my own.
2. The Italian critic Debenedetti suggested that Svevo's insistence on Joyce's ignorance of psychoanalysis was intended to minimise his own indebtedness to Freud (cited in Lavagetto, 1975, p. 43).
3. In a letter, Steiner (1999) proposes that Svevo intuitively anticipated in *Senilità* such psychoanalytic concepts as projective and introjective

identification, possibly influencing Weiss's nascent theorizing—
object-relations theory *avant la lettre*.
4. A reference to Edoardo Weiss's dismissal.

References

Accerboni. A.M. (1992). Scrittura e psicoanalisi: La sfida di Italo Svevo
[Scripture and psychoanalysis: The challenge of Italo Svevo]. In:
Origini e svilluppi della psicoanalisi applicata [Origins and evolutions
of applied psychoanalysis]. Lavarone: Centro Studi Gradiva.

Ellmann, R. (1982). *James Joyce*, 2nd edition. New York: Oxford University
Press.

Freedman, B. (1931). Italo Svevo: psychoanalytic novelist. *Psychoanalytic
Review 18*: 434–8.

Freud, S. (1901a). On dreams. *Standard Edition 5* (pp. 629–714).

Freud, S. (1901b). The psychopathology of everyday life. *Standard Edition
6* (pp. 1–290).

Freud, S. (1916–1917). Introductory lectures on psychoanalysis. *Standard
Edition 15–16*.

Furbank, J.N. (1966). *Italo Svevo, the Man and the Writer*. London: Secker
& Warburg.

Gatt-Rutter, J. (1988). *Italo Svevo: A Double Life*. Oxford: Clarendon.

Lavagetto, M. (1975). *L'impiegato Schmitz* [Schmitz the employee]. Torino:
Giulio Einaudi.

Palmieri, G. (1994). *Schmitz, Svevo, Zeno* [Schmitz, Svevo, Zeno]. Rome:
Bompiani.

Robison, P. (1970). Svevo, secrets of the confessional. *Lit Psychol 20*:
101–14.

Steiner, R. (1999). Who influenced whom? And how? [Letter]. *International Journal of Psychoanalysis, 80*: 367–74.

Svevo, I. (1927). *James Joyce*. S. Joyce, translator. San Francisco, CA: City
Lights, 1972.

Svevo, I. (1930). *Confessions of Zeno* [1923]. B. de Zoete, translator. New
York, NY: Knopf.

Svevo, Letizia (n.d.). *Iconographia Sveviana*. Trieste: Studio Tesi.

Svevo, Livia (1990). *Memoir of Italo Svevo* [1950]. I. Quigley, translator.
Marlboro, VT: Marlboro.

Weiss, E. (1970). *Sigmund Freud as Consultant: Recollections of a Pioneer in
Psychoanalysis*. New York, NY: Intercontinental Medical Book Co.

CHAPTER TWO

A father's abdication

Lear's retreat from "aesthetic conflict"

James V. Fisher

The author explores the potential contribution of Shakespeare's King Lear *to psychoanalytic thinking, linking a reading of the play focused on the emotional tensions inherent in the parental function of endowing ("heriting") the next generation with the developmental struggle characterized by Donald Meltzer as the "aesthetic conflict". Following Meltzer's definition of passion as the "consortium" of Bion's emotional links, love, hate, and the urge to know (L, H, and K), the author develops an understanding of "aesthetic conflict" linked with the tension inherent in that constellation. It is suggested that L and H split off from each other and from K become attempts to possess and control, while K split off from L and H becomes an attack on dreaded emotional links, oscillating between attempting to ignore them and attempting to overcome them. The author suggests an affinity between Bion's K-link and what in* King Lear *is pictured as a capacity to "see feelingly" in the context of the struggle to*

An abbreviated version of this paper was presented at the International Conference "A developmental view of the psychoanalytic method" in Florence in February 2000. This version reproduced, with permission, from *International Journal of Psychoanalysis*, 81: 963–82 (2000). © Institute of Psychoanalysis, London.

give the object its freedom. This way of characterizing "aesthetic conflict" is linked with a fresh look at weaning as a lifelong developmental process, which in turn leads to a reconsideration of the psychoanalytic models of the dynamics of mourning.

Introduction

In *King Lear* Shakespeare exposes his audience to a fierce, unrelenting dramatic exploration of one of the important functions of the father, a function for which our language, the English language at any rate, has no adequate word. It is a function that is in one way quite familiar as a correlate to the notion of *inheriting*, a function that we roughly paraphrase as "passing on" to the next generation, although that does not quite capture the parental role at the heart of Lear's agony in Shakespeare's play. "Endowing" perhaps comes closest. This parental function has as its counterpart the struggle of the child to inherit its heritage.

The drama of *King Lear* turns on the emotional tensions inherent in this parental function of endowing. Or perhaps it would be more accurate to say of this play that it offers us an arresting portrait of a father who seeks to escape the emotional turmoil of this parental responsibility of endowing, "heriting" (to invent a term), perverting it instead into an abdication, an abdication that disturbs and confuses the relationship between the generations. We might term it a "conditional endowment". That is at least one reading of this intense, complex play, a reading that I hope will allow Shakespeare's observations to throw some light on the developmental achievement required for this parental function.

I want to be clear that in this paper I am interested in the potential contribution of *King Lear* to our psychoanalytic thinking and not in offering a literary critical interpretation. Nor is this a study in aesthetics, not explicitly anyway, and I shall not explore, let alone defend, the use of the term *aesthetic* in this discussion. Of course we would have little hesitation in characterizing *King Lear* as a work of art, an aesthetic object, and perhaps therefore this paper might be seen as having implications for the relationship between psychoanalysis and the arts. Although throughout the history of psychoanalysis issues to do with aesthetics have elicited interest, aesthetics has not generally been seen as a source for the development of clinical theory and practice. This might have been predicted from Freud's comments introducing his paper, *The "Uncanny"*:

> It is only rarely that a psychoanalyst feels impelled to investigate the subject of aesthetics, even when aesthetics is understood to mean not merely the theory of beauty but the theory of the qualities of feeling. He works in other strata of mental life and has little to do with the subdued emotional impulses which, inhibited in their aims and dependent on a host of concurrent factors, usually furnish the material for the study of aesthetic. (1919, p. 219)

The idea that aesthetics has to do with "subdued emotional impulses" may come as a surprise to those inside as well as those outside the psychoanalytic community. But, although the question of the relation of emotional intensity to our experience of something we describe as "aesthetic" is interesting, perhaps more relevant to our psychoanalytic interest is the question of, to use Freud's phrase, the *qualities of feeling*. In terms of a theory of the quality of feeling, Ronald Britton has articulated the relevant distinction regarding works of art as the difference between those that aim to express psychic reality and those that seek to evade it. He links this qualitative distinction with the difference between genuine dreams and daydreams, between phantasies based on, or accompanying, actual experience and phantasies conjured up to deny experience (1998, pp. 109–19). Art defined in terms of its capacity to give shape to psychic reality offers a vital resource for our understanding of the human experience we encounter in our consulting rooms.

In this paper I want to explore something of the emotional turmoil of one of Shakespeare's most disturbing plays, noting a few of the points at which the characters, and thus inevitably the poet himself, seem to me to be struggling with questions that Donald Meltzer has taught us to think about in terms of the notion of "aesthetic conflict" (Meltzer & Williams, 1988). My aim will be to explore the extent to which this concept of "aesthetic conflict" and Lear's struggle with the endowing or "heriting" role of the father can illuminate each other. The framework for this exploration will be found in a notion of "passion", understood in the intersection between the language of *King Lear* and Bion's schema of emotional engagement—the impulse to love, the impulse to hate, and the impulse to know (*L, H,* and *K*). That is, passion experienced as the tension inherent in the constellation of these three schematic elements.

In my reading of *King Lear* I am inviting the reader to consider the possibility that Lear's intention to bequeath his kingdom to his daughters is not the act of generosity that Lear tries to portray it as. I am suggesting that, instead, it is an abdication of and a retreat from a father's ultimate responsibility. Even worse, it is a perversion of the responsibility of "endowing" or "heriting" marked by cynicism and confusions that affect, and infect, those who would inherit. I am also suggesting that approaching this theme of the father's role via the notion of "aesthetic conflict" will make possible a revisiting of two of the most basic concepts in our psychoanalytic vocabulary— weaning and mourning—to see how our understanding of them is affected by this most intriguing of Meltzer's clinical and theoretical contributions. This will provide a context and a framework for a view of "endowing" and inheriting as important and difficult developmental processes.

While we unburdened crawl toward death

What do we make of Lear's announcement of his purpose at the opening of this play?

> 'tis our fast intent
> To shake all cares and business from our age,
> Conferring them on younger strengths, while we
> Unburdened crawl toward death. (1.1.37–40)[1]

In one sense it seems ordinary enough. As an old man, a king, and father of three daughters, two of whom are married and the third entertaining two fine suitors, Lear proposes to divide his kingdom, a third to each daughter as her dowry, her inheritance. "Crawling toward death", Lear says he wants "to shake off all cares and business from our age" to confer them on "younger strengths". It sounds quite reasonable, does it not? His aim, he says, is to prevent future strife. But leaving aside for the moment the fact that he has reserved a "third more opulent" for his favourite, his youngest daughter Cordelia, it seems this father has not considered the possibility of future strife between him and his daughters. He appears to assume that he and they will be of one mind. Like Shakespeare himself who went to great lengths in his own will (Honan, 1998, p. 396), Lear's wish, it seems, is to try to control, as much as he can, the fate of his endowment.

Shakespeare will no doubt have read Montaigne's essay "Of the affection of fathers to their children" in Florio's 1603 English translation (Montaigne, 1993; cf. Salingar, 1986, pp. 124–55). In this essay, Montaigne urged aged fathers to distribute their wealth to their children, castigating miserly old men for forcing their sons to desperate means by refusing to give up. It is almost as if Shakespeare takes this essay as a text for his own development of the Leir/Lear story well known in his day. Interestingly, Freud suggested that Shakespeare intended in the story of Lear to inculcate the "wise lesson" that "one should not give up one's possessions and rights during one's lifetime" (1913, p. 300). Although one can see how the play might be read in that way, I want to consider how behind issues of possessions and rights we might discover the issue of the need for us to be able to acknowledge our distinct place in the intimate relationship between the generations.

In *King Lear* there is tension not only about when the father hands on the inheritance but also to whom. The traditional answer to the latter question was the rule of primogeniture. We are drawn irresistibly into the tension of this question by the brief dialogue between the Earls of Kent and Gloucester, which immediately precedes the scene in which Lear announces his abdication. Gloucester introduces his second son, Edmund, to Kent with a provocative account of his conception:

> . . . though this knave came something saucily into the world before
> he was sent for
> yet was his mother fair
> there was good sport at his making, and the whoreson must be
> acknowledged. (1.1.20–3)

Not only is Edmund a second son, he is a bastard son. His father's apparently affectionate humour has just enough of an edge of hostility to it that we are quite prepared for this son's tirade against the "injustice" of this rule of the legitimate "first-born". We are almost sympathetic when he schemes to get the inheritance he feels is rightfully his. In fact Edmund's plot against his elder brother Edgar is devious and will end in the blinding and ultimately the death of his father as well as his own death at the hands of the elder brother he would displace. This story of Gloucester resonates with Lear's struggle with the next generation, a counterpoint so to speak: a blind and doomed father; an immature and gullible first-born who has to learn what it means to inherit, to become a son; and an envious second-born bastard who is doubly cursed.

Lear has no sons. And the picture of the first- and last-born is reversed, the first-born daughters, Goneril and Regan, are portrayed as envious and scheming, the last-born daughter, Cordelia, somewhat naïve and immature, although there is evidence of something that makes her the true heir of her father. Her capacity to "inherit" involves a developmental process that we do not see portrayed in the play. However, we do see it portrayed in the story of Edgar, the first-born son who has to learn what it means to inherit one's heritage. Were we to pursue the question of the developmental process involved in "becoming a daughter" or "becoming a son" (Adams, 2000), we would need to follow Edgar's development as Shakespeare portrays it, juxtaposed with Lear's struggle. But it is the father's struggle that I am interested in for the moment.

Not technically bound by the law of primogeniture since he has no sons, Lear proposes a "love test", a test to determine merit, a meritocracy where the coin is a daughter's love for her father. In fact it was increasingly common in the sixteenth century for the father to be seen as capable of disposing of his property as he saw fit, rewarding or punishing his children at will (Stone, 1979, pp. 112–13). The absence of the principle of primogeniture presents parent and child with difficult emotional issues in that the parent must choose who shall inherit what. Janet Adelman observes:

> It makes sense that the central anxieties of this [absence of a rule of primogeniture]—anxieties about sincerity and insincerity, about bribery and misplaced trust—should be played out in relation to daughters, especially daughters whose impending marriage threatens the fantasy that they love their fathers. (1992, p. 296)

It is as if Lear's "love test" is meant to ease some of this anxiety. Those who love most should receive most:

> Tell me, my daughters—
> Which of you shall we say doth love us most,
> That we our largest bounty may extend
> Where nature doth with merit challenge. (1.1.48, 51–3)

It sounds as if Lear were serious about this meritocratic picture and is about to "extend his bounty" in accordance with what each daughter "earns" by her love of her father.

But this apparently open competition to determine who deserves most disguises Lear's wish to control both his "gift" and the recipients of his beneficence. The love test has been prejudged and one daughter is to be favoured. Is this one meaning of Lear's earlier saying that in the publication of his daughters' dowries "we shall express our darker purpose"? (1.1.35) Lear's desperate wish to control emerges even more clearly as we become aware of just what this father means by his demands for "love". By the time of the final rupture between this demanding father and the two daughters who were prepared to make the required declaration of love, we are in no doubt that he judges their love by their capacity for obedience and gratitude.

Later, as the tension builds between this father with his unruly entourage and Goneril, the daughter in whose home he is now a "guest", Lear is outraged by her challenge to his authority. He bitterly rejects her as no daughter of his in an attack reminiscent of his disinheriting of Cordelia:

> Degenerate bastard, I'll not trouble thee:
> Yet have I left a daughter. (1.4.245–6)

Surely Regan, his last hope for an obedient and grateful heir, cannot be a bastard! But when she casually says she is "glad" to see her father, Lear growls that she had better be glad to see him, since if she were not, she might be her mother's child but not his:

> If thou shouldst not be glad,
> I would divorce me from thy mother's tomb,
> Sepulchring an adulteress. (2.2.318–21)

And when she suggests that the kind of vicious curse with which he has abused his eldest daughter will soon fall on her, Lear must idealize this child of his or be left childless. He protests desperately that it is not in her "tender-hafted nature" to oppose him:

> Thou better knowst
> The offices of nature, bond of childhood,
> Effects of courtesy, dues of gratitude.
> Thy half o' the kingdom hast thou not forgot,
> Wherein I thee endowed (2.2.366–70).

For Lear the child's response to its endowment, the indication that this child is a genuine offspring and not a bastard, is dictated by the "bond of childhood", the natural state of obedience and gratitude. Disobedience is bitterly disappointing to the fathers in this play, but what inflames their rage is the ingratitude. "To his father, that so tenderly and entirely loves him", moans Gloucester. And when Lear calls Goneril "degenerate bastard", he cries:

> Ingratitude, thou marble-hearted fiend,
> More hideous when thou show'st thee in a child
> Than the sea-monster. (1.4.245, 251–3)

The curses become even more pitiless as we hear this father appealing to the goddess Nature to destroy his child's capacity to have a child:

> Suspend thy purpose if thou didst intend
> To make this creature fruitful
> Into her womb convey sterility,
> Dry up in her the organs of increase,
> And from her derogate body never spring
> A babe to honour her. (1.4.268–73)

Before we can draw breath and shake our heads in incomprehension at the viciousness of this father's curse, Lear rages:

> If she must teem,
> Create her child of spleen, that it may live
> And be a thwart disnatured torment to her.

> Turn all her mother's pains and benefits
> To laughter and contempt, that she may feel
> How sharper than a serpent's tooth it is
> To have a thankless child. (1.4.273–5, 278–81)

I have quoted this profoundly disturbing outburst of Lear's at some length because it throws the experience of the "ingratitude" of the daughter (or the son) into sharp relief. But why should ingratitude be so intolerable to these fathers? It is as if Lear's volatile rage seems to point to an underlying tension just waiting to be triggered, a tension I want to try to understand.

Of course the lack of gratitude in the recipient of any genuine benefice is sad, and on occasions even offensive to us. But on the other hand, the expectation of gratitude by the benefactor is also sad, even offensive to us, to say nothing of the demand for gratitude. Commentators have often remarked on Lear's tyrannical childishness, either as the archetypical geriatric whose narcissistic rage is provoked by his terror of the helplessness of old age (Hess, 1987, pp. 210–12), or as the archetypical baby whose rage is aroused when his omnipotent arrangements to "wean himself from the kingdom of his mother" are not obediently followed (Williams & Waddell, 1991, p. 33). Goneril certainly does not see it as a matter of gratitude to this "Idle old man,/That still would manage those authorities/ That he hath given away". For her it is obvious that "old fools are babes again" and she is in no doubt that one ought to be prepared to reprimand as well as coddle such babies (1.3.17–21).

Here I want to suggest that the demand for gratitude and the absolute despair and rage at its apparent absence point us in the direction of what Meltzer has called the "aesthetic conflict". In order to give an account of why I think Shakespeare is describing in this play what Meltzer has defined as a retreat from "aesthetic conflict", I want to return to the so-called "love test" at the opening of the play.

We are shocked when Lear reacts to his youngest daughter's apparent lack of gratitude with a violent disinheriting of her. Of course this plain-speaking Cordelia does offer a brusque picture of a daughter's love being divided in two when she marries. The new husband will carry

> Half my love with him, half my care and duty.
> Sure I shall never marry like my sisters
> To love my father all. (1.1.102–4)

Lear seems at first stunned: "So young and so untender?" Taking this as a challenge Cordelia responds with alacrity: "So young, my lord, and true" (1.1.107–8). Lear fairly explodes in a curse, disinheriting this favourite daughter: "Thy truth then be thy dower".

> Here I disclaim all my paternal care,
> Propinquity and property of blood,
> And as a stranger to my heart and me
> Hold thee from this for ever. (1.1.109, 114–17).

As if to drive home his hatred of reality contrary to his wishes and his rage at anyone who dares speak the truth he would not hear, Lear instructs his sons(-in-law), the Dukes of Cornwall and Albany, to "digest" Cordelia's share of the kingdom, her dower, her inheritance. Of this disinherited daughter he virtually growls: "Let pride, which she calls plainness, marry her" (1.1.130). Whether it is indeed Cordelia's pride which stops her from indulging her father in his demand for this expression of love and gratitude as the price of her dowry is an interesting question. However, at this point I want to suggest that Lear has caught hold of an essential component of the developmental process that he cannot bear.

Interestingly, when Lear says that Cordelia calls this "plainness", despite the fact she does not actually use that word in the play, we get the impression that this is not the first instance of his daughter insisting on being "true". It suggests an ongoing struggle in the intimacy of this father–daughter relationship about control and freedom—a struggle, that is, about the reality, the truth, that a father's child is both *his* and *not his*. The child's "endowment" is to be a person, separate, to some degree enigmatic, in some ways unknown, and always ultimately unknowable in the absence of a willingness to be known. It does not mean, of course, that Cordelia cannot be grateful. But it does mean one cannot demand her gratitude. Lear as father is struggling with something he cannot quite comprehend, something which he does not want to know and about which he wants to hear no "plain-speaking".

This theme of plain-speaking is carried through the play by three linked characters. Kent, Lear's loyal courtier throughout the play, is the first to echo Cordelia's being "true", speaking the truth to the King at the risk of his life:

Be Kent unmannerly
When Lear is mad. What wouldst thou do, old man?
Think'st thou that duty shall have dread to speak,
When power to flattery bows? To plainness honour's bound
When majesty falls to folly. (1.1.146–50)

These are strong words and for them Kent is banished. One hears echoes of Coriolanus in his rage banishing Rome, as if one could banish the reality one does not want to know, the truth one refuses to acknowledge. The third character in this trio of plain-speakers, and the only one who has licence to speak the uncomfortable truth, is the Fool. But even the Fool is threatened with whipping by the King when he seems to go too far, for example when he laughs that Lear made his daughters his mothers, gave them the rod and dropped his britches (1.4.163–75).

In an important sense the plain-speaking Cordelia, Kent, and the Fool are joined unwittingly in their resolution to face reality by Edgar in his guise as "Poor Tom". Feigning madness as a "Bedlam beggar" allows him to observe in Lear's madness an encounter with the truth of emotions. In this, I suggest, he comes to a maturity that makes it possible for him to "inherit his heritage", learning through that experience what it means to become the "next generation". His final speech at the end of the play, as we shall see, suggests a capacity to acknowledge one's place and responsibility in the ordered linking of the generations (5.3.323).

I want to invite you to think of this plain-speaking, this seeking the truth and seeking to be true, as having an affinity with the affectional link that Bion called K, the desire to know. It is linked with the capacity to think and reflect that Bion saw as the basis for the mother's ability to contain her infant's overwhelming emotion. Similarly I want to explore the affinity of the process of development Shakespeare describes in this play with the experience Meltzer has termed the "aesthetic conflict". That is, I want to ask: what is the truth of intimate relationships that Lear cannot face, and what is the nature of intimate relationships implied in the *K*-link within the tension of the *L*, *H*, and *K* constellation?

Bion's schema of aesthetic experience

In order to describe the structure of what Meltzer calls "aesthetic conflict" I need to indicate a central assumption that underpins the notion. Readers familiar with *The Apprehension of Beauty*, Meltzer's most elaborate exposition of his thinking about the aesthetic dimension in psychoanalysis, will be aware of some of the complexity of his thought (Meltzer & Williams, 1988). My aim here is not to offer anything like a comprehensive examination of the issues that arise when we approach psychoanalytic theory using the language of aesthetics. We shall have to ignore here, for example, some urgent and critical questions about the relationship between knowledge and aesthetics. The romantic notion that there is some link between truth and aesthetic experience is an idea that for the purposes of this paper we shall simply have to assume. Instead I want to offer a characterization of the notion of "aesthetic conflict" that is concise and clear enough for us to be able to examine its potential usefulness for understanding human development, and particularly the developmental achievement I am suggesting is necessary for "heriting" and "inheriting".

Meltzer's description of "aesthetic conflict" assumes that the aesthetic object and the aesthetic experience can be defined in terms of the "qualities of feeling" and he makes explicit use of a schematic theory about the qualities of feeling. At least that is the way I read his discussion, although he himself does not offer a systematic elaboration of this assumption. The aesthetic object on this reading becomes that which evokes a particular configuration of emotional engagement, the elements of which are defined by use of Bion's schema of *L*, *H*, and *K* (broadly the emotional links of loving, hating, and the impulse to know). It is an assumption that widens the scope of the concept of the aesthetic, linking aesthetic experience with the totality of emotional engagement (assuming that Bion's schema "*L*, *H*, and *K*" is meant suggestively and typologically, not definitionally, to indicate the range of the kinds of affective engagement) (Bion, 1962, pp. 42–9). Significantly, it also allows us to specify the retreat from "aesthetic conflict" as the retreat from this totality of emotional experience.

In Bion's own account he characterizes passion as "all that is comprised in L, H, K" or "the component derived from L, H, and K" (1963, pp. 4, 12). However, I think Meltzer's account moves the theory on when he describes the "nub of the matter" as what he calls the "consortium" of Bion's schema of emotional engagement. That is, Meltzer describes "passion", the experiential expression of the aesthetic impact of the aesthetic object, as the consortium of Bion's three elements of emotional engagement. I think that opens the way to a new dimension in Bion's schema, the possibility that L, H, and K each have a different quality when integrated as a totality of emotional engagement from the quality each has when isolated from the others. As such it is a remarkable insight with unexpected consequences for our view of developmental processes as well as the related analytic process itself.

In *The Apprehension of Beauty* it first occurs, almost one might say "in passing", as Meltzer is describing the first aesthetic impact of the mother in his imaginative account of the latter months of intra-uterine life. When he says that this aesthetic impact is responded to passionately, he adds parenthetically that "passion" is "used in the sense of an integration of love, hate and the thirst for knowledge: Bion's plus L, H, and K" (Meltzer & Williams, 1988, p. 60). Near the end of the book he offers a more explicit account:

> The most adequate description of "passion" would seem to be that our emotions are engaged in such a way that love, hate and the yearning for understanding are all set in motion. The *quantity or intensity can be disregarded*. It is the *consortium* that is essential. Many objects and events arouse one or the other; we love this, hate that, wish to understand the other. Our passions are not engaged. Our interest is in abeyance; we wish to engage with the object of love, to avoid or destroy the object of hate, to master the object that challenges our understanding. But when we encounter something that engages our *interest*, when we see it as a fragment or instance or sample of the beauty of the world, we wish to ascertain its authenticity, to know it in depth. And at that moment we encounter the heart of (its) mystery, along with the severe limitations in our capacity for knowledge. We enter upon the realms of science and art, the cathedral of the mind hidden in the forest of the world. (Meltzer & Williams, 1988, pp. 143–4; my italics)

We need to be careful here, as Meltzer is developing a technical concept using ordinary terms in a particular way. It is quite a radical innovation to describe "passion" in the sense of the "consortium" of Bion's *L, H,* and *K.* And it points to the reality that the constellation of these three elements involves tension, in the first instance because *L* and *H* are antithetical. Although Meltzer also refers to an "integration" of these three elements, I do not think we should imagine some homogenized mixture of *L* and *H,* for example, that results in a tepid emotional link with the object. I am suggesting we imagine a constellation, a consortium, in which love, hate, and the wish to know are not diminished by being linked, but rather are held in a potentially creative tension, always threatening to disintegrate, intensifying as they move towards *–L, –H,* and *–K.*

We see just how radical this idea is when we consider Meltzer's suggestion that we do not think of passion primarily in terms of quanity or intensity. This "quantitative" notion of passion is how the term is usually understood, indeed how Bion himself used it: "I mean the term to represent an emotion experienced with intensity and warmth though without any suggestion of violence: the sense of violence is not to be conveyed by the term 'passion' unless it is associated with the term 'greed'" (1963, pp. 12–13).

We characteristically speak of someone as "more" or "less" passionate, and of "heightened" or "subdued" passion, all measures of the quantity of the intensity of emotion. But in order to follow Meltzer's discussion of "aesthetic conflict" we must hold these usual quantitative notions at bay in our minds while we focus on what it would mean to think about aesthetic experience in terms of the tension of the constellation of *L, H,* and *K.*

On the other hand it is important to keep in mind these ordinary quantitative uses of the term *passion.* In particular I want to consider this quantitative sense of passion associated with each of *L, H,* and *K* separately. We know, for example, about a "passionate" love that longs to be one with its object, even lusts passionately after the loved object. And there is a "passionate" hatred, such as we have seen in *Lear,* which wants to wound and even destroy its object. And, I suggest, there is also a "passionate" urge to know, almost a drive, that wants to control and possess its object. As Meltzer himself observes, something that challenges our understanding can lead us to want to "master" it.

Isolated from the other two kinds of emotional engagement, each of the three, *L*, *H*, and *K*, has its own kind of intensity. In this quantitative understanding of "passion" the *K*-link is particularly interesting in that it can become a wish to master in two different senses. In the first, knowing can become an acquisitive accumulation of knowledge about those objects. I want to learn more and more and want to master my subject (object of my knowledge). This is what Bion and others refer to as "knowing about". Here knowing subtly evades, or at least seeks to evade, the influence of *L* and *H*. It passionately seeks to be dispassionate in the sense of knowledge for its own sake. It is as if there were a fear that *K* might become drawn back into a link with *L* and *H* and the purity of the urge to know would thus somehow be contaminated.

In the second sense, a wish to master this fear of a link with *L* and *H* leads to a more radical aim. Faced with this fear of the influence of the two emotional links of love and hate, *K* can become degraded into a wish to master these emotions themselves, an urge to master *L* and *H*. That is, in the wish to isolate the *K*-link from *L* and *H* there is an oscillation between attempting to ignore these dreaded emotional links and attempting to overcome them.

Meltzer's description of passion as the "consortium" of *L*, *H*, and *K* is immediately helpful in thinking, for example, about *King Lear* and the question of development in the play. Of course one can reasonably hold the view that Lear himself does not develop, does not learn anything in the course of the play (cf. Booth, 1983, p. 162). However, while Shakespeare might not locate development in one character, facing us instead with thinking about it in the complex dynamics of the play, we can watch Lear struggle with tension between *L*, *H*, and *K*. We have already seen this father as unbearably "passionate", in the quantitative sense of intensity, in his hateful cursing of Goneril. Does this result from his now being an old man who needs someone to control what he himself cannot control?

O, sir, you are old:
Nature in you stands on the very verge
Of her confine. You should be ruled and led
By some discretion that discerns your state
Better than you yourself. (2.2.335–9)

Regan tells her father that he has need of those "that mingle reason with . . . passion" (2.2.423). Foakes (1997) glosses "mingle reason with your passion" as "apply cool judgement to your passionate outbursts". He goes on to suggest that the play challenges the conventional wisdom of Shakespeare's age, which assumed that reason was given to human beings to control their passions, quoting Sir John Davies's lines in his *Nosce Teipsum* (1599) on the fall of Adam and Eve: "Ill they desir'd to know, and ill they did,/ And to give Passion eyes, made Reason blind". But, he concludes, "the play shows a more complex relation between reason and passion" (Foakes, 1997, p. 253).

If Foakes is correct in this reading of *King Lear* might we then want to link this more complex relationship between reason and passion, between thinking and feeling, with some implications of Meltzer's innovation in Bion's schema? Might we, for example, say that the *K*-link, the desire to know, isolated from *L* and *H* can become a desire to master disturbing emotions, the application of reason, one might say, to violent "passions"? If so it might begin to account for the common idea that "reason", the impulse to know, and the wish to understand are all dispassionate, opposed in fact to passion. On this view the wish to know is not an emotional link at all.

Integrated with the emotional links of *L* and *H*, the wish to know becomes the opposite of the wish to master. It involves instead respect for the object and the recognition that the wish to master and possess the object leads away from any possibility of genuine knowing. Genuine knowing is possible only when the other makes her- or himself available to be known. It is predicated on that freedom of the other and is therefore, as the Biblical sense of "knowing" suggests, a kind of intercourse.

We see in *King Lear* a good example of how the tension between joy and pain resulting from the emotional links of love and hate involves one in an ambivalence that seems to demand a process of splitting in order to avoid an irresolvable impasse. Lear repeatedly tries to split these emotions in his relationships with his daughters. And when this splitting finally fails, the only option is to attack these emotions themselves in order to avoid the pain of ambivalence. He does this in part by attacking emotions as feminine, as if by giving them a gender he can link his anger with his masculinity, using "reason" to control these emotions which otherwise would control him:

And let not women's weapons, water-drops,
Stain my man's cheeks . . .

You think I'll weep,
No, I'll not weep. [*Storm and tempest*]
I have full cause of weeping, but this heart
Shall break into a hundred thousand flaws
Or e'er I'll weep. O fool, I shall go mad. (2.2.466–7, 471–5)

One might think of Lear's fear of madness here as linked, not with
an excess of emotion (an excess of passion as some commentators
describe it), but with his desperate attempt to control the storm of
his emotions. We could picture madness as the attack on his capacity
to think, a destructive attack on the "consortium" of L, H, and K. He
is exposed to "thought-executing fires" by his daughters' ingratitude
as he faces his inability to think about the emotional chaos into which
he has been driven (3.2.4). He may be referring to the execution of
thought by the fire of his love and his hatred or to the carrying out
of his omnipotent wish to call down thunderbolts to "singe his white
head". In a sense both describe an attack on thinking.

One of Lear's most poignant views is that he is suffering from
hysteria. Shakespeare's language suggests the poet had some knowledge of contemporary medical opinion, for example Janet Adelman
quotes Edward Jordan's *A briefe discourse of a disease called the
suffocation of the mother* (1603):

"This disease is called by diverse names amongst our Authors.
Passio Hysterica, Suffocatio, Prasocatio, and Strangulatus uteri,
Caducus matricis, etc. In English the Mother or the Suffocation of
the Mother, because most commonly it takes them with choking in
the throat: and it is an affect of the Mother or wombe" (pp. 5–6); the
suffocation is caused by "the rising of the Mother wherby it is
sometimes drawn upwards or sidewards above his natural seate,
compressing the neighbour parts" (p. 6). (Adelman, 1992, p. 300)

Again Lear pictures the emotions attacking him as feminine and does
his best to control them. He is sure that these uncontrolled emotions
make us "not ourselves" and says to himself: "[I] am fallen out with
my headier will" (2.2.299). He must regain control:

O, how this mother swells up toward my heart.
Hysterica passio, down, thou climbing sorrow.

Thy element's below . . .

O me, my heart! My rising heart! But down! (2.2.246–8, 310)

The Fool amusingly compares Lear trying to control these emotions with a fishwife who, having baked a pie with eels not yet dead, has to bash them with a stick: "Down, wantons, down!" (2.2.311–14). This desperate wish to master emotional reality might be thought of as a form of what Bion called –K, or the K-link split off and isolated from the emotional links of L and H. But why is there a persistent tendency towards a degradation of K to an impulse to master, control, and possess? I want to suggest that there is always an inherent tension present in the consortium of L, H, and K. Love, split off from K and H, degrades into what Bion called –L, seeking to merge with and possess the object. Hate, split off from L and K, degrades into unmitigated hatred, seeking ultimately to destroy the object. Both split-off opposing impulses lead to an impossibility of knowing.

On the other hand, knowing held in tension with the emotional links of love and hate requires that the object remain always outside the orbit of either the impulse to possess or to control and destroy. Meltzer describes this as the "enigmatic" quality of the object:

> The tragic element in the aesthetic experience resides, not in the transience, but in the enigmatic quality of the object . . . The aesthetic conflict is different from the romantic one in this respect: that its central experience of pain resides in uncertainty, tending towards distrust, verging on suspicion. The lover is naked as Othello to the whisperings of Iago, but is rescued by the quest for knowledge, the K-link, the desire to know rather than to possess the object of desire. The K-link points to the value of the desire as itself the stimulus to knowledge, not merely as a yearning for gratification and control over the object. *Desire makes it possible, even essential, to give the object its freedom.* (Meltzer & Williams, 1988, p. 27)

The quest for knowledge rescues the lover from the need to possess and control, and thus ultimately to destroy, the beloved. But we see how unstable this "consortium" of emotional links with the object is when we consider the anxieties attendant on the discovery that the wish to know leads to an acknowledging of the freedom of the object. This letting go, this giving the object its freedom, can itself be experienced as a threat to the emotional links with the object, a fear that the freedom means that the love will be lost, and thus the hate increased. If the wish to know the beloved means giving the beloved his or her freedom, will that not be the end of love? The tension in the consortium of *L*, *H*, and *K* lies in the seeming incompatibility of these emotional links with each other. It is almost impossible to sustain this constellation of emotional links with the object, and the attempt can feel unbearable. This is what Meltzer has called the "aesthetic conflict".

In order to put this tension in a developmental context we need to look again at two familiar processes—weaning and mourning. They are both so familiar that it seems almost pointless to ask what weaning is and what mourning accomplishes. Nevertheless, I think Meltzer's description of the "aesthetic conflict" in terms of Bion's schema puts both weaning and mourning in a fresh light, especially when we think about them in the context of Shakespeare's *King Lear*.

Weaning and mourning: Thy truth then be thy dower

Weaning is usually understood to be "weaning from" something, archetypically the baby from the mother's breast. In my attempt to follow Shakespeare's examination of the father–daughter relationship in the Lear plot and the father–son relationship in the Gloucester plot, I am exploring the possibility that the father's role, the responsibility I am referring to as "endowing", can be seen in the context of the lifelong process of weaning. But that requires us to rethink just what the process of weaning is. I will be brief as I mean only to call attention to something implicit in the notion of weaning.

Melanie Klein pointed out in a paper on weaning for a general audience that there was an earlier meaning that had the sense of a "weaning to" in addition to the sense of "weaning from" (Klein, 1936, p. 304). The *OED* basically ignores that Old English usage that never took hold in the language, although there is a clear intuitive and indeed logical link between the two senses. The process of becoming accustomed to the loss of something, being weaned *from* it, can, and often does, involve being accustomed to the presence of something else, what we might call being weaned *to* it. However, if we focus too quickly on what we might call the replacement object I think we may miss something of the nature of the need to relinquish something.

One only needs to be weaned *from* something where there is a desire for it, if only the desire that accompanies having become accustomed to it. And where there is desire there is a question about the capacity to tolerate the emotional turmoil of the gap between desire and gratification, the turmoil of wanting-in-anticipation-of-having. In the mother–baby relationship the mother may foster an illusion of omnipotence in the baby, an illusion that the baby's desire creates the reality it seeks, for example in her feeding "on demand". And it might even be argued that this illusion itself is functional in the earliest stages as it fosters a sense of agency in the infant. My focus here is the simple observation that, insofar as weaning involves the baby having to face the reality that wanting is not the same thing as having, weaning is not limited to the relinquishing of the breast (or bottle). Consider Melanie Klein's early, common-sense observation in that paper on weaning:

> In so far as the baby never has uninterrupted possession of the breast, and over and over again is in the state of lacking it, one could say that, in a sense, he is in a constant state of being weaned or at least in a state leading up to weaning (1936, p. 295).

And not only is the baby in a constant state of being weaned, leading up to the moment we generally recognize as weaning. Coming to terms with reality that wanting is not the same thing as having is a struggle that does not end with the moment when we relinquish the breast in a literal sense. To see that we need to take account of a potential confusion.

There is of course a point when the breast or bottle is gone irrevocably, as Melanie Klein went on in that paper to point out. The loss of the breast is complete. But this fact, this irrevocable loss, can itself foster another illusion in the baby, an illusion doubtless shared by the mother to some degree. I am referring to the illusion that the breast *per se* is the object of the baby's desire. However, as soon as one begins to think about what the baby wants, the question of the object of desire becomes more complex. Reflection leads to an awareness that what the baby is wanting is satisfaction of its hunger sensations, or warmth, or something to satisfy its urge to suck, and so on. Thus, for example, if the baby's desire is to suck, a dummy might do, but if the desire is to be fed, it will not do.

Meltzer suggests that essentially both Freud and Melanie Klein have a "tragic" view of the critical developmental achievements, whether the resolution of the Oedipus complex or the attainment of the depressive position. They are tragic views, he suggests, because both look back at the relinquished object instead of forward to the possibility of an enriched object that this relinquishment makes possible (Meltzer & Williams, 1988, p. 27). Might we also think of the potential confusion of the means of satisfaction of desire with the object of desire as "tragic"?

Weaning involves a relinquishing. But a relinquishing of what? In a sense it is the relinquishing of the breast, the irrevocable loss of the breast. However, it is obvious that it is not a relinquishing of the desire to be fed, or for warmth, or even to suck. I suggest that what the baby is called on to relinquish is the *belief* that it controlled and possessed that object, that means of the gratification of desire. In this belief, this omnipotent illusion, desire is unconsciously equated with reality. There is no gap between "I want" and "I have".

In effect this unconscious equation of desire and reality obviates dependence on anyone. Weaning in this expanded sense is a lifelong developmental process of giving up omnipotent illusions, a lifelong process of coming to terms with the truth of one's condition. Lear seems to be struggling with a weaning in this expanded sense, a relinquishment of his illusion of omnipotence, when he says to the blinded Gloucester, whom he does not yet recognize and seems to confuse in his madness with his hated daughter:

> Ha! Goneril with a white beard? They flattered me like a dog and told me I had the white hairs in my beard ere the black ones were there . . . They told me I was everything; 'tis a lie. I am not ague-proof (4.6.96–8, 103–4).

Not "ague-proof", not immune to shivering or fever, says Lear "when the rain came to wet me once and the wind to make me chatter, when the thunder would not peace at my bidding" (4.6.100–2). The rage of Lear's frustrated omnipotence has subsided as he recognizes the difference between wanting and having. Cavell (1987) suggests that Lear's capacity to acknowledge his own vulnerability, humanity, and mortality, seems linked with blind Gloucester's recognition of him. "Is't not the King? . . . O, let me kiss that hand!" Lear says: "Let me wipe it first, it smells of mortality" (4.6.128).

Whether Lear feels the pain of acknowledging his mortality in his madness is difficult to gauge. We expect him to feel his grief and sorrow most poignantly in the reunion with Cordelia at the end of the play when he is faced with the reality of the consequence of his omnipotence, and to some degree he does. We expect that *mourning* is at the core of the experience of weaning, and it is this experience of mourning that makes weaning a process of growth leading to the development of the mind.

We know that mourning is a painful process involving grief and sorrow for that which is lost and as such is a basic building block of psychoanalytic thinking (e.g. Judd, 1995). And we know about the sequence of stages of mourning (Parkes, 1972). However, when we ask ourselves what it is that mourning accomplishes, how it is that the process of mourning comes to an end and we move on, we find that the answer is not so clear. In fact I think there are three distinct psychoanalytic models of the dynamics of mourning, and I want to comment briefly on each of them in order to ask how the concept of "aesthetic conflict", understood in terms of the tension of the unstable consortium of L, H, and K might inform our picture of the process of mourning.

Freud's "exhaustion" theory of mourning

Freud puzzled over the dynamic process of mourning, especially that "we do not even know the economic means by which mourning carries out its task." May I remind you of his account in "Mourning and melancholia", although in many ways his assumption of a neurophysiological model focused on the distribution of energy makes it seem somewhat quaint to us now? As usual Freud's intuition captures features that are worth thinking about if only to help us clarify our own views. He begins by asking what the work that mourning performs consists in. He suggests that reality testing shows that the loved object no longer exists and demands that "all libido shall be withdrawn from its attachments to that object" (1917, p. 244).

The difficulty of this demand to withdraw libido from the attachment to the loved object, and what requires the "work" of mourning, is that people never willingly abandon a libidinal position.

Although opposition to this work can lead to hallucinatory wishes seeking to deny the loss, Freud suggests that respect for reality normally wins the day. But this work of mourning takes time: "Each single one of the memories and expectations in which the libido is bound to the object is brought up and hypercathected, and detachment of the libido is accomplished in respect of it" (1917, p. 245).

Freud seems aware of the puzzling nature of what he is saying, why this "hypercathecting", this intensifying of attachment so to speak, should lead to the detachment of the libido. His conclusion is appropriate to his energy model: "We may perhaps suppose that this work of severance is so slow and gradual that by the time it has been finished the expenditure of energy necessary for it is also dissipated" (1917, p. 255).

I am inclined, in the light of this description, to call this theory of the work of mourning the "exhaustion" theory. The mourning comes to an end as it exhausts itself in this prolonged painful process and the mourner turns to other, living, objects as subjects for libidinal attachment. His conclusion about this work of "severance" is even more explicit in his little paper "On transience": "When it has renounced everything that has been lost, then it has consumed itself, and our libido is once more free" (1916, p. 307).

Even were we to accept this energy model of the work of mourning, we are left with a puzzle in that it seems to suggest that once this process is complete there is no longer a libidinal attachment to the lost loved object. But what then is the libidinal status of the object which he describes in "Mourning and melancholia" as installed inside the ego as a result of mourning? Perhaps libidinal attachment is reserved for external objects and, at least for Freud, it makes no sense to talk of libidinal attachment to what we now would call "internal objects". In reference to external objects the loss of the object has become the withdrawal, in effect the loss, of desire. This is not the disaster it might at first seem, since desire arises from the ashes of that loss like the Phoenix, liberated from the object, "once again free".

We have here the perfect antithesis of Meltzer's picture of the need to give the *object* its freedom. In Freud's view of mourning, it is desire that must be given its freedom.

Klein's theory of mourning as the predominance
of love over hate

Mourning is central in Klein's ideas, and as with Freud's account, requires only a brief summary here. She pictures the process of mourning as a struggle involving ambivalent feelings towards the lost loved object. Greedy and destructive phantasies combined with the experience of the loss of the loved object give rise to deep and disturbing conflicts in the mind of the mourner. But what allows the mourner to progress from a state of mind in which good and bad aspects of the loved object must be kept split out of fear that hatred will undermine or overwhelm the loving feelings to a state of mind in which it is possible to tolerate the anguish of ambivalent feelings? That is, what allows for the move from a paranoid-schizoid to a depressive position? In her view the problem with the splitting in the paranoid-schizoid position is that it makes impossible the bringing together of these contrasting aspects of the lost object, "good" and "bad", loved and hated: "While the separation of these contrasting *aspects*—felt in the unconscious as contrasting *objects*—operates strongly, feelings of hatred and love are also so much divorced from each other that love cannot mitigate hatred" (Klein, 1940, p. 349, n. 2).

For love to be able to mitigate the hatred, the mourner is dependent on the survival of, in Klein's language, good internal objects.

The fear in mourning is that hatred may gain the upper hand, a devastating fear because the loss of the external loved object "shakes the mourner's belief in his inner good objects as well" (Klein, 1940, p. 355). This fear of having lost the *internal* good objects as well as having lost the loved-and-hated external object is a fear of having lost all possible resources. The only hope of diminishing the ambivalence, and thus diminishing the threat to the loving feelings for the lost loved object from the feelings of hatred, lies in "reinstating" the good *internal* objects in the process of mourning.

This bivalent theory would seem to depend on it being the case that there is good reason to trust one's reparative and constructive feelings over one's envious, destructive feelings. In Bion's shorthand it involves the mitigation of *H* by *L*. We could say that not only is Klein's view tragic in the looking back to the lost loved object, it is also a view premised on a profoundly optimistic assumption. In fact she makes clear that in her view there is no ambivalence regarding internal objects. "Ambivalence," she says, "refers to object-relations—that is to say, to whole and real objects" (1940, p. 350).

One might say a similarly optimistic assumption underlies Klein's picture of the shift from the paranoid-schizoid position to the depressive position, the move from a self-interested concern for one's own welfare to a concern for the welfare of the loved object. The possibility of such a shift is central in her thinking, but how is it that it happens? I think Meltzer is correct when he suggests that Melanie Klein does not describe the *modus operandi* of the shift (Meltzer & Williams, 1988, p. 28).

It is only in Bion's development of psychoanalytic theory that we have an account that points beyond the potential impasse of ambivalence. It offers an alternative to simply relying on some predisposition of human love to outweigh human hatred, and it suggests the *modus operandi* of PS↔D.

Bion's *L, H,* and *K* and a theory of mourning

Of course Bion's schema of the three central affective links is not itself explicitly a theory of mourning. But perhaps it is possible to see how Bion's conceptualization of the function of the desire to know linked with love and hate radically relocates the agony of mourning. In part, this relocating, I suggest, involves the recognition that mourning for the lost loved object brings one back to the agony of the emotional attachment to the present loved object. But how is it that we would speak of *mourning* in the *presence* of the loved object?

We have seen that in Meltzer's notion of "aesthetic conflict" understood in terms of the consortium of the emotional attachment, the object remains necessarily outside the orbit of any demand for possession and control. This leads to two closely related experiences. The first is an agony that resides in that psychic reality that the object is outside my control and my ability to possess it, leaving me, Meltzer suggests, "in uncertainty, tending towards distrust, verging on suspicion". As we have seen he describes this as the "enigmatic" quality of the loved object (Meltzer & Williams, 1988, p. 27). And if the lover is rescued by the quest for knowledge, it is not a rescue from uncertainty. The rescue, if that is what we want to call it, is in fact the achievement of a new capacity to tolerate uncertainty. Bion following Keats called it "negative capability". And the *desire* that leads to this capacity, the desire that makes possible, is our desire to know the loved and hated object, a *K*-link integrated with *L* and *H*.

This struggle to allow the object its freedom is an essential dynamic of the *K*-link, the wish to know. Or perhaps we should say it is the struggle to acknowledge the freedom of the object, since its freedom is not within our gift. It is part of our omnipotent illusion that *we* could give the object *its* freedom. It is in this sense that I want to suggest that the *K*-link also involves a process of mourning, but not just a mourning for the lost loved object. It is also a mourning for the omnipotence which in love or hate, or in the ambivalence of *L* and *H*, seeks to possess and control, the belief that one could possess and control the object and still have an object to possess and control.

The *K*-link exposes one to the experience of uncertainty, the not knowing whether or when the freedom to go separate ways will also be a freedom to come together again. Intimacy is the gift of that freedom. Mourning the abandoned omnipotence is a mourning for an intimacy that was an illusion. As Othello discovered too late, and as Lear seems almost to have grasped in his madness, love as the desire to possess and hate as the desire to control both end in the final absence, the death of the loved object.

One vital consequence follows from this way of thinking about the process of mourning. Building on the work of Freud and Klein, we can say that the process of mourning leads to an internalization or introjection of the lost loved object in the form of an alteration in the ego that we think of in terms of an internal good object. But building on the work of Bion and Meltzer, we can also say that the internal good object, like the external object, must be given its freedom if we are to sustain a *K*-link with it. Introjective identification is not a chimera. But neither is the good internal object at our beck and call. As our creative artists know, and as we all struggle to learn, we do not possess and control our muses. Their presence is a gift.

In other words the dynamic Meltzer described as the "aesthetic conflict" is at the heart of the developmental struggle to move beyond our infantile omnipotence. As such it is at the core of the process of weaning in the wider sense I have been describing. It is also a way of characterizing the struggle I suggest Shakespeare portrays in Lear's attempt to be a good father to his daughters, seeking to "endow", to "herit" them. I want to conclude by returning to Shakespeare's description of that struggle to point out a few of the things I think we can learn from *King Lear* about the "aesthetic conflict".

I see it feelingly

In a moving encounter between Lear in his madness and Gloucester in his blindness near the end of the play, the two fathers are struggling to discover and acknowledge the reality of what has happened. I have already referred to that moment when Gloucester recognized Lear and would kiss his hand, a hand that "smells of mortality". He cries to Lear: "Dost thou know me?" And Lear responds:

> I remember thine eyes well enough. Dost thou squiny at me? No, do thy worst, blind Cupid, I'll not love. (4.6.132–4)

It is as if Lear fears Gloucester's "squint", a fear that being seen is being known, as Stanley Cavell argues in one of the most penetrating essays on this play (1987). But known as what, for what? How is it that being seen, being known, might make him (acknowledge his) love? In his seemingly mad associations and disconnected ramblings, Lear paints a picture all the more powerful in opening our eyes to thoughts from which we want to turn away. The role of eyes and seeing runs through the play like a bright thread catching the light (Alpers, 1963). The references are too numerous to detail here, but the more one looks the more ubiquitous they seem to be.

In this scene Lear persists, almost taunting this father who had been blind to his son's love for him: "read this", "read", "no eyes in your head", "yet you see how the world goes". Gloucester's response could stand for the struggle of these blind fathers, both him and Lear: "*I see it feelingly*". How can one see feelingly? How can one think about emotional turmoil "feelingly"? How does one see the world feelingly?

The ambiguity of Gloucester's words invites us to think, to wonder. Might we hear him saying, "I see by my touch, feelingly"?

Perhaps. Or is he saying, "I see passionately, emotionally, feelingly"? One distinctive mark of drama is the opportunity for the author to station a character strategically to see something for us, on our behalf as it were. Edgar, this son whose father was so quick in his suspicion of him, has been observing his blind father since agreeing to lead him to Dover where he wished to kill himself.

Shakespeare invites us to observe this unbearably painful scene through the eyes of this son to whose love the father was blind:

> Edgar (*aside*): I would not take this from report; it is
> And my heart breaks at it. (4.6.137–8)

He would not take it from report, he would not trust his "knowing-about" this scene of recognition. But it is. He knows it, because he sees it, feelingly. And so might we. But it would not be by *knowing about* Edgar's view of this scene, or indeed anyone else's. Might there be some imaginative intercourse in our mind, some knowing in creative tension with our emotional experience of loving and hating, which might allow us to *see it feelingly* as Edgar does?

You will see that I am taking this exploration of the theme of seeing—the portrayal of two fathers who were blind when they could still see, blind to emotional reality—as Shakespeare's exploration of what Bion called the *K*-link. Like Meltzer's picture of the "aesthetic conflict", Lear's conflict is marked by pain residing in his uncertainty, distrust, and suspicion in his attempt to "endow" his daughters. But is Lear "rescued" (to use Meltzer's term)? Indeed, does he want to be?

Shakespeare's version of Lear's conflict offers us a moving portrait of him in the storm, and of the storm in him, a storm into which he feels exiled by the ingratitude of his daughters. This father, half recognizing that something is wrong with his wish to control and possess what he seeks to give to the next generation, is at a loss to understand just what it is that is wrong. All he knows is the storm of his rage mirrored by the storm outside:

> this tempest in my mind
> Doth from my senses take all feeling else,
> Save what beats there, filial ingratitude. (3.4.12–14)

Lear ricochets between the feelings he would evade, terrified that continuing to think about his emotions, especially his rage at the ingratitude of his daughters, will drive him mad. His aim must be, he concludes, to stop thinking, at least to stop "thinking feelingly":

> No, I will weep no more. In such a nigh,
> To shut me out? Pour on, I will endure.
> In such a night as this? O, Regan, Goneril,
> Your old, kind father, whose frank heart gave you all—
> O, that way madness lies, let me shun that;
> No more of that. (3.4.17–22)

I have already suggested that Lear's fear of madness can be seen as linked, not with an excess of emotion, an excess of "passion", but with this desperate attempt to stop thinking feelingly. It entails an attack on his mind and his capacity to think feelingly, and thus is a destructive attack on the "consortium" of L, H, and K. The forms of perversion and confusion are numerous and if we had time it would be interesting to look in detail at Shakespeare's portrayal of Lear's madness.

But what I want to emphasize here is the wish to see, to think, to understand that can be traced through the storm scenes right up to the end of the play like a bright thread. Shakespeare marks it first, as we have seen, as "plain-speaking", the wish to be true, to speak truthfully whatever the consequences. It is an interesting version of what Bion describes as the mother's capacity to think about the turmoil of the baby's emotions projected into her. Would Shakespeare describe it as the mother's capacity for plain speaking, her emotional truthfulness with her infant? Were Shakespeare to have had as much influence on our psychoanalytic vocabulary as Bion has had, would we be speaking of the mother not as "container" but as the "Fool" to "His Majesty the baby". It is an intriguing image.

In the storm when Edgar disguised as "Poor Tom" begins to take on the role of the fool, Lear becomes curious about Poor Tom as a source of knowledge, especially when he sees him in a state similar to his own. What has happened, Lear asks, that Poor Tom has been reduced to this wretched state of nakedness and madness, pursued by the "foul fiend"? "Didst thou give all to thy two daughters? And art thou come to this?"

The audience may laugh at Lear's obvious self-reference. Such self-reference is funny as well as sad. But we might also want to note Lear's wanting to know. He wants to understand how his own attempt to endow his own daughters has come to such disaster, so he turns to one who like him has "come to this". But when plain-speaking Kent tries to tell Lear that "Poor Tom" has no daughters, Lear is incredulous. His wish to know at this point is still under the influence of his hatred for his ungrateful daughters, K is perverted by H in our schema. He shouts to this truth-telling Kent:

> Death, traitor! Nothing could have subdued nature
> To such a lowness but his unkind daughters. (3.4.69–70)

We could pursue this wish to know through all the subtleties Shakespeare gives it, especially in reference to Lear and Edgar. For example, how Lear persists in wanting to talk with "Poor Tom" whom he calls his "philosopher", his "learned Theban", "good Athenian", "noble philosopher". Again it makes us laugh, this caricature of learning. But we also feel Lear's desperation to understand how his desire to possess and control has become his being possessed and controlled himself, mad and impotent.

We see Lear in a struggle with something in him that would scorn this seeing or knowing feelingly, the Lear who shouted to his daughter Goneril, when, unable to control his (feminine) emotions, he burst into uncontrollable weeping:

> Life and death, I am ashamed
> That thou hast power to shake my manhood thus,
> That these hot tears, which break from me perforce,
> Should make thee worth them. . . .
>
> Old fond eyes
> Beweep this cause again, I'll pluck ye out (1.4.288–91, 293–4).

Better blind than see feelingly. This brutal attack on his capacity to see is in reality an attack on the unbearable emotions that torture him and an attack on his mind and his capacity to think. Even at the very end in his reunion with Cordelia his beloved, Lear cannot bear her tears. It is a scene in which it is difficult not to hear a grieving husband discovering, or rediscovering, the pain of the loss of his wife.

Does he think at last he can possess his beloved, hidden away in a walled prison where the knowledge of reality cannot penetrate?

> Come, let's away to prison;
> We two alone will sing like bird i' the cage . . .

> Wipe thine eyes;
> The good years shall devour them, flesh and fell,
> Ere they shall make us weep! (5.3.8–9, 23–5)

It is as if Lear senses but can never quite realize a knowing, a desire to understand, that can acknowledge the freedom of the loved object. As a father he could not trust that he might be loved, and of course might also not be loved—this is anxiety that comes with the reality that love is a gift, a gift that may or may not be given. His perversion of "endowing" into an abdication, which appeared to make the daughters' inheritance a gift, disguised the reality that what he sought was possession and control of his children. It was in that sense the opposite of endowing, confusing and perverting it for his own gratification.

In the end the daughter who seems genuinely to have loved him, Cordelia, seeks to restore him to the throne that he abdicated. Why? There may be many answers to that question, but one implication that strikes me is something that is also portrayed in the closing speech of the play where Edgar is about to take up his heritage. It is as if both these children have come to recognize the reality of the generations and can therefore assume their place as "generated" and as "generators".

> The weight of this sad time we must obey,
> Speak what we feel, not what we ought to say.
> The oldest hath borne most; we that are young
> Shall never see so much, nor live so long. (5.3.322–5)

Hanna Segal, writing about the analysis of an old man (1958), discusses a report from his son about his father's death at 85, some eleven years after the analysis had ended. The son reported that on the day he died his father asked his wife where their children were and what they were doing, saying that before it had not seemed real to him but now it did. Segal speculates about this preparation for death:

The preparation consisted in "placing his objects in reality". I think it signified a relinquishing of omnipotent control and allowing these objects to live on without him. It also probably had the significance of placing them correctly in his internal world, without coercion or control. (1981, p. 181)

One might even say that there is a kind of paradox in the "aesthetic conflict". In this case a paradox in the struggle as a parent with one's wish to possess the loved child, or control the hated, while aware of an urge to know them in a way that rescues both parent and child from this gratifying, and destructive, possession and control. It seems the capacity to "endow" or "herit" one's son or daughter necessarily involves the capacity to give them their freedom, an endowing that means one does not abdicate one's position as parent. The correlate of the acknowledging of the freedom of the other to come or go is that it locates both parent and child in the reality of the separate generations. That is truly an endowing. It is an endowing based upon one's desire to see feelingly, to know feelingly these offspring. It is an endowing that makes possible the gift of love.

But perhaps it is also true that *King Lear* grips us because in this play Shakespeare portrays the tragedy for Lear and others that this unstable consortium of emotional links is an aspiration never quite achieved. Perhaps in seeing and knowing this play feelingly, we ourselves hear its plain-speaking to us.

Acknowledgement

I would like to thank Alberto Hahn, Noel Hess, and Mary Adams for their helpful comments on an early draft of this paper.

Note

1. All references to the text of *King Lear* cite the act, scene, and line according to Foakes (1997).

References

Adams, M. (2000). Becoming a daughter: intimacy and weaning in patients with the "dead mother" syndrome. Paper presented at: A developmental view of the psychoanalytic method: theoretical and clinical studies of Dr Meltzer's contributions to psychoanalysis, Florence, 17–20 February.

Adelman, J. (1992). Suffocating mothers in *King Lear*. In: *Suffocating Mothers: Fantasies of Maternal Origin in Shakespeare's Plays*, Hamlet *to* The Tempest (pp. 103–29, 293–312). London: Routledge.

Alpers, P. (1963). *King Lear* and the theory of the sight pattern. In: R. Brower & R. Poirier (Eds.), *In Defense of Reading* (pp. 133–52). New York: Dutton.

Bion, W.R. (1962). *Learning from Experience*. London: Heinemann.

Bion, W.R. (1963). *Elements of Psycho-Analysis*. London: Maresfield.

Booth, S. (1983). King Lear, Macbeth, *Indefinition, and Tragedy*. New Haven, CT: Yale University Press.

Britton, R. (1998). *Belief and Imagination: Explorations in Psychoanalysis*. London: Routledge.

Cavell, S. (1987). The avoidance of love: a reading of *King Lear*. In: *Disowning Knowledge in Six Plays of Shakespeare* (pp. 39–123). Cambridge, UK: Cambridge University Press.

Foakes, R.A. (Ed.) (1997). *King Lear*. Walton-on-Thames, UK: Nelson.

Freud, S. (1913). The theme of the three caskets. *Standard Edition 12* (pp. 191–301).

Freud, S. (1916). On transience. *Standard Edition 14* (pp. 305–7).

Freud, S. (1917). Mourning and melancholia. *Standard Edition 14* (pp. 237–58).

Freud, S. (1919). The "uncanny". *Standard Edition 17* (pp. 219–56).

Hess, N. (1987). *King Lear* and some anxieties of old age. *Br J Med Psychol* 60: 209–15.

Honan, P. (1998). *Shakespeare: A Life*. Oxford: Oxford University Press.

Judd, D. (1995). *Give Sorrow Words: Working with a Dying Child*, 2nd edition. London: Whurr.

Klein, M. (1936). Weaning. In: *On the Bringing up of Children*. Reprinted in: *Writings of Melanie Klein 1921–1945*, Vol. 2, (pp. 290–305). London: Hogarth.

Klein, M. (1940). Mourning and its relation to manic–depressive states. *International Journal Psychoanalysis, 21*: 125–53. (Reprinted in: *Writings of Melanie Klein 1921–1945*, Vol. 2 (pp. 344–69). London: Hogarth.)

Meltzer, D. & Williams, M.H. (1988). *The Apprehension of Beauty: The Role of Aesthetic Conflict in Development, Art and Violence*. Strath Tay: Clunie.

Montaigne, M. de (1993). *The Essays: A Selection*. M.A. Screech, translator. London: Penguin.

Parkes, C.M. (1972). *Bereavement: Studies of Grief in Adult Life*. London: Tavistock.

Salingar, L. (1986). *Dramatic Form in Shakespeare and the Jacobeans*. Cambridge: Cambridge University Press.

Segal, H. (1958). Fear of death—Notes on the analysis of an old man. *International Journal Psychoanalysis, 39*:178–81.

Segal, H. (1981). Postscript 1980: fear of death. In: *The Work of Hanna Segal: A Kleinian Approach to Clinical Practice* (pp. 181–2). London: Jason Aronson.

Stone, L. (1979). *The Family, Sex and Marriage in England, 1500–1800*. New York: Harper & Row.

Williams, M.H., & Waddell, M. (1991). *The Chamber of Maiden Thought: Literary Origins of the Psychoanalytic Model of the Mind*. London: Routledge.

CHAPTER THREE

"The music of what happens" in poetry and psychoanalysis

Thomas H. Ogden

The author presents a close reading of a Frost poem and a detailed discussion of an analytic session. Using specific examples from the poem and from the analytic session, he then offers some thoughts concerning the relationship between the way he listens to the language of the poem and the way he and his patient speak with and listen to one another. The author illustrates in this reading of the poem and in the way he speaks to his patient that he is not primarily engaged in an effort to unearth what lies "behind" the poem's words and symbols or "beneath" the patient's report of a dream or of a life event. Instead (or perhaps more accurately, in addition), he attempts to listen to the sound and feel of "what's going on", to the "music of what happens". This is achieved to significant degree in the analytic setting by means of the analyst's attending to his own reverie experience.

> There are the mud-flowers of dialect
> And the immortelles of perfect pitch

Reproduced, with permission, from *International Journal of Psychoanalysis, 80*: 979–94 (1999). © Institute of Psychoanalysis, London.

And that moment when the bird sings very close
To the music of what happens.
(Heaney, "Song", 1979)

In this paper I will be asking the reader to do a somewhat different sort of work from that which other analytic writers and I usually ask of the reader. In the course of this discussion, I will ask the reader to listen to his or her listening, that is, to listen to the ways he or she listens and hears me listening to an analytic session. I will try to stay out of the reader's way as he or she does this work and only at the end of the paper will I offer some thoughts about what I currently think listening to and saying a poem have to do with listening to and speaking with a patient in analysis.

Before turning to Frost's (1928a) "Acquainted with the night" and to a session from the twelfth year of an analysis, I will make a few introductory comments. Over the course of the past fifty years, there have been a number of important shifts in the theory and practice of psychoanalysis. Among them is an increasing awareness that the most interesting and productive avenues of analytic enquiry seem no longer to be adequately addressed by the question, "What does that mean?"—that symptom, that set of dream images, that acting out, that rageful response to the sound of the analyst's coughing, and so on. An enquiry into personal meanings has become inseparable from an understanding of the unconscious intersubjective context in which those meanings are generated. Consequently, the question "What does that mean?" has gradually expanded in such a way as greatly to increase emphasis on such questions as: "What's going on here?" "What's happening between us consciously and uncon-sciously and how does that relate to other aspects of the patient's (and the analyst's) past and present experience, both real and imagined?" With this shift in our conception of the analytic process comes the need for a commensurate change in the way we use language to speak to ourselves and to our patients. It seems to me important that we develop a capacity to use language that does justice not only to the task of understanding and interpreting the conscious and unconscious meanings of our patients' experiences, but also, our use of language must be equal to the task of capturing and conveying in words a sense of what it is "that's going on here" in the intrapsychic and intersubjective life of the analysis, the "music of what happens" in the analytic relationship.

This paper is offered as a contribution both to the understanding of the shift I have mentioned in our understanding of the nature of the analytic process and to the development of our capacity to use language in a way that is adequate to that shift. In the course of this paper, I will look at the ways in which a poem grapples (often with great success) with the challenge of getting into the language the full richness, complexity, and movement of living human experience. (See Ogden, 1997a–e; 1998, for previous contributions to the exploration of the use of language in psychoanalysis.)

In what follows, I will not be offering an analytic interpretation of a poem, nor will I attempt to provide a piece of criticism that treats the analytic session as a literary "text". To do so would be to sap the vitality from both the poem and the experience in analysis. Instead, I will address the experience of the Frost poem and the analytic experience each in its own terms. I have made no conscious effort to select a poem that "fits with" or "speaks to" the aspects of human experience that are most alive in the analytic session or vice versa. I urge the reader to read the Frost poem aloud several times before proceeding to my discussion. Frost's best poems come to life through the play of the sounds and meanings of the words and the feel of the words in our mouths as we "say the lines" (Frost, 1962, p. 911).

While there has been some discussion in the analytic literature concerning aspects of the relationship between poetry and psycho-analysis (for example, Edelson, 1975; Hutter, 1982; Jones, 1997; Martin, 1983; Meares, 1993), as far as I have been able to determine, there has been to this point no contribution to either the literary or the analytic literature that has undertaken to offer a close reading of a poem, a detailed description of an analytic session, and some thoughts about what the two have to do with one another.

"Acquainted with the night"

When "Acquainted with the night" was published in 1928, Frost was in his early fifties and already had achieved extensive recognition as a poet, not only in the USA, but also in Europe. Frost and his family, however, were in a state of exhaustion brought on in large part by Frost's frequent travelling for purposes of reading and lecturing and from the many moves that the family had made (from New

Hampshire to New England to Massachusetts to Michigan and back again to New England) as Frost pursued his ambition to be not only one of the "great poets", but also a widely read poet. When this poem was written, Frost's wife, Elinor, and their children were in poor health, their daughter Marjorie seriously ill. Frost's third child had died a decade earlier only three days after her birth.

Acquainted with the night

I have been one acquainted with the night.
I have walked out in rain—and back in rain.
I have outwalked the furthest city light.

I have looked down the saddest city lane.
I have passed by the watchman on his beat.
And dropped my eyes, unwilling to explain.

I have stood still and stopped the sound of feet
When far away an interrupted cry
Came over houses from another street,

But not to call me back or say good-by;
And further still at an unearthly height,
One luminary clock against the sky

Proclaimed the time was neither wrong nor right.
I have been one acquainted with the night.

The opening line, an apparently simple sentence, is remarkable for the complexity, subtlety, and self-sufficiency of the language. It is not at all apparent how to read this line. Depending on where the reader places the emphasis in the words "I have been one", a different "sentence-sound" (Frost, 1914, p. 675) is made, each with its own meaning. The line, as I have lived with it and struggled with it, seems to me to be most enigmatically alive when one says it with equal lack of stress on any one of its words. The enormity of the force of the restraint of the language of this first line is palpable and sets the tone for the rest of the poem.

Even the syntax (which is "the nerve and bone structure of language" [Steiner, 1989, p. 159]) of the first sentence contributes to its sombre vitality: grammar is pushed to its limit, is unobtrusively

broken just a bit, and is newly created. It is as if the structure of
language itself is unable to contain "some strange resistance within
itself . . . As if regret were in it and were sacred" (to borrow from
Frost's [1928b] "West-running brook"). The "grammatically correct"
form of the first line would read: "I am one who has been acquainted
with the night". A new grammar (both broken and newly made) is
required that dissolves the immediacy of "I" (or "I am" or "I am one")
in the present, and instead creates an unlocalizable past that is
present and a present that is somehow already past: "I have been
one"—and still am? Or have been until recently? Or used to be, but
am uncertain about whether I am now?

The sounds and rhythms of the first six lines of the poem
are mesmerizing and are inseparable from the connective tissue of
the overarching metaphor of the poem: the poem as a walk. The
poem is not a poem about a walk: the poem is a walk. The alternating
unstressed and stressed syllables of the iambic metre[1] all but
disappear into the larger two-stride "sentence-sounds" of walking-
and-breathing-and-thinking-while-walking. The speaking voice
naturally breaks the sentences into two parts:

I have been one . . . acquainted with the night.
I have walked out in rain . . . and back in rain.
I have outwalked . . . the furthest city light.
I have looked down . . . the saddest city lane.

This "walking poem" (in a style reminiscent of the "walking poems"
of Dante and Wordsworth) manages to get into the language what
it sounds like and feels like to be alone, talking to oneself "in one's
head" and in one's body (in the sensations and rhythms of breathing
and walking and being). The sound of the voice in this poem is not
the sound of story-telling or of the narration of experience; it is
a sound that is as close as I have encountered in any poem to the
background sound of being.

The voice in the first two stanzas manages to encompass not only
sadness and loneliness, but also irony and a dark humour, that seem
to protect the poem and the poet from the embarrassment of
excessive earnestness of voice.[2] There is pleasure taken (and perhaps
shelter found) in playing with words: "walked out" in line 2 becomes
"outwalked" in line 3. The walked is both "in rain" and "reined in".

"Looked down" in line 5 carries a double meaning of seeing (experiencing) the sadness in the city lane/line and at the same time, the sense of defeating (looking down) the sadness in a battle of I's/eyes (eyes locked in a struggle that ends when one or the other turns away, averts his gaze).

Frost seems unable to resist the mischievous use of the phrase "And dropped my eyes" ("I's") at the beginning of line 6, the only line in the first two stanzas to begin with a word other than "I". At the same time, this phrase "dropped my eyes" is part of one of the most desolate, and yet thoroughly matter-of-fact, moments in the poem:

> I have passed by the watchman on his beat.
> And dropped my eyes, unwilling to explain.

The speaker is not only unwilling to explain, he is unable to explain. The poem itself is what stands in the place of an explanation.

A subtle shift occurs in line 7, which is felt largely through the disruption of the sound and rhythm of this walking-and-thinking-and-breathing poem: "I have stood still and stopped the sound of feet". The words "stood still and stopped the sound of feet" require that the voice pause after "still" and "stopped" and finally come to a halt mid-sentence at the end of the line. This stopping of the sound of feet (both anatomical and metrical feet) at the end of line 7 is achieved without the help of a period, a semi-colon, or even a comma: for a moment words cease; the rhythm of walking ceases; the sounds of thinking and breathing cease.

> I have stood still and stopped the sound of feet
> When far away an interrupted cry
> Came over houses from another street,
>
> But not to call me back or say good-by;

Out of the silence comes an interrupted cry, which has a disturbing, uncompromising otherness to it. It is not a cry intended for the ears of the speaker, but it is nonetheless a sound that changes him, becomes a part of him, as it seems to give voice to inarticulate feeling. The word "interrupted" (both harrowing and utterly indifferent) is for me the most unexpected and newly made word in the poem. (What is an interrupted cry?) The sound of the word "interrupted" itself interrupts the more flowing phrase that immediately precedes it ("And far away") and the one that follows ("Came over houses from another street").

In this part of the poem (lines 7–10), the experience of being acquainted with the night gathers into itself new sounds and meaning. The soft rhyming of "night" (in the title and in the first line) and "not" in line 10 ("But not to call me back or say good-by") unobtrusively links the two. Being acquainted with the night is becoming an experience of being "acquainted with the not": the "not" of the empty space, the interruption in the middle of the cry; the "not" of the force disrupting the rhythm of the poem; the "not" that is the "strange resistance" that will not be reined in by the rules of grammar and the laws of time; the "not" of the "I"/eye that is dropped and refuses to see or to be seen. But at the same time, the "not" that is being created in this poem is the "not" of imaginative possibility, a space in which something new, something never before heard (the poem itself) comes into being. The not/night of this poem has a reticence about it; the reader will be allowed to glimpse it, hear it fleetingly (in the interruption of the cry and of the rhythm of the words), but the reader will only know/no it as an acquaintance, never as a friend.

The poem concludes in a surprising way:

And further still at an unearthly height,
One luminary clock against the sky

Proclaimed the time was neither wrong nor right.

I have been one acquainted with the night.

The final four lines of the poem are mystifying, and more than any other part of the poem, defy paraphrase. The speaker in these lines seems to marvel at the vast indifference and vast beauty of the night sky. He seems no longer to ask or to expect that the sounds of the night should acknowledge his presence ("to call me back or say good-by"). But at the same time the language is doing something quite different. The poem in these lines personifies, makes human, the "luminary clock against the sky" (a clock-tower as metaphor for the moon or vice versa?), which talks (proclaims) to him (or is it proclaiming to nothing but the night sky?). And what the luminary clock momentously proclaims is the lack of moment, the lack of significance of the temporal movement, rhythms, and punctuations of life ("the time is neither wrong nor right"). Moreover, the proclamation is delivered not in a hard, mechanical cadence, but in the very human, softly flowing rhythms of what Frost describes as the "living sounds of speech" (Frost, 1915, p. 687).

The "I" that begins the final line is a very different "I" from the "I" that began the poem. It is an "I" that has earned the right to say "I have been one acquainted with the night", I have been one acquainted with the sound of solitary walking-thinking-breathing-being, acquainted with feelings of sadness and remorse and shame that cannot be explained, acquainted with the loneliness and unexpected curiosity stirred by the sound of an interrupted cry, acquainted with the feeling of humility and wonder engendered not only by the indifference of the night, but also by the way in which that strange inhuman otherness is created in language that is derived from and saturated with the uniquely human living sounds of speech.

All of this, all that the poem is, is unobtrusively gathered together into the sound of the word "night", which is the final sound of the poem. I say final sound and not final word because "night" sets in motion cascading resonances and disruptions of sound (largely through a variety of forms of rhyming) from every part of the poem. In addition to the rhyming of the final word/sound "night" with the "I" that opens the poem (and the six that follow), there are a half-dozen line-ending rhymes with "night", several internal rhymes (by, eyes, neither, time), as well as a number of soft internal rhymes (for example, night/not/nor). These echoes continue to reverberate in one's ear long after the final word is said. In this poem of cycles, of endings that are beginnings, there can be no final word.

An analytic session

From my consulting room I could hear Ms S, a woman in her late thirties, close the door to the bathroom in my office suite. In the twelve years that we had been working together in a five-session-per-week analysis, it was only in the previous year or so that Ms S had begun occasionally to use the office bathroom. As I waited for her, I recalled an event that had occurred five or six years earlier when on leaving the bathroom, Ms S had realized that she had failed to button some of the many buttons on her trousers. In reality, there was no danger of them falling down, but she experienced intense feelings of embarrassment when she noticed the unfastened buttons. I remembered having suggested to Ms S that she might have felt that the bathroom was a place where both she and I were undressed (although at different times) and it may have felt as if we had been undressed together in that small room. My interpretation seemed heavy-handed and formulaic in retrospect. This "bathroom incident" was followed by several months of profound emotional withdrawal on the part of the patient. At that time, I was practising at a different office building. I recalled, more in visceral sensation than in visual imagery, what it felt like when the office next to mine was occupied by my closest friend, J, and how empty that building had felt when her office was rented to someone else after her death.

These thoughts and feelings, which began as I heard the bathroom door close, left me feeling diffusely anxious. When I met Ms S in the waiting room, there was an unexpected and uncomfortable formality about it.

Once in the consulting room and on the couch, Ms S began without a pause to tell me that she had had a dream the previous night that she was looking forward to telling me. She said that it was an unusual dream in that it was about the two of us and a friend of hers and not about female students of mine. (For years she had imagined that my students were far more interesting and likable to me than she was.) The dream seemed to her to be a very important one.

In the dream, *your office has very white walls. You have a collection of ten statues in the closet behind your chair. You've had them there all along, but you've never known quite what to do with them. It's you, but you don't look like you. Each of the statues is a talisman. One represents Victory and another Courage. I forget what the others represented. You've taken them out over the years. My friend, R, is there and I'm glad that the two of you are meeting one another. She tells you a story of my swimming in an ice-covered lake. There is a really nice feeling in listening to her tell you the story. I laugh and say, "I wouldn't do that now." You take out a statue which has real green grass growing in it. I think it's a woman cooking, a woman making things. I forget what happens next, but at the end, R and I leave the office. In the dream I think that this is my lot in life . . . I will have friends, but not a love relationship with a man. I've begun to accept being alone . . . I know how difficult I am to be with.*

I was struck by the simple directness of the dream. Things of significance were being taken out of hiding. Feelings were being accurately named. Her practice of swimming in an ice-covered lake, which was portrayed (rather optimistically I thought) as a thing of the past, seemed to refer to the patient's chronic state of psychological detachment in which she is unable to know what she thinks or feels or experiences in her body. Ms S had relied heavily on histrionic imitations of feeling and on efforts to elicit feelings of anger from me by means of endless provocations. Her ability to get me angry would momentarily relieve her profound feelings of psychological deadness. The naming of the statues in the dream reminded me of the fact that the patient's mother, who was twenty years old when she gave birth to Ms S, was so ambivalent about having a baby that she was unable or unwilling to give the patient a name for almost a month after her birth.

After telling me the dream, Ms S said that she missed the excitement of expecting magic from me each time she came to her sessions. (She was referring to her previously unconscious wishes that "the treatment" would involve my giving her my thoughts [in fantasy, parts of my vitality and sense of self], which would magically transform her into a person who felt alive, albeit, with my feelings.) She told me that in the dream *the statues did not feel like magic charms that would give her victory or courage or anything else. They were interesting pieces, particularly the one with the grass growing in it*. She said that that statue gave her the feeling that, unlike the other statues, it was not an object "left over from some ritual performed by an extinct culture"; rather, it felt like "part of an event that never stopped happening and is still happening". She said that she had the thought as she was telling me the dream that I might have been awarded the statues for achievements in my life. But the thing that felt new about the dream was the fact that she did not get stuck, as she often has, in making a story in which she is the outsider trying to steal my life, my achievements, my family, and my friends. She said that in this dream, although there was a sense of her being resigned to being alone for the rest of her life, she did at least bring her own friend and her own interests and curiosity.

While the patient was talking to me about her dream, I was feeling quite off-balance not knowing what to make of what was happening in the hour. Ms S seemed to be making analytic use of her dream, but it seemed to me quite possible that she was being compliant in coming up with what might have felt to her like "the right answer" (i.e. my answer) to the dream. I felt that there was a good deal in the dream that I could comment on. For instance, the statue of the woman with grass growing in it might allude to the patient's increasing sense of her own fertility, her own ability to make things with her mind (perhaps even our imaginary baby), as well as an enhanced sense of groundedness in her own femininity. This and several other possible interpretations that went through my mind felt flat to me and so I remained silent rather than saying something for the sake of saying it. I found my mind wandering to thoughts about a patient whom I would be seeing later in the day. That patient had been in a great deal of pain and turmoil at the end of our most recent session. I felt concerned about her and eager to hear how she was feeling.

Ms S went on to describe more fully the feeling of hopelessness that she experienced at the end of her dream. She then told me that for several weeks she had been extremely frightened of driving in the rain because she could not see clearly despite the fact that she had twice changed her windscreen-wiper blades. She had been afraid that she would be killed in a "head-on collision". (This brought to mind for me the fact that the patient's father, before Ms S was born, had been in a very serious car accident. He had been chronically depressed up to that point, but the accident seemed to exacerbate the depression. From very early on in her life, Ms S felt that she had served as her father's confidante and [in unconscious fantasy] his therapist, his mother, and his wife.) The morning of the session under discussion, the patient had been told by her car mechanic that her windscreen had opacified slightly and needed to be replaced. I began without being aware of it to think about the fact that the elder of my two sons, who was living in New York City at that time, would be coming home for a visit in a few days. I was very much looking forward to seeing him and was going over in my mind the details of the arrival time of his flight and the need to tell him that I would meet him at the baggage claim area. Despite the fact that we had for years met at the baggage claim area when he came to visit, I felt at that moment in the session a great sense of urgency to remind him. I felt put upon by him, which seemed odd to me. I realized that my disgruntlement with my son disguised my fear of not finding him or of my getting lost. I also realized that the fluorescent lighting of the airport that I was picturing was associated with my visceral memory of feelings of sadness, emptiness, and fear as I had waited in the airport late one night several years earlier for a flight to New York to visit my father who was gravely ill and hospitalized.

As I refocused my attention on Ms S, my partial understanding of the reveries that were occupying me (particularly my irrational annoyance with my elder son) led me to be more consciously aware of the sourness and disguised fearfulness that I was experiencing at that moment and, in retrospect, had been feeling throughout the session. I think it was my tone of voice more than the content of my interventions that conveyed the emotional change that I was undergoing as a consequence of my increased self-awareness.

A little later in the hour, Ms S said that even though she was feeling that she had a place here in my office today and had even used the office bathroom, she had felt that when I met her in the waiting room, I seemed surprised that it was she who was there. I was quite startled by the simple straightforwardness of the patient's observation. I had the somewhat disturbing feeling that for quite some time in this session, and probably in previous sessions, the patient had been "ahead of me": she was looking forwards (through her windscreen and looking forward to telling me her dream) while I was looking backwards (to the "bathroom incident" of a half-dozen years earlier and to the death of a friend). What had previously been for me intellectualized ideas and subliminal feelings and images, now began to take on a stark clarity and emotional immediacy. My thoughts and feelings about the trip East to visit my father became an "analytic object" of a different sort at this juncture. I recalled crossing the street at night in the bitter January cold of New York City with my wife and sons after having visited my father in the hospital. My elder son was seventeen years old at that time and was only a year away from going to college. I had been aware of the intense sadness that I had been feeling about the approach of the time when he would be leaving home, but until that moment in the session with Ms S, I had not been as fully aware that during that trip East I had been experiencing his leaving as if it were he (and I) who were dying, and not my father.

Despite the fact that it has required much time and many words to describe this reverie experience, these thoughts, feelings, images, and sensations occupied only a short period of time in the session. Ms S went on to say that she had made a decision as she entered my office today not to fold up and put under her head the blanket (which I keep at the foot of the couch) as she had done for the previous month or so: "When I put the blanket on top of the pillow [to remedy back pain], my voice comes from my throat. My voice is fuller and comes from my chest when I don't use the blanket to prop up my head. I wanted to see today what would happen if I didn't use the blanket in that way. As I'm talking about this, I'm so curious about whether you noticed the change. It's only what you think or see or feel that counts. Why do I still need that from you?" This question was followed by a silence of about a minute. I then said to the patient that I thought that she had been feeling great pride and excitement about hearing the fullness of her voice and the richness of her mind in being able to dream a mysterious and interesting dream and to think creatively about it. I added that I thought that she had noticed with disappointment that she had interrupted herself as she began to feel that I was the only one in the room who had a mind and that it was crucial that she get me to give her my thoughts. Ms S replied that she had been aware of feeling anxious as she was telling me earlier in the session that she enjoyed thinking and speaking in a way that felt creative to her. She said that even though she had been aware of what she was doing, she could not stop herself from turning to me in the way that she had. I suggested that she might be afraid that if she were to feel that she has become a person in her own right, and not simply a carrier of parts of me, it would mean not only that the analysis would come to an end, but that we would lose all connection with one another in an absolute way, almost as if one or the other of us had died. (I was thinking not only of the feeling in my reverie that my elder son's growing up was equivalent to his dying and to my feeling utterly lost, but also of the reverie involving my experience of the absence in my life [the empty office] following J's death. Also in my mind was the patient's fear of being killed in a "head-on" collision [a fatal collision perhaps in fantasy resulting from her having her "head on", that is, from her being able to think and feel her own thoughts and feelings].)

Ms S cried and after several minutes said that what she was feeling now was gratitude to me for having talked to her in the way that I had and for her ability to talk to me in the way that she had today.

She said that she did not want to say more because she was afraid of crowding out what she was feeling with space-filling words.

The patient and I were silent for the final few minutes of the hour. In that time I experienced a quiet feeling of love for Ms S of a sort that I had never previously experienced with her. It was a love that had a sadness about it. I became aware in the course of the silence that I felt appreciative of the unconscious effort on the part of Ms S in this session to teach me (by showing me) about the struggle in which both of us were engaged to live with the sadness and loss and pride and excitement and sheer inevitability of movement towards separateness that is inherent in growing up and becoming a person in one's own right.

The patient began the following meeting by saying, "I've never met anyone like you before." I laughed and Ms S joined me in this laughter. The laughter felt full of affection, as well as having a sense of comic relief, as the two of us looked at ourselves (as if from a distance) after a very long period of strenuously and earnestly toiling with (and at times against) one another. I said, "Maybe you felt that you met me for the first time in yesterday's session. Meeting me in that way is not the same as having a meeting with me."

In the weeks that followed, we talked about the idea/feeling that you can't leave a place you haven't been to. It was only after Ms S had met me that there was the possibility of her ever considering leaving me.

Discussion

Space does not permit a detailed discussion of the moment-to-moment movement of the analytic process in the clinical material just presented. In what follows, I will limit my focus primarily to a discussion of the ways in which I made use of overlapping states of reverie of analyst and analysand in an effort to "catch the drift" (Freud, 1923, p. 239) of the leading edge of anxiety in the transference–countertransference and to make use of this understanding in the formulation of transference interpretations and other interventions.

I will use the term "reverie" (Bion, 1962) to refer to the analyst's (or the analysand's) daydreams, fantasies, ruminations, bodily sensations, and so on, which I view as representing derivatives of unconscious intersubjective constructions that are jointly, but asymmetrically, generated by the analytic pair. These intersubjective constructions, which I have termed "the analytic third" (Ogden, 1994a; 1994b; 1995; 1996a; 1996b; 1997c; 1997d; 1997e), are a principal medium through which the unconscious of the analysand is brought to life in the analytic relationship. Almost always, the analyst's reveries initially seem to him to represent his own mundane, idiosyncratic everyday concerns, fantasies, ruminations, memories, bodily sensations, and so on, which have little, if anything, to do with the patient. In fact, the analyst's reveries regularly feel to him to be distractions and preoccupations ("his own stuff") that reflect the ways in which he is not being an analyst at that moment, i.e. the ways in which he is not giving focused attention to what the patient is saying and doing.

The session (and the beginning of the subsequent session) that I have presented began when I heard the bathroom door close behind Ms S. My reverie concerning the "bathroom incident" seems in retrospect to have reflected my unconscious wish to view the patient and the analytic relationship as if Ms S, and my relationship with her, had remained timelessly suspended in that earlier period. The experience of this reverie, which included a sense of profound absence in my life resulting from J's death, left me diffusely anxious and contributed to my feelings of woodenness when I met Ms S in the waiting room.

The dream that the patient presented at the beginning of the hour (again in retrospect) seems to have involved a sense of several important ways in which Ms S had changed in the course of analysis: she no longer swims in an ice-covered lake, that is, she no longer lives in a frozen state of autistic encapsulation—"I wouldn't do that now". Instead of being perpetually engaged in a futile effort to steal life parasitically from me in order to compensate for her own feelings of deadness, she had developed, to a significant degree, a capacity to be fertile and to make things (the living green grass) that felt real and alive to her. There was also in the dream a feeling that the patient was beginning to feel prepared to consider the possibility of the end of the analysis (suggested by her leaving me in my office at the end of the dream).

My response to the dream as Ms S was telling it to me was in part to appreciate its simple directness. However, despite the patient's capacity to be interested in and curious about her dream and her ability to make analytic use of it (for instance, in her comments about the ways in which she no longer felt single-mindedly intent on getting me magically to transform her), the possible interpretations of the dream that occurred to me felt hackneyed and emotionally flat. As I look back on this moment in the session, I seemed to have felt anxious about acknowledging that the patient had matured psychologically in the course of the analysis and that she was trying to tell me that she was for the first time daring to imagine leaving me (albeit with sadness and disappointment).

As the patient was talking about her feelings about the dream, my own thoughts turned to a patient who clearly needed me and who was hardly at all concerned with the eventual termination of her analysis. In this displacement, I was (unconsciously) longing to return to a time in the past when Ms S needed me in a more primitive and desperate way than she currently depended upon me.

Although I was unable to hear it at the time, Ms S's fears about the opacified windscreen seemed to have reflected her ambivalence about looking ahead. At that point in the session, I began to ruminate anxiously about meeting my elder son at the airport and felt (irrationally) burdened by the task of having to remind him where we would meet. I also experienced fleetingly (more in the form of a subliminal image than a narrative) a combination of fear, sadness, loneliness, and emptiness as I remembered the night that I waited for a plane at the airport to visit my father when he was very ill.

As my focused attention returned to Ms S, the combined effect of the reverie experiences that I have described led to an increasing awareness of the anger, sourness, and disgruntlement that I had unconsciously been feeling towards Ms S throughout the session. I also became aware that the anger served to protect me against feelings of fearfulness and sadness.

My own increased self-awareness and partial understanding of what was occurring, was, I think, conveyed to the patient by my tone of voice more than by the content of what I said (my "tone of meaning but without the words", Frost, 1942). The patient, somewhat later in the session, was able to tell me that I seemed not to have expected to see her when I met her in the waiting room. Her comment startled me and helped me to consolidate my conscious and subliminal reverie experiences. I became much more fully aware of the way in which I had been unconsciously holding on to the past relationship with the patient while she was (ambivalently) attempting to look forward to her maturity, fertility, and independence. The patient's observation led to an enrichment of my own reverie experience, which in turn enhanced my ability to be more fully present with the patient. I "recalled" a moment of understanding that had occurred years earlier, but nonetheless was in a sense occurring for the first time in the session with Ms S. I (re-)experienced that moment of recognition in which I realized that it was my father, and not my elder son or I, who was dying. My son was growing up and leaving home (leaving me), but this was for both of us a form of being alive (a form of life that was full of sadness and feelings of loss as well as a sense of pride, excitement, and possibility) and not a form of deadness.

The links between these understandings and what had been occurring in the session with Ms S now felt palpably real and immediate. Ms S spoke about feeling that she was speaking with a fuller voice because she had decided not to prop up her head with my blanket (that is, not to use me to prop herself up in a way that made her voice and her sense of self sound and feel thin and insubstantial). However, Ms S then found herself slipping back into a feeling that she needed parts of me with which to make up for missing parts of herself.

Speaking from (but not about) my reverie experiences, in conjunction with the rest of what I understood about what had been happening during the hour, I spoke with Ms S at the end of the meeting about her fear that having a mind and a voice and a life of her own would result in an end to the relationship with me that would feel so absolute as to feel like one or the other of us had died. The session ended with the patient's expression of gratitude that the two of us had been able to think and talk to one another in the way that we had. Not wanting to supplant a feeling that felt real with space-filling words, Ms S was silent for the final few minutes of the hour. During that silence I felt a form of love and sadness that I had not previously experienced with Ms S.

In a sense, the session ended and became the beginning of something new in the opening moments of the following day's session when Ms S said, "I've never met anyone like you before." I experienced her comment as both humorous and rich with wonderful ambiguities. After we laughed together, without planning to do so I said to Ms S that I thought she must have felt that she had met me for the first time in the previous day's session. I added that meeting me in the way that she had is not the same as having a meeting with me. There had been very little playfulness in the analysis up until this point and so it was a new and welcome experience to both Ms S and to me to find ourselves taking pleasure in spontaneous play with words and feelings and ideas.

Afterwords

In this final section, I will offer some specific comments about what, to my mind and to my ear, the experience of saying and responding to "Acquainted with the night" has to do with the experience of listening to and speaking with Ms S in the analytic session that I have presented. Before beginning that discussion, however, it is important to make explicit the context for the comparison of the use of language in poetry and in psychoanalysis that I will offer. A critical divide separates the two activities: psychoanalysis is a therapeutic activity while reading and writing poetry are aesthetic activities. An attempt to draw one-to-one correspondences between the two, represents, I believe, a form of reductionism that obscures and distorts the essence of these two quite different human events.

Analysts attempt (with varying degrees of success) to use language in the service of communicating with the patient in a way that is maximally utilizable by the patient in his (always ambivalent) efforts to achieve emotional growth. For the analyst, the attempt to achieve aliveness in his use of language is in the service of bringing feelings and ideas to life in words that will advance the analytic process. A conscious or unconscious effort on the part of the analyst to be "poetic" (that is, to create beautiful, pithy, artistic forms with words) in his patterns of speech and choice of words in the analytic dialogue almost certainly reflects a form of narcissistic countertransference acting in. Such acting in will severely impede, if not destroy, the analytic process unless the analyst is able to recognize what he is doing, and subject his thoughts, feelings, bodily sensations, and behaviour to analytic scrutiny. The poet, on the other hand, is answerable only to the art that he is attempting to create. His failures are lines that lack vitality and imagination and are devoid of feeling.

In the work with Ms S, I was attempting to listen and to be attentive not only to what Ms S was talking about, but also to the effects created by the way she and I were using language. This way of attending to language determined to a large degree the forms and qualities of my ways of being and talking with Ms S, that is, my "analytic technique" (a very dry-sounding name for a very lively thing). In the session described I attempted not simply to "translate" what Ms S was saying by making interpretations in the following form: "Your feeling at the end of the dream of being resigned to spending the rest of your life without a love relationship with a man represents your unconscious disappointment and anger about the fact that you feel that you and I will never have a romantic relationship." I am aware that this interpretation is heavy-handed, but what I am attempting to focus on here is an interpretive posture that treats the patient's words and sentences, images and ideas, excessively like symbols to be seen through and presented to the patient.[3] Such an approach to the language of interpretation (either of a poem or of analytic experience) presupposes that feelings and ideas are there "behind" the repression barrier "in the unconscious" waiting to be mined (brought to mind) and exposed to the light of day, brought into the light of conscious attention and secondary-process thinking. When I speak of "translating" or "decoding" symbols, I am referring to a rather mechanical form of listening to patients that involves a unidirectional movement from symbol to symbolized, manifest to latent, conscious to unconscious, as opposed to a form of listening that is responsive to the rich reverberations of sound and multi-layered meanings that lie at the heart of both poetry and psychoanalysis. Of course, all interpretation of verbal symbols and the emotional context in which they are created involves, in one form or another, a search for a meaning/content that is unspoken and perhaps unspeakable. In this sense, all interpretive listening involves to some degree "listening through" the language. I am suggesting, however, that interpretation becomes dryly explanatory ("this means that") when the emphasis on the "listening through language" is excessive. Moreover, I believe that the unspoken and the unspeakable are present (sometimes in their absence) in the language that is spoken, in the manner in which it is spoken, in the sounds of the words and sentences, in the feelings elicited in the listener, and (in the analytic setting) in the behaviour and bodily sensations that accompany what is being said.

In the analytic session presented, I made use of a set of reveries that at first were only subliminally available to me (more sensation than thought). I treated my reveries neither as distractions from the "real" work of analysis nor as packets of pure unconscious meaning. Rather, I treated my reverie experiences (to the degree I was able to achieve and maintain awareness of them) as an indirect (association-al) method of talking to myself about what was occurring uncon-sciously between Ms S and me. This way of approaching reverie experience reflects a perspective that does not view the unconscious as residing behind my reveries or at the end of a chain of reverie associations, but as coming to life in the movement of feeling, thought, imagery, and language of the reverie experience itself.

It is necessary at some point for the analyst to recast his reveries into a more highly organized, verbally symbolized form of talking to himself (and eventually to the patient) about the affective meaning of the reverie experience as it pertains to and is derived from what is going on at an unconscious level in the transference–countertransference. This act of bringing one's experience into a verbally symbolized form is not a necessary part of saying poems. At times, the reader might find it useful and interesting to attempt to talk to himself about what is going on in the language of the poem (as I have done in my discussion of the Frost poem), but the reader of a poem may prefer to allow the poem to remain in the form of a predominantly sensory experience that need not and perhaps cannot be transformed into a verbally symbolized response to the poem. In fact, the impossibility of doing justice to a poem in one's efforts to paraphrase it reflects something of what goes into our distinguishing poetry from other forms of imaginative use of words (for example, in novels and short stories where plot and character development carry far greater significance than they do in lyric poetry).

Towards the end of the analytic session that I have presented, on the basis of my (always tentative) understanding of my reverie experience, I said to Ms S that I thought that at that moment growing up felt both dangerous and exciting to her. It seemed that the independence involved in being an adult felt to her as if it necessarily brought with it the end of all connection with me, a disruption that felt as absolute as the death of one or the other of us. In saying this, I was not telling Ms S what she really felt, or what lay under or at the back of what she thought she felt. Rather, I was making use of metaphorical language in an effort to draw one aspect of her experience into relation to another in a way that created something new: a way of seeing and experiencing herself that had not previously existed.[4]

Just as my listening to Ms S did not primarily involve an effort to get "behind" what she was saying (in the sense described above), my way of listening to the Frost poem was not most fundamentally an act of "translating" or "decoding" symbols. For example, I was approaching the poem in a way that was cognizant that the night at times seemed to serve as a representation of the darkness of despair and at other times seemed to represent the mysteriousness of the vast otherness that surrounds us and of which we are a part. But in the reading of "Acquainted with the night" that I presented, I was primarily engaged in an effort to listen to the sound and feel of what the language was doing as I said the lines. For example, in the final four lines of the poem, the language gracefully, celestially keeps turning in on itself in a way that seems to have no end. Even as the speaker seems to be marvelling at the vast, nonhuman otherness of the night sky, the language is doing something quite different in personifying (making human) the "luminary clock against the sky", which speaks (proclaims) the arbitrariness of time while the language of the proclamation (the poem itself) is alive with the very human, very beautiful rhythms and cadences of "the living sounds of speech". The beauty and mystery of the human and the nonhuman weave in and out of one another like the sides of a Möbius strip.

It seems to me that one of the most fundamental similarities between Frost's "Acquainted with the night" and the fragment of the analysis of Ms S is the way each achieves its emotional force through what Frost called "feats of association" (quoted by Pritchard, 1994, p. 9). In other words, both the poem and the analytic session generate powerful resonances and cacophonies of sound and meaning. I have discussed how in the Frost poem the final word/ sound, "night", gathers into itself, through resonances of sound and sense, all that the poem is, all of its exquisitely beautiful sounds and all of its aridity, all of its flowing, ethereal parts ("One luminary clock against the sky") and all of its disrupted parts where the ear "stands still" in sadness and in wonder when "an interrupted cry/Came over houses from another street".[5]

Ms S's comment, "I've never met anyone like you before," is no less alive in its associative richness than is the interrupted cry in the Frost poem. Her statement set in motion remarkable feats of conscious and unconscious association that in so many ways drew upon what was most alive in the current moment and in the preceding session and made of all of it something new through her use of language. (See Boyer, 1988, for a discussion of the relationship between unresolved transference–countertransference feelings in one analytic session and the opening moments of the subsequent meeting.)

Italo Calvino (1986) has commented that the rhyming of words in poetry has an equivalent in prose narrative where "there are events that rhyme". I would add that in the analytic setting, there are conscious and unconscious feelings, thoughts and other intrapsychic and intersubjective events that rhyme, "that echo each other" (p. 35). For example, Ms S's word/idea/sound "met" had lively connection with ("rhymed with") her observation (in the previous session) that when I met her in the waiting room, she felt that it was not she whom I expected to meet. Ms S's dream involved a "meeting": a friend of hers (perhaps an aspect of herself) met me for the first time and made a comment that caused the patient to laugh in a good-natured way that felt to me closely associated with the laughter at the beginning of the following session. In addition, Ms S's comment about meeting me held an important resonance with still another "meeting", the imaginary meeting with my son in my reverie in which he and I would be meeting at the airport as if we had never met there before. These reverberations were not sequential, but instantaneous and generated a comically poignant moment in which both Ms S and I experienced an intensified sense of being present together (but as separate people) in that moment.

This "rhyming" of the word/idea "met" in these different forms of the experience of meeting made for a rich and lively ambiguity and expressiveness. Ms S's highly compact statement suggested that she was meeting me in the sense of seeing me, knowing me as a separate person for the first time; that she was meeting me in the sense of being equal to me (able to meet the force of my presence); that she was meeting me in the sense of making a rendezvous with me, perhaps a romantic meeting. Her comment conveyed in an instant all of these feelings/meanings and more.[6]

The sound of Ms S's voice assured that the "like you" in "I've never met anyone like you before" conveyed tender feelings of fondness for me (of "liking me") and not simply a comparison of me with other people whom she had met.

And then there is the word "be", unobtrusively tucked into "before", which brings the experience of being to the fore. Ms S was in an important sense bringing herself into being in the course of developing a voice of her own with which to speak.

I have rarely received a more loving and interesting gift than the one Ms S gave me wrapped in the words "I've never met anyone like you before".

Perhaps what is most fundamental to both poetry and psychoanalysis is the effort to enlarge the breadth and depth of what we are able to experience. It seems to me that both poetry and psychoanalysis at their best use language in a way that encompasses a full range of human experience from "the most awful and the most nearly unbearable parts to the most tender, subtle, and loving parts, a distance so great". Both poetry and psychoanalysis endeavour to "include, connect, and make humanly understandable or humanly unununderstandable so much" (Jarrell, 1955, p. 62, speaking of Frost's poetry).

The movement of sounds and cadences of loneliness and sadness and possibility in "Acquainted with the night" and the movement of feelings of anger, fear, sadness, disappointment, and love in the session presented from the analysis of Ms S, represent efforts to generate experiences in which poet and reader, analyst and analysand, might become more fully capable of living with, of remaining alive to, the full range and complexity of human experience, even in the face of "humanly understandable" conscious and unconscious wishes to evacuate, pervert, subvert or in other ways attempt to kill the pain. Perhaps, the almost irresistible impulse to kill the pain, and in so doing kill a part of ourselves, is what is most human about us. We turn to poetry and to psychoanalysis in part with the hope that we might reclaim (or perhaps experience for the first time) forms of human aliveness that we have foreclosed to ourselves.

Notes

1. Iambic metre is composed of two-syllable units ("feet") in which an unstressed syllable is followed by one that is stressed.

2. In a letter to his close friend, Louis Untermeyer, Frost (1924) wrote "Irony is simply a kind of guardedness. So is a twinkle. It keeps the reader from criticism ... Humor is the most engaging cowardice. With it myself I have been able to hold some of my enemy in play far out of gunshot" (pp. 702–3).

3. Searles has observed: "Surely many a neurotic patient in analysis ... finds himself maddened on frequent occasions by his analyst's readiness to discount the significance of the patient's conscious feelings and attitudes and to react to preconscious or unconscious communications as if these emanated from the only 'real' and 'genuine' desires and attitudes" (1959, pp. 282–3).

4. Metaphor (in contrast to the process of decoding the unconscious meanings of symbols) inherently creates an unfilled space of possibilities between the two elements that are being drawn into a relationship of similarity and difference, and not into a relationship of equivalence.

5. The juxtaposition in this paragraph of my experience with Ms S and my experience with the Frost poem underscores for me another difference between my analytic and poetic experience. The former involves a relationship of a dozen years in which millions upon millions of events (in psychological and external reality) occurred (for example, experiences of a great variety of grades of intimacy and psychological distance, of anger and love, of hopefulness and immense frustration). An experience with this poem, even though it is a poem that I value greatly, cannot possibly capture the range and depth of experience of a twelve-year relationship. I think that it is perhaps partly because of this difference in the experiences, that my responses to the poem tended to be centred more on the universal elements of experience (which are made immediate and personal by the poem), while the focus of my analytic attention tended to be on what was most specific and unique to my experience with this patient in this analytic hour.

6. These "feats of association" related to (actual and fantasized) meetings and partings give renewed vitality to the concept of "overdetermination" (Freud, 1900, p. 283), revealing it to be more verb than noun, and to have as much reference to the future as it does to the past. In the analytic fragment under discussion, it seems

to me useful to view over-determination as a process in which meanings and feeling tones come into being and accrue in such a way that the experiential outcome cannot be foreseen and is forever in motion: "like giants we are always hurling experience in front of us to pave the future with" (Frost, 1939, p. 777). The over-determined, from this perspective, always has a good deal of the "yet to be determined" about it.

References

Bion, W.R. (1962). *Learning from Experience*. New York, NY: Basic Books.

Boyer, L.B. (1988). Thinking of the interview as if it were a dream. *Contemporary Psychoanalsis, 24*: 275–81.

Calvino, I. (1986). *Six Memos for the Next Millennium*. Cambridge, MA: Harvard University Press.

Edelson, M. (1975). *Language and Interpretation in Psychoanalysis*. Chicago: University Chicago Press.

Freud, S. (1900). The interpretation of dreams. *Standard Edition 4–5*.

Freud, S. (1923). The encyclopaedia articles. *Standard Edition 18* (pp. 235–59).

Frost, R. (1914). Letter to John T. Bartlett, 22 February. In: R. Poirier & M. Richardson (Eds.), *Robert Frost: Collected Poems, Prose and Plays* (pp. 673–9). New York: Library of America, 1995.

Frost, R. (1915). The imagining ear. In: R. Poirier & M. Richardson (Eds.), *Robert Frost: Collected Poems, Prose and Plays* (pp. 687–9). New York: Library of America, 1995.

Frost, R. (1924). Letter to Louis Untermeyer, 10 March. In: R. Poirier & M. Richardson (Eds.), *Robert Frost: Collected Poems, Prose and Plays* (pp. 702–4). New York: Library of America, 1995.

Frost, R. (1928a). Acquainted with the night. In: R. Poirier & M. Richardson (Eds.), *Robert Frost: Collected Poems, Prose and Plays* (p. 234). New York: Library of America, 1995.

Frost, R. (1928b). West-running brook. In: R. Poirier & M. Richardson (Eds.), *Robert Frost: Collected Poems, Prose and Plays* (pp. 236–8). New York: Library of America, 1995.

Frost, R. (1939). The figure a poem makes. In: R. Poirier & M. Richardson (Eds.), *Robert Frost: Collected Poems, Prose and Plays* (pp. 776–8). New York: Library of America, 1995.

Frost, R. (1942). Never again would birds' song be the same. In: R. Poirier & M. Richardson (Eds.), *Robert Frost: Collected Poems, Prose and Plays* (p. 308). New York: Library of America, 1995.

Frost, R. (1962). On extravagance: a talk. In: R. Poirier & M. Richardson (Eds.), *Robert Frost: Collected Poems, Prose and Plays* (pp. 902–26). New York: Library of America, 1995.

Heaney, S. (1979). Song. In: *Selected Poems, 1966–1987* (p. 141). New York: Noonday, 1990.

Hutter, A.D. (1982). Poetry in psychoanalysis: Hopkins, Rossetti, Winnicott. *Int Rev Psychoanal 9*: 303–16.

Jarrell, R. (1955). To the Laodiceans. In: *Poetry and the Age* (pp. 34–62). New York: Vintage.

Jones, A.A. (1997). Experiencing language: some thoughts on poetry and psychoanalysis. *Psychoanal Q 66*: 683–700.

Martin, J. (1983). Grief and nothingness: loss and mourning in Robert Lowell's poetry. *Psychoanal Inq 3*: 451–84.

Meares, R. (1993). *The Metaphor of Play: Disruption and Restoration in the Borderline Experience*. Northvale, NJ: Jason Aronson.

Ogden, T.H. (1994a). The analytic third: working with intersubjective clinical facts. *International Journal of Psychoanalysis, 75*: 3–19.

Ogden, T.H. (1994b). *Subjects of Analysis*. London: Karnac/Northvale, NJ: Aronson.

Ogden, T.H. (1995). Analysing forms of aliveness and deadness of the transference–countertransference. *International Journal of Psycho-analysis 76*: 695–709.

Ogden, T.H. (1996a). The perverse subject of analysis. *J Am Psychoanal Assoc 44*: 1121–46.

Ogden, T.H. (1996b). Reconsidering three aspects of psychoanalytic technique. *International Journal of Psychoanalysis, 77*: 883–99.

Ogden, T.H. (1997a). Some thoughts on the use of language in psychoanalysis. *Psychoanal Dialog 7*: 1–21.

Ogden, T.H. (1997b). Listening three Frost poems. *Psychoanal Dialog 7*: 619–39.

Ogden, T.H. (1997c). Reverie and metaphor. *International Journal of Psychoanalysis, 78*: 719–32.

Ogden, T.H. (1997d). *Reverie and Interpretation: Sensing Something Human*. Northvale, NJ: Jason Aronson.

Ogden, T.H. (1997e). Reverie and interpretation. *Psychoanalytic Quarterly, 66*: 567–95.

Ogden, T.H. (1998). A question of voice in poetry and psychoanalysis. *Psychoanalytic Quarterly, 67*: 426–48.

Pritchard, W. (1994). Ear training. In: *Playing it by Ear: Literary Essays and Reviews* (pp. 3–18). Amherst, MA: University MA Press.

Searles, H. (1959). The effort to drive the other person crazy—an element in the aetiology and psychotherapy of schizophrenia . In: *Collected Papers on Schizophrenia and Related Subjects* (pp. 254–83). New York: International University Press, 1965.

Steiner, G. (1989). *Real Presences*. Chicago: University Chicago Press.

CHAPTER FOUR

From symbols to flesh:

the polymorphous destiny of narration

Julia Kristeva

The author analyses certain aspects of the narration of a generally taciturn hysterico-phobic obsessional patient as they appear in the transference relationship, pinpointing its phallic mastery and the sadistic impact of the domination over the audience/analyst that underlies this mode of discourse. She examines them in relation to Proust's À la recherche du temps perdu, *discussing the place of perversion in analytic listening and interpretation. She then outlines some of the key structuralist and formalist views of narration as a form of syntactic structure expanded by the resolution of an enigma via a hero's ordeal, arguing that if syntactic structure exists, it consists neither of affirmation nor of negation but rather of interrogation. The author notes that what makes psychoanalytic theory radically different from other interpretive theories is the co-presence of sexuality and thought: psychoanalysis reinforces the formal description of a signifying act by the unconscious psychosexual conditions of its possibility. She then discusses*

This paper was presented at the Joseph Sandler Research Conference on "Qualitative methods in psychoanalytic research", London, 4–5 March 2000. Translated by Paula Barkay. Reproduced, with permission, from *International Journal Psychoanalysis*, 81: 771–87 (2000). © Institute of Psychoanalysis, London.

*the poetic narrative of Nerval and also that of Proust, which is dominated
by the acting out of perverse fantasy, the resulting polyphony of various
psychosexual registers, its philosophical and metaphysical impact and its
relevance to the analyst's own interpretive acts when formulating stories
within the countertransference relationship.*

Free association is not only a narration

On the eve of a holiday, one of my patients complained that I was
abandoning her, off to enjoy myself without her. I thought that this
patient was expressing her feelings of *Hilflosigkeit*, helplessness and
distress, resulting from her conflicts with her parents, their divorce,
which was traumatic for her, and from her conviction that she was
neither likable nor capable of love. However, she went on to say:
"What I miss when I don't see you is the story-telling. I was not aware
of this need, but realized that if I miss a session, or you are away, I
not only spend time dishing out stories to friends, but also I talk
during staff meetings at the hospital, and give endless accounts of
patient cases. It is as if I compensate for not being able to tell you
my own story. And I bore to death colleagues who find me more
and more peculiar, as heaven knows I have never been very talkative.
It is only now that this is all happening."

This patient was a young psychiatrist who was undergoing
psychoanalytic training. She was far from verbose—unlike those
hysterics who, for example, consume "airport literature": unrepen-
tant *Scheherezades* whose dissatisfied libido spills over into a flood of
barely coherent words. Rather, this woman's discourse was usually
tightly constructed, and somewhat conceptual and guarded, but
attuned to her unconscious, and capable of striking insights. (I would
describe her as a depressive with a phobic obsessional armature.)
The fact that she understood the importance of narration for her
seems to me to be a new stage, perhaps a decisive one, in her analysis.

It is from this highly specific viewpoint that I shall approach
the problematic of narration, leaving aside its other aspects and
usage, which can also be relevant to psychoanalysis. I shall ask first,
therefore, what is the role of narration in free association? To which
mental structure does it belong within the multiple aspects of the
patient's mental life?

I will not take into account the possible variations of narration in the discourse of hysterics, nor in that of obsessives, phobics or psychotics, even though this is an essential consideration. The basis of my approach, particularly in cases of hysteria and its relation to temporality, is drawn from Freud's remarks on Dora. He stresses the inability of the hysteric to maintain continuous linear narration, as the tale of hysteria gets bogged down between the "rocks" and the "sandbank", as if its "stream" is being "choked", "leaving gaps unfilled", possibly even "true amnesias", "gaps in the memory . . . formed secondarily so as to fill in those gaps" (Freud, 1905; Kristeva, 1996a). Furthermore, while I agree that narration is an integral part of free association, I also contend that free association is not solely about narration, but that it comprises other enunciative modalities. To touch briefly on this diversity, I would draw on the knowledge of the types of discourse coming out of the literary analysis of genres, such as structuralism or stylistics.

Brief narratological aide-mémoire

Following on from the Russian formalists (Chklovski, Eiklenbaum, Propp, etc., and Todorov, 1988), French structuralists studied the canonical forms of narration (e.g. Lévi-Strauss's study of myth, Roland Barthes's study of the novel, the work of French semiologists centred around Greimas, etc.—see, for example, Kristeva, 1970). From this work two main conclusions were reached. Every tale follows the ascending/descending, questions/answers logic of an ordeal: initiation of the ordeal, with the creation of a binary set of agents (furthering or hindering the action) that surround the hero— development of the action—*dénouement*. This curve of logic forms part of a larger and more universal structure, which it modifies, and which is none other than the logic of the sentence—a subject, a verb, and an object. The hero is the grammatical subject, the action is the verb, the *dénouement* of the plot is the object. The story thus becomes an extension of the logic of the sentence, modulated by the logic of binary conflict (between the hero's "good" and "bad" companion) and a quest.

If we accept this general model, then several other sorts of enunciation become interwoven with it. This occurs to the extent that in the history of narration (from the myth, to the modern novels of Joyce and Kafka, and to the *nouveau roman*); these other discourses, generally considered more elliptical and poetic, blur the linearity of the narration, as well as its temporal linearity. The tale, in its pure form, is compromised by elliptical sentences or, conversely, by sentences overburdened with subordinate clauses and hyperbolic metaphors. As a result, the narrative plot is often difficult, if not impossible, to spot. The interest of both narrator and reader rests on impressions and feeling, pain and pleasure, the intensity of which is conveyed by over-condensation. In this way, one can end up with ellipses, such that the meaning of the story, or even of a sentence, remains unclear, "not recoverable" in linguistic terminology, thus requiring the participation of the reader to complete the missing meaning with their own creativity. (This is the case with some of Mallarmé's texts such as *Un coup de dés* [A throw of the dice] or with Joyce's *Finnegan's Wake*.) In other writers, without noticeable grammatical distortions, the over-use of sensorial metaphors and multiple subordinate syntactical clauses producing sentences of two or three pages, changes the pace of memory and attempts to re-establish contact with regressive states, hallucinations or dreams. I have proposed that Proust's "poetical" narration in *Remembrance of Things Past* should be read in this way, suggesting to see there (as the author himself thinks) an attempt to reinstate actual sensorial experience by means of a narrative technique, completed with other processes, which Proust calls "transubstantiation" (I shall return to this point) (Kristeva, 1996b). Sometimes, as with Nerval, these modifications of narrative logic reveal states of melancholia, even psychotic decompression.

"Pre-narrative envelopes", between anxiety and language

Let us now return to narration in psychoanalysis. If one accepts that the object with which analytic listening works is indeed fantasy, the question could be formulated as follows: *what is the discourse of fantasy?* If fantasy is an imaginary "act" or "scenario", as many writers have maintained, is the narration its sole discourse, or simply one of the discourses, or its *optimal* discourse?

Recent observations, inspired by cognitive psychology, seem to confirm the Kleinian concept of "protophantasy" found in babies (I am keeping to Susan Isaacs's spelling of phantasy with a "ph" to emphasize the primary, archaic aspects of these formations), meaning a "quasi-narration" that articulates drives and desires, which are aimed at the object (the breast, the mother) to ensure the survival of the young, phobic, and sadistic ego.

There have indeed been observed "representations of events" or "cognitive affective models" in children of less than a year of age, which are to take at once the shape of a "pre-narrative envelope" (see Nelson & Gruendel, 1981; Mandler, 1983; Cellérier & Ducret, 1992; Stern, 1993). It is about subjective, mainly affective, reality, which takes on the logical properties of the drive, such as desire (or motivation), aim, satisfaction temporality, repetition, associations of memories, curves of dramatic tension equivalent to a primitive plot, etc. This pre-narrative envelope amounts to an emotional experience, both physical and subjective, based on the drives in an interpersonal context. In other words, it is a mental construct that emerges from the real world: an "emerging property" of thought. Thus, there are multiple brain "centres" that specialize in the control of numerous mental events (sensations, instinctual needs, motor function, language, time, place, etc.) or parallel distributed processing (PDP). They manage this early in life to co-ordinate at a higher level, establishing precisely their integration into a unified event endowed with a structure close to that of narration. Is narration an elementary structure of the object relation, and of the phantasy on which it is based? This is the hypothesis proposed by some cognitive researchers.

In the same way that generative grammar (Chomsky) has postulated the existence of an innate grammatical language competence (with a minimal matrix containing the subject, the verb, and the object), which is later used in the many grammatical performances of the different languages, we can observe here a tendency towards the notion of a basic, if not innate, narrative structure, which would be activated with the early drive interactions of the newborn. The "pre-narrative envelopes" are accompanied by "analogous representations", which are neither pure real-life nor pure abstraction, but intermediary between the two. From this perspective, phantasy becomes an analogous representation of the narrative envelope that is lived in virtual time.

This theoretical advance seems very compelling, but only if one adds that the analytic experience on which it claims to be based demonstrates, moreover, how far phantasy (and thus the pre-narrative envelope itself) belongs in an emotional context, without which the sequence of the actual phantasy cannot occur. More specifically, the phantasy acts as such within and through the destructive oral drive, from which it cannot be dissociated. In other words, the pre-narrative sequence characterizing the formal logic of phantasy depends on the possibility of expressing, or not, this destruction. On the one hand, it must be manifested in the child, and on the other, the mother must recognize it, aware of the hidden hand of the death drive. The case of little Dick, now well-known, is a shining example of this destruction, of this "negativity" (Klein, 1930).

Kleinian and post-Kleinian theory, which has indicated the existence of thought phantasy [pensée phantasmatique], developed it not through pinpointing the logic of early narrative, but rather through emphasizing *primary anxiety*, which becomes the prerequisite of thought, if and only if it is recognized and replayed by the object (by the mother or, at best, the analyst). Let us keep for the moment this excess of anxiety, as we shall return to it when considering the changes in the canonical narrative structure.

Moreover, analytic experience shows that protophantasy, as a "pre-narrative envelope" of an "emerging property", requires *words from the other* to construct itself permanently as phantasy. While it is true that Klein insists on the pre-verbal and affective aspects of the narrative envelope that constitute fantasy, she also links it, through the analytic setting, to the verbal interpretations of analysts, who in their own words, lead the pre-narration to phantasy *sensu strictu*. Because this narrative, which is the therapist's named, verbalized phantasy, interpreting the *acted out* phantasy in the child, brings the emerging thought of the child to a new third level: one that might be described as symbolic, in which *primary anxiety*, thus recognized and reconstituted in the account of the analytic interpretation, finds the best conditions for the child's narration to take over, before other thought processes follow on.

Sign-syntax-interrogation: From the depressive position to the phallic stage

Let us pause momentarily at a difficult point that appears to have been ignored in the cognitive research I have just mentioned. I am referring to the role of verbalization in the crystallization of the actual "pre-narrative envelope" particular to archaic mute fantasy in the narration of fantasy. We know, through the works of Hanna Segal, of the importance of the "depressive position" in the passage of "symbolic equations" to real symbols: in other words to the acquisition of language considered as made up of linguistic signs (Segal, 1957). It should be noted that Segal is concerned with isolated symbols but not with language as a grammatical structure, syntax or as judgement.

My own experience leads me to add to this Kleinian understanding of symbols the importance of the phallic stage, which appears to me critical in consolidating symbolism and thought cathexis in the patient. I could maintain that, from a certain point in the psychic and neurological maturational process, the castration complex steers both the boy and the girl to phallic identification with the father. We learn from Lacan that the paternal phallus is not only the penis organ, but a representation of the father's symbolic authority over the family triangle. The appropriation of the phallus by the boy and the girl appears to be the fantasy prior to incest with the mother and the murder of the father, which are typical of the Oedipal complex (with different variations related to sex differences that I cannot elaborate upon now). The tumescence and detumescence of the penis, its "guilty" visibility (there is a word-play in the French *cutable* [*coupable*]: cut-able but also guilty) make the processes during the phallic stage similar to those of a psychosomatic computer. It is as if the phallus, during the phallic stage, becomes the psychosomatic support in this binary process on which are based the language signs and the structures of meaning (presence/absence, positive/negative, 0/1).

This consolidation of symbolism during the phallic stage occurs along with another manifestation of logic, also linked to phallic identification. It is the psychical curiosity that (Freud had suggested) was rooted in the first ever *question*, "where do children come from?" Even though this curiosity is supposed to exist from birth in the protophantasy of the baby, it is through the phallic stage and the consolidation of linguistic symbolization observable at this stage that it is able to articulate itself as an *interrogation*, involving causality and goal.

Affirmation and *negation* are implicit in the linguistic sign: every sign is already a sentence or a *holosentence* ("Mummy" means "I want my Mummy" or "I don't want Mummy"). On the other hand, the curve of the quest, which implies a narration composed of an enigma, an ordeal, and a solution, is a more complex construction. It is dependent, even more than statements of wishes or pleasure, on the capacity of the subject to overcome the phallic trial to reach the Oedipal triangle. It is strange that Freud, who was interested in the judgement of existence and attribution (Freud, 1925) and who pinpointed their dependence on rejection, on the one hand, [*Ausstossung, Verwerfung*], and on the symbol of negation, on the other, [*Verneinung, Negativität*], did not follow through with a consideration of interrogation. It is a familiar issue though, notably when he deciphers it in Oedipus's discursive position, "Who am I? Where do I come from? Where I am going?" This is the exposition of the enigma representing Oedipus in front of the Sphinx, and which underlies the very possibility of telling the *story* of this central hero of psychoanalysis.

Last but not least, if narration presupposes a *question* to which it is the answer, this also means that by narrating we are in an *interlocution*, almost a transference. Indeed, the *act of questioning* is addressed to the second person and tells it implicitly:

> I do not assume necessarily that you have the same knowledge as me, but I merge our psyches. I assume there is a part of me in you, and I await from it the answer to the question formulated by the other part, or an adherence to the story that I create in answer to my question—unless it is a refusal. (Kristeva, 1996a)

(For more on Oedipus, or phallic monism, see Kristeva, 1996a; 1996b.) The "human questioning reality" that the philosopher considers essential (Heidegger, 1968, p. 48) and to which the narrative answer is concomitant, might be, for psychoanalysis, attached to the phallic trial introducing the Oedipal stage.

We can see, therefore, that with the narrative story we are at a level of symbolism that includes not only symbols, not even just sentences with their implication of affirmation and negation, but more particularly the capacity to question and answer. This has the advantage of psychic curiosity ("Where do children come from?") and the positioning of the other as symbolic interlocutor: this curiosity and this other are psychic acquisitions consolidated by the elaboration of the phallic trial in the Oedipal phase.

If we accept that the theory of the unconscious, whatever the modern ramifications, does possess a unity, one could define it, it seems to me, as the co-presence of sexuality/thought.[1] Psychoanalysis adds the *sexual and subjective conditions of interaction* that underlie the stages or structures of thought that Piaget, on the one hand, and the cognitive theorists, on the other, reveal in the child. While our British colleagues, with Klein, insist more readily on the pre-Oedipal side of the acquisition of symbolic functioning (notably its dependence on the depressive position and its reparation value) we, the French (perhaps because we are Southerners or Latins?), tend to rehabilitate the role of the phallic libido in the investment of symbols and the later developments of thought.

One can maintain, therefore, that the capacity to pose questions (questioning utterances), and the narrative aptitudes of early childhood, are closely linked to the active phallic identification of the subjects. From this same perspective, one could put forward the claim that the "phallicism" of the hysteric woman can take the shape of excitement in the story-teller, the uninterrupted narrative "logorrhoea" celebrated by Joyce in Molly's monologue in *Ulysses*. Conversely, the failure of this phallic identification, its doubts and impasses, can take on the shape of a story bogged down or weighed down by gaps and amnesia, transgressing linear temporality, as was the case with Dora, according to Freud.

My patient, with whom I had started this paper, and who claimed to be bisexual or homosexual, with strong tendencies towards phallic competition, seemed to me, at that time in the analysis, to have started *working through* her "phallicism". In this way, instead of the acting out typical of the beginning of the analysis (conflicts with her parents or her bosses in the hospital, car accidents caused by speeding to prove that she was as "powerful" as a man, careless dressing, or caricaturing male dress), now she would find affirmation in a narrative word, painstakingly constructed, perhaps too much so, and wanting too much to please. "It's by telling stories that I can stand firm," she would tell me. "What is strange is that I also tell on the couch, where I can also hold myself firmly, but in a different way, not standing up, but in an under-water position."

I will leave these words of my patient here to move from the canonical narration and the phallic gratification it provides, to this variation of narration that is free association. The invitation to "say everything that comes to mind" brings out an obviously narrative discourse in the patient, with all that is implied about the reparation of the depressive position, as well as phallic curiosity and seduction—I hope to have convinced you about this. But free association also involves random words, elliptical phrases, not to mention shouts, whispers, snatches of non-existent languages, secret idiolects, and silences. This is part of my patient's "under-water position"—attempts to communicate split-up or archaic psychical states, where the object relations are minute, unstable or non-existent, and where phantasy (if there is any) is centred around *painful or ecstatic self-perception*, where action and its object are suspended, if not absent. This brings back to mind the Freudian concept of "primary narcissism". It seems to me that the therapeutic power of free association lies precisely in the combination that it brings about between, on the one hand, narration, as I have just outlined as definitively phallic and, on the other, primary processes such as displacement and condensation. The latter, while quite often presented as linguistic signs (words or phrases), are not strictly speaking "signs", but function as "indicators" ("index" according to Peirce) of feelings and affects, or according to Hanna Segal, of "equations", even "thing-presentations" rather than "word-presentations" (according to Freud's terminology). Narration on the couch is comprised of these two facets, and we are bound to listen to both if we want to follow our patients in their dives into the unconscious as well as in their ascents towards the dramas of eroticism and its elaboration. Nevertheless, within these non-narrative shreds, in these "indexes", "equations" or "thing-presentations" a specific psychical experience is deciphered: the patient attempts to regain with words—these "things"—that are for them the feelings of affects or drives. I shall give two examples from literature of the risk to the psyche and to life, represented by this departure from canonical narration, and about the seduction it holds for us.

Nerval: The impossible story and/or the suicide

"El Desdichado" is one of Nerval's (1808–1855) last writings. It was written in 1853 and published in 1855 (see Kristeva, 1989). Attentive reading of the sonnet shows that it is made up of elliptical phrases, isolated words, even proper nouns or foreign nouns, over-charged with allusive connotations. It is as if to maximize esoteric value, but above all to take refuge in the secret of pain (death of the mother, loss of the mistress). When the intensity of this trial seems sufficiently revealed, the poet succeeds in building complete sentences in the last tercets, which are finally a real mini-story and cut through the accumulation of the previous elliptical affirmations, negations, and questions:

> Am I Cupid or Phoebus, Lusignan or Byron?
> My brow is still red from the kisses of the queen:
> I have slept in the cave where the siren turns green,
> I've twice, yet alive, been across the Achéron,
> Modulating and singing on Orpheus's lyre
> The sighs of the saint and the cries of the fairy.

I put forward the hypothesis that the "I" affirms itself at the same time as the story finally becomes possible. This provisional affirmation of the speaking subject allows the poet to go beyond his melancholic state: the narration, a somewhat maniacal enunciation, after devastating melancholia? The conflicts with his father who never gave Nerval support after the death of his mother, his heartbreaks, and his disappointing relationship with his physician, Dr Blanche, lead him soon afterwards to this final triumphant narrative to hang himself from a Parisian street-lamp. Nerval"s other texts, notably those in prose, bore witness in a different way to his difficulty in maintaining linearity and the curiosity of the narrative thread—captivating for the reader, who is invited by these stories into delicious dream-like states. These fragmented narratives, dispersed into star-like shapes, testify to a depressive pain, which never stabilized within a gratifying phallic identification.

Transubstantiation according to Proust

In a very different way, the writings of Marcel Proust in *Remembrance of Things Past* (see Kristeva, 1996b) put us in touch with a much more abundant narrative but nevertheless one with a highly modified canonical structure: lengthening of sentences, over-abundance of metaphors, overplay of characters between themselves and with the character of the author, etc. I venture that these changes in the narrative have as their basis, or purpose, to cross through repression where the language of canonical narration operates, thus enabling a real surge of sensorial experience—its "indexation" or its "equation" found within words, or even, according to the Freudian model, in a return of "word-presentations" to "thing-presentations". Proust himself points to this exorbitant change of language in his narrative— "words" becoming "things"—explaining that the purpose of litera- ture is to create the "transubstantiation" proclaimed by the Catholic Mass. (I would remind you that, contrary to Protestant belief, Catholics believe in the transformation of the substance of the bread and the wine into the total substance of the body and blood of Jesus.) Proust was Jewish on his mother's side and Catholic on his father's— one and the other but rather neither one nor the other—agnostic and sarcastic. He uses this metaphor of transubstantiation to indicate that through the art form of the novel he attempts to transfer his own body as well as the body of the world within the framework of narration. And he invites us to read his narration as the real presence of his affects, drives, and desires. I have attempted to comment elsewhere on this unusual encounter of metaphysics, religion, and literature—which calls out to the psychoanalyst (Kristeva, 1996b). It is already, under the pen of Proust, a beginning of analysis: notably an analysis of the phantasy of equation between things and words, celebrated by "transubstantiation". Relevant to the theme of the meeting today is the fact that Proust's protean narrative, both lacunal and poetic while stubbornly continuous, testifies to a fragmentation of the psychic apparatus, and to its recomposition in the pleasure of sadomasochism, which compensates for depressive pain and even the autistic burial suggested on some pages.

Proust or the power of sublimation

Freud has left us with a vision of literature which as he undoubtedly recognized preceded analytic discovery because of its proximity to the unconscious, but which remains mainly dominated by the pleasure principle. One finds also this vision in some of Lacan's formulations, who detects in the "imaginary" an avoidance of "truth". From there on, psychoanalysts have tended to consider writings as a denial of trauma or, more modestly, of conflict, as an escape towards the fetish. The power of sublimation is often neglected as a retake of the trauma, emptying out and evidencing trauma. The narrative is woven from the words of natural language, to signs, which Proust tries to bring as close as possible to the indescribable, to feelings and to drives, from which, by necessity, he protects himself as well. Sublimation is not necessarily a process of working through, even though many passages of *Remembrance* testify to a conscious awareness of the ambivalent link that makes the asthmatic child cling to his mother, for example, or of the homosexual bedrock of jealousy, etc. We come across this in analytic treatment; before any "understanding" or "intellectualization"; the mere fact of naming affect in order to return it to the other/the analyst is a mediation/meditation that mitigates its death instincts, and renders them bearable, livable, perhaps even agreeable and pleasant. Proust protects himself differently from the patient, since by naming the taste of the madeleine savoured with Mamma, or tripping on the paving-stones of St Mark's in Venice echoing the paving of the courtyard at Guermantes, he embraces previous rhetorical codes. He appropriates George Sand, the favourite author of his mother, Jeanne-Clémence Weil-Proust, as well as the character of the incestuous miller/mother in Sand's *François le champi* [François the waif] who is named . . . Madeleine. He competes with seventeenth-century classical art, with the portraits of La Bruyère, with the scandal-mongering of Saint-Simon, with Mme de Sévigné and what he calls her "Dostoevsky side" . . . At the same time he appraises himself against the literary market, and the editorial and journalistic worlds of Paris to see what they expect from "a great French writer" at the beginning of the century. And, in the alchemy of this style wrapped around the drives, he constructs an object—the book—that one must qualify as deceitful and artificial. One needs to go underneath the reproach made by the average reader of being "snobbish" or "dandyish", in order to detect an important level, and one perhaps indispensable to the work of sublimation, of its omnipotence and of the universal ambition contained in this style.

This extravagance does not in any way prevent the writing from being a framework of unconscious truth, particularly as this work of sublimation, which makes the unbearable attractive, and also eternal—this conspiracy of trauma, of asthmatic pain or homosexual guilt, never fails to put into "narrative themes" the very conflicts that make it possible. In other words, the conflict of the parental imagos, the maternal imago in particular, appears to be the source of what Proust calls "the involuntary memory", which one can compare to "unconscious memory". I have been able to observe that, following the death of his mother in 1905, the first sketches of *Remembrance* in the 1908 Carnet accomplish a mourning process that takes place using, among others, substitution figures: certain maternal relation-ships with women from the aristocracy who surrounded him, such as Mrs Straus, *née* Halévy (wife of Georges Bizet and mother-in-law of Proust's classmate, Jacques Bizet). She supports him and offers him the carnet which will be the first sketches of *Remembrance*, and which bequeath to Oriana her blonde hair, her red velvet dresses, her childish and melancholic face. Or also the Comtesse de Chévigné, *née* Laure de Sade, of pure aristocratic blood this time, recognizable by her hooked nose and her bird-like head, which will become the distinguishing features of Guermantes. These are distant and alive mothers, who will be joined from 1914 by the discerning and devoted Céleste Albaret, indispensable servant and privileged confidante of illnesses and of a few orgies. They allowed for the recurrence of the traumatic situation that Proust experienced in the close proximity to his mother, and the escape from this osmosis by an admission of his homosexuality on one hand, and by narrative writings, on the other. The new narrative took over the unfinished poetico-biographical novel, *Jean Santeuil*, as well as his essay project, "Against Saint-Beuve", which the author had planned before his mother's death. The later form of narrative writing in *Remembrance* has the delicacy of metaphors, matched only by the unforgiving aggression of the plots, notably when relating to maternal characters and femininity—even as far as femininity in men: his homosexuality which is, according to Proust, a sign of both election and comic defect; an indelible excuse for tenderness, sarcasm and scandal-mongering.

Transgression of the forbidden, in which identification with the maternal figure maintained him, reinforced this process of recollection, which allows the writer to reinvent childhood and to reveal, by "word-presentations", the "thing-presentations" themselves. This occurs in a way such that the cruelty of the narration goes hand in hand with "incarnated" language. Proust uses the term "transubstantiation", as I have already mentioned. Metaphors and hyperbolic syntax are specifically the Proustian "technique", but they are for him very obviously *a necessity of life*: as writing a narrative is now the only life possible, the very assurance of biological survival. The purpose of the reshuffling of tired signs of language is to crush the obsessional inhibiting aspects of social language, the so-called "mother-tongue", to bring it closer to the drive of desire. Proust calls this enigmatic sphere "Being", which he wants to reach by the extravagant means of a transfigured language. This "Being" is not so much in reference to Plato as to Schopenhauer, whom Proust knew about, if only through his course on philosophy at the Sorbonne. A "Being" which for us, the reader of the conclusion of *Time regained*, would be the unconscious, and also, perhaps beyond him, strictly speaking an excessive ambition to escape the subjective to reach the pre-psychic modality of human experience.

How could literature, made up of words and imagining the human universe, be able to reach "that"? If not by this monstrous modification of language and narration that overwhelms us with feelings and, further, takes us to an uncontrollable universe that would be "off the subject". Such is, in any event, Proust's ambition. Obviously, psychoanalysis has attempted to understand this excess as a heroic attempt to pull away from the traumatic separation from the object—difficult, if not impossible, separation and individuation, which Proust experienced in the context of asthma and homosexuality, and which he directs to a context of language and story transformation.

This experience led him to discover and to translate, in modern terms, what philosophy, and before it mysticism, have named "flesh". In other words, a kind of weaving between the drives and the undecidable web of human ties, significant connections that the subject does not control, and which escape us. From this perspective the Proustian unconscious is a version of the "flesh".

An example: The madeleine

It is thus like a sort of *dream* and simultaneously as an "intertext" (returning to other known texts by the author) that I propose to read the narrative episode of the "madeleine", or that of the "Vinteuil's sonata". The famous pages on the madeleine begin, as one will remember, with the strong idealization of the narrator's mother. After remembering that she reads him novels by George Sand before putting him to bed, Marcel regrets losing the colour of his childhood memories, the "dramas of his going to bed", with the exception of a "patch of yellow wall" in the night. And with the exception, immediately afterwards, of a dull day brightened up by the oral memory of tasting tea with a madeleine, enjoyed with this mother/reader, which led the child to oceanic pleasures, unnamable, for ever lost. All his attempts to recall and describe them failed, until Marcel, having become narrator, carried out a displacement in time and space: another taste of tea reaches him, this time no longer in the company of his mother but that of his paternal aunt, Léonie. In place of his mother, who had aroused in him an unnamable excitement, there is now a different figure, more distant, almost neutral, who enables the trauma to be verbalized: *I am unable to say what happens from mouth to mouth with Mamma, but I can speak of it if I replace Mamma with Aunt Léonie.* This association, which must be called "metonymic", glides from one woman to another, from one place to another, from one time to another, opening a complex chain of associations that are bearable from now on: visual, olfactory, etc. Words are suddenly possible, they restore the whole countryside, the village, details of the house and garden. As if to mark the importance of the metonymic distancing in a dynamic of memory and naming, Proust compares this upsurge of memories that he thought had faded away for ever to those Japanese papers which take on fabulous shapes when they are put in water. "Estranging" himself from Mamma by going to Aunt Léonie, and even as far as Japan, if necessary. Such will be the conditions in which pleasure becomes describable! Bear in mind, however, that Aunt Léonie is not only a strategy to remove Mamma to a safe distance, she is a rather degraded example of femininity, a more or less imaginary invalid, and a Sunday Mass gossip, not spared by the author's sarcasm. Moreover, it is on this aunt's couch that Marcel experiences his first amorous frolics with a female cousin; and, even more seriously, it is Aunt Léonie's furniture that the narrator will bequeath to a brothel—as, in reality, after his parents' death, the writer gave the family furniture to a brothel, for men this time, that of Le Cuziat.

You see that my reading of the episode of the madeleine, which removes us from an idyllic tea-time, which lulled so many schoolchildren throughout the world learning French, mobilizes both the *texts* that underlie *Remembrance* and the biography of the writer. We observe, in the very laboratory of writing, that what allows the symbolization of trauma—in this instance, the osmotic links with the mother—passes through a mobilization of opposing drives (Mamma/Aunt Léonie); love and desire are inverted into rejection, hate, anger, perhaps putting to death. We are at the heart of perversion and profanation underlying the Proustian sublimation by narration.

Trauma and perversion

Biographical testimonies and the text of *Remembrance* make me think that the fusional relationship was traumatic to the extent that Proust had first to go through somatic compliance in order to acquire some ego autonomy. I interpret his asthma as an abreaction to the ambivalent love/hate around the "body" itself, which is also indistinctly that of the subject *and* the mother-object; asthma as a laceration or flagellation (to take up Proust's own fantasies) of the other on the actual body of the subject. Ultimately, with the relative de-inhibition of homosexual desire, it will be the scenography of blasphemy that will take over from the asthmatic symptom. *I don't attack myself, I don't suffocate myself merged with Mamma, I desecrate Mamma herself.*

I associate perversion with profanation, because it seems to me that the universe that we touch here with Proust perhaps goes beyond that of psychoanalysis. I think that with his "transubstantiation" of language and his meditation on the inherent sadomasochism of the social pact, Proust reaches an important metaphysical level, that of profanation, which is concerned with the destruction of the divine image. Obviously, this is also a psychoanalytic preoccupation, not least because the divine image is rooted in paternal law: but the stakes of this demolition, including perversion, seem to me to go well beyond our clinical field. For what is the divine image? The divine is not dependent only on the father who guarantees the ideal and the forbidden. Beyond the theory of the unconscious, and anthropology and archaeology as well, I would say that for the psychoanalyst the divine appears to be the metaphor of the capacity to represent—which characterizes human nature at the highest level: of our capacity to hallucinate/image/talk/symbolize. When Ancient Greeks identify Being and Thought, when monotheism celebrates a single God—to stay within the approach to the Divine of our own culture—it seems to me that they consider a reality which, under the guise of philosophical or religious speculation, nevertheless still confronts the analyst. From our point of view as analysts, it is about an extremely complex, heterogeneous, and multilayered capacity that is the *aptitude for representation*. According to the Freudian model, it comprises the unconscious, the preconscious, and the conscious, while current psychoanalytic reality does not cease specifying its heterogeneity: hallucination being the representation of words or things, "alpha" or "beta" elements, semiotic and symbolic pictograms, in my terminology and so on. Is not psychoanalytic treatment the very attempt to consolidate the entire range of precisely this heterogeneity of the aptitude for representation, to amplify psychic life to the optimum, to remove inhibition and resistance, and enhance their sublimation and elaboration?

Proust went far in this direction, and he reached the point at which he achieved a true fragmentation of the apparatus for representation, of the psychical apparatus itself, without this fragmentation collapsing in the asymbolism of psychosis. This particular fragmentation is at the same time a major risk to the subject's psychic integrity, and an extraordinary source of exaltation. When Proust writes that "thoughts are substitutes for sorrow", or that "sorrow is the only way through which certain thoughts first reach us", he is referring to the depressive states, at those moments of separation from the loved object, the maternal object, in the first instance. But he hears, more fundamentally, the anxiety of the collapse of the psychical apparatus under the attack of this "work of the negative" as Green puts it, which explores and disintegrates all unity—of the ego, of the other, and the very units of language itself. The work of the negative comprises drives, desires, and their symbolization, all three woven in a revaluation of the identical being, even of the living being. But

Proust adds straightaway that there are several clusters of ideas "some of which are immediate sources of joy". By this he means the great exaltation brought about by writing, that manic enthusiasm, if you like, which overwhelms the subject if he does not give into disintegration, when he succeeds in transforming it into a pluralistic verbal framework that is nevertheless assembled into a narrative, into a certain coherence or verbal unity of the *narrative works*.

The framework that emerges is no longer the ordinary system of everyday language, since we are witnessing a metaphoric hyperbole, syntax swarmed with clauses that are sometimes undecidable, of characters that lose their shape and are confused in rough sketches, but which also reflect each other, as Proust says, in the definitive text (thus, who is Swann, who is Bloch, who is the narrator, and Albertine, Odette, Oriane, etc.?). The writer has from then the feeling and thought, which are a true *experience* of holding the divine—in the sense of possessing the *aptitude for making sense*, both in the possible eclipse, and its threatening nullification, and in its polyphonic magnificence, in its "rose window". We understand now the meaning of Proustian imagery comparing narrative work to a cathedral. You will recall that Proust first compared his text to a "robe", another revealing indication of the femininity of the subject and all characters in *Remembrance* before firmly placing it in the ambitious hopes of the "cathedral" and its "stained glass windows".

An atheism

This rivalry with Catholicism must not be understood as treason to Judaism, to which Proust often refers, and from which he seeks the bright enlightenment of Zoharic wisdom as far as in the steeple of St Mark's in Venice. I would see rather—in this reference to the cathedral—a search for support, to justify that strictly personal experience he achieved as he came through depression and perverted polymorphism, which is simply the possibility of *representing the bursting of the One*; to juggle with the plurality of meanings, to assemble in the unity of the work a sort of polytheism of feelings, transformed into images and monstrous signs and protean forms, uncontainable by any aspect of conscience but that the artist—that "subject on trial"—could for ever attempt to hold. Indeed, an infinite search, and in this sense a "search" ("remembrance") "of things past", a search for the most explosive possible verbalization, which is, nevertheless, communicable.

Kant understood the sublime to be similar to a reconciliation of "the thing in one" with imagination, at the intersection of beauty and ugliness, and beyond. Unlike him, Proust with his profoundly ironic and iconoclastic mind, built on the sublime as another means of exploring or rather, exploding, the divine, on the edge of the risks that threaten psychic integrity, as do all the great adventures of contemporary art—and also as an appropriation of the divine within an alchemy of the verb of which the writer is explorer and builder/unbuilder. He thus attains a level of atheism that has perhaps no other reality than that of aesthetic experience, which is the counterpart of analytic experience. Sartre used to say that atheism is a "cruel and long-winded enterprise". Proust proves it to the letter; by the bursting of the ego, full of desire spreading as far as sadomasochism, by the shattering of meaning while still contained in the polyphony of his poetic narrative, of his "cathedral" narrative.

Proust's writing has the further advantage of testifying, in a tone that is both tender and sarcastic, as much about the cruelty of the social contract—what the writer calls "public opinion"—as about the untenable sadomasochism of desire—all Proustian "love" dissolves into jealousy, when not into weakness and hate. The sacredness of social ties, like the sacredness of eroticism, is decimated by Proust's pen into a true "theatre of cruelty", from which the author does not come out appalled as after a reading of Artaud or other poetic texts. On the contrary, he laughs about it. Why? Because the "tool" of the performance is preserved, amplified, and exalted. The language is a pleasure: the tale is a triumph. In place of shattered illusions (love is an illusion for Proust, as is jealousy) is the joy of narrating the collapse of all identity, as well as the collapse of the story—derisory yet maintained. This *turnaround from depression and perversion* in apology for the *capacity to represent the very collapse of units*, of values and senses is perhaps the greatest gift Proust offers his reader. And the psychoanalyst, who appears to have advanced since Freud, in the accompaniment, if not in the displacement, of psychosis and autism. Proust's experience gives us the *mots justes*, which incite us, the analysts, to find a form of interpretation to lead to more vivacious, more sensitive verbal creation, more attuned to what the tie to the other means in terms of cruelty and joy, abuse and disillusionment.

To succeed where the autistic person fails

A very symptomatic dream told by Proust, that of the "second apartment", describes a dream-like experience of a purely sensorial nature: it is mainly about auditory sensations which, as the dream goes on, move surreptitiously towards visual sensations. A second dream then appears, more frontal, so-called "of the first apartment", which contains characters and speech, and which seems managed in a very Freudian way, notably in respecting the logic of inversion and ambivalence that we know from *The Interpretation of Dreams*. The grandmother turns into the manservant, pain turns out to be a wish for proximity ... would it be to this man, etc.? As in Plato's cave, fire starts by enlightening auditory darkness, before this increasing visibility gives way to words, "signifiers" that articulate "ideas". The "second apartment", however, remains buried in pain and in the unmentionable, and only emits sounds from inanimate objects—a real sensorial cave, even more buried than the Platonic to which the text apparently alludes.

I put forward the hypothesis that there is a *latent compensatory autism* featured in this dream of the "second apartment", out of which the frontal dream, but even more the work of writing cumulative metaphors and syntactic clauses, aspires to bring out the intensity, and succeeds. I suggest that the writer, and certainly the writer Proust, "succeeds where the autistic fails" (see *Le temps sensible* mentioned above), echoing Freud's famous comment that he "succeeds where the paranoid fails". I understand Freud's sentence as follows: on the one hand the paranoid is precisely the one who is incapable of connecting with the other, since he projects his destruction and fear on to the other, in such a way that the other appears if, and only if, the paranoid perceives and thinks of him as an aggressor. On the other hand, the analyst, without repressing this projected aggression that is the link with the other, succeeds in untying this projective/ introjective cycle, in calming the persecuting anxiety, by posing as the other for the patient, since he has begun to hear the patient as other than himself, and he opens up from then on the possibility of ties with others in the patient's fantasy and real life. The writer, for his part, is not foreign to this economy, in that his imaginary work on the *character* as alter ego, or as strangeness, belong to the register of projection/introjection: let us recall the couplings of Swann/Charles Haas, his main prototype, which threads its way surreptitiously through the text, Swann/Bloch, Swann/the narrator, the narrator/Charlus, and also the narrator/Albertine/Albert, etc. But the author adds another capacity, which consists in translating his "autistic" sensitivity, invading and resisting words, through a chain re-shaped from usual signs into metaphors and syntax, but also in unbelievable, exorbitant, and immoderate stories. Remember the giants that surround *Time Regained* such as the Duc de Guermantes on his stilts, because their "space" incorporates "time" in their memory? Following the example of these monstrous characters, the language itself becomes ambiguous, polymorphous, leading the reader's conscience, with endless subordinate sentences, to states of *mnesic* over-competence, but also states of forgetfulness, of non-sense, to confused states—dream-like as they produce anxiety and joy.

How does this naming of the unnameable drives or the sensorial become possible? How can the writer succeed where the autistic fails? Therein lies the Proustian perspicacity in the space of perversion.

The only way to withdraw from this persistent envelope of autism is the violence of desire assumed as such: against the "part object", detached from the mother, and which remains to be subjected to ordeals of suffering until put to death. One example of this is the Proustian ritual that consisted of piercing rats with hatpins; this represents the breast, the penis or faeces belonging to the mother, or rather the conglomeration that is the amalgamated mother and son, against which the writer persists as if both trying to bring about separation and refuse it. In the same way, in the flagellation scenes that Proust observed through the keyhole of a brothel for men, the feminine body is eclipsed, protected in some way, and it is a man's body that is branded with unbearable pain by flagellation, which reminds one of the child's asthma and, at the same time, of a passivity that is all-feminine, a suffering in impotence, in the vengeance he wishes to inflict on the one (female in the text) who abandons him to enjoy pleasure without him. A beginning of alterity . . .

The memoirs of Céleste Alberet—a well of biographical information but relating also to the laboratory of writing—testify to the passage from voyeurism of the story-teller. The author reaches home late after these inadmissible outings; however, he does share them with his governess—Céleste is a pseudo-analyst, she pretends to look shocked but does not lose sight of the details of the reasoning and the words of her employer–patient. Proust confides that beyond the pleasure of seeing the suffering of the flagellated businessman, it is the whole picture that holds his attention, the spatial and visual management of the scene, as if this first *scopic* grip of the drive temporarily appeases him. It is only afterwards that he can start using words, not about the pain–pleasure but about the whole picture. Proust begins, before his analyst/governess, to search for words, trying them out, changing them, to make his first rough attempts out loud, not by kneading the body of the businessman, but by kneading the body of language this time, shaping and unshaping it. Apparently harrowing work for the governess, who says that she comes out of it "battered" and "exhausted". What of perversion in this trajectory? What is the narrator's erotic object that has taken over from the voyeur? Homosexual object? Maternal object disguised under the mask of the homosexual and the governess? Probably both at once. But also, and right through this journey, the true erotic object of the sublimatory act is none other than the signifier/language. A sentence of Proust, of magnificent lucidity, and which is rarely cited, describes this sublimation: "I had to carry out the successive parts (of the memory, of sensation) in a somewhat different matter, in a distinctive and new way, transparent, with a special sonority, compact, fresh as a daisy" (see Kristeva, 1996b).

This "matter", "fresh as a daisy", which is the matter of poetic language and the Proustian story is, of course, without matter, all sonority and meaning, poetry and narrative. Yet, it is no accident that Proust calls it "matter": the bloody body of the rat and the businessman hide in it as does the voyeur's body of pleasure, like the child's shiver while drinking his tea through the madeleine or inhaling the scent of vetiver or lilac. Proustian narration, as the language of grandiose sublimation, has absorbed the sensitive, and for that very reason it is also "fresh as a daisy", if we are willing to read it in the way the author invites us, and not like a crossword, or a chronicle or conceptual essay. Thus, he spontaneously finds, and not just to please the Daudet family and be accepted by it, a term from the Catholic Mass, "transubstantiation", to qualify this immersion of the signifier in the drives and feelings that is the aim of his writings, which does indeed seem to be a *suspension of repression*. *"I know well that words are neither things nor feelings, nor affects, but nevertheless they can get sufficiently close as to merge with them"*. Risk or ecstasy? Transubstantiation.

The analyst talks

I am persuaded that the analyst's free-floating attention proceeds by identification with the unconscious and, further, with what Merleau-Ponty calls "the flesh"; flesh of the person, flesh of the world, he says. Identification with the flesh of the patient, which is the foundation of art—so rare but which we sometimes attain—to name this bi-univocal immersion that is transference and countertransference. Exchanges between unconscious and unconscious, pre-psyche to pre-psyche, dolphin communication, if you wish, to strongly suggest that this is about the "semiotic", the pre-verbal, which nevertheless mobilizes our capacities for rhetoric to give it a communicable formulation. The analyst does not dispose of enough time for rhetoric refinement. Nevertheless, he shares the economy of writing that is an accomplice of the flesh, in the way the "comprehension" of the patient is a process of identification with him and of a mellowing, possibly a removal of censorship. We are familiar with these two moments of sensorial and drive overflow that follow transference and countertransference, and its juncture with the work of formulating the interpretation. They cannot be better described than within that sentence of Proust, cited above, which evokes the author's entry into a transparent and sonorous "matter", fresh as a daisy. These are moments of interpretive grace that rarely occur, but which do exist and which make psychoanalysis distinct from all other therapeutic experiences.

It seems to me important, on the basis of Proust's writing, to reflect on the sadomasochistic parts of narration that are concealed in the analytic interpretation—narrating the patient's phantasy.[2] Analytic listening is in itself a violent act. I appropriate the patient's utterances, I identify with their suffering and pleasure, I am stirred by their words and hear with them in the same music. There is a part of perverted pleasure in this identification, which inevitably takes the way of part-objects and the ambivalence of the drives and desires in the transference and countertransference. But a further violence is added. I detach myself from this free-floating attention in order to name a meaning. My interpretation, because it is verbal, has to remain limited with regard to tone, the *Stimmung* of the listening. But it is the more so, because of the "theoretical" choice that stands out unconsciously in my spoken interpretation; since I chose to reveal this regression, oral or anal, or depressive, etc., and not another. Aulagnier (2001) has emphasized this violence of interpretation, which is doubtless a saviour; in the way that it exactly imposes a meaning, automatically limited, on the chaos of the drives, and that it favours psychic integration. It has been possible to locate the risks of giving allegiance to the analyst's wish that this violence carries, as well as its valency of suggestion. We have not, perhaps, emphasized sufficiently the mobilization involved in the analyst's own perversion. If it is true that, by interpreting, I turn myself into an other or an object for the analysand, it is nonetheless true that this structure that benefits the patient is taken from the perverted part of my personality, which manages to "capture" the other in the stride of sadomasochism.

When I make my patient the object of a case history, the narrative object develops in the ambivalence of love/hate, as in the sharing of the tea and the madeleine between the narrator and his mother, and as in the effort of naming this communion/communication. In fact, the patient's unconscious is aware of this as he violently demands interpretation, but as soon as he is given one, he suffers from it just as violently, since every interpretation, even the most correct one, reifies patients, objectifies them, and can in the end "analify" them. When Freud recommends silence as a means of analytic intervention, it is also probably to relieve this reduction of the patient to a perverse object, which might remain with the abusive interpretation, and to open up, in consequence, the time for the psychical working through.

Lacan seems to have been aware of this when he stopped interpretation. But here we touch on the reversed symmetrical pole. Systematic silence turns the analysand into a passive or decathected object, and sometimes triggers on the part of the patient an over-interpretation without a reference-point, which precipitates them into paranoia. It is left to us to modulate the two attitudes and direct the patient to become himself his own narrator, without needing, by the end of the analysis, our interference or even our sanction.

The reading of Proust, and the narrative experience more generally, would enable us, the analysts, to maintain tact, benevolence, care for others, while remembering precisely the permanence of sadomasochism. The reading of *Remembrance* leads us, I believe, to a maximum level of cruelty and a maximum level of delicacy. I am convinced that this is precisely what happens in analysis. If the analyst is not aware that he interprets by mobilizing this cruelty towards the patients, to the extent that he manages to identify with their pre-psyche, with their part-objects and with themselves, then he is only giving out superficial psychological help. Conversely, the knowledge that interpretation is an act of cruelty leads us to carry it out with the utmost kindness and tact. The care is in the delicacy of the story-telling. It cuts gently into the flesh and thus optimizes the capacity for representation, which is exactly the therapeutic means of Freud's legacy. One should recommend the reading of some literature in the syllabus of candidates, particularly that of Proust, so that they can master the art of delicacy that is narration.

Notes

1. The following passage is a substantial development of my idea that the Freudian theory of the unconscious is a theory of the co-presence of sexuality and thought:

    Psychoanalysis neither biologizes nor sexualizes the essence of man but emphasizes the copresence of sexuality and thought. It is on this point that cognitivist theories could make an interesting contribution, for they constitute an attempt to construct a theory of thought in relation to biological and sensorial development. But this is also their limitation, for they pretend to do without sexual development.

    I have already pointed out that Freudian psychoanalysis was founded on the asymptote between sexuality and language and that this gap between the two was readable in the first observations Freud made concerning hysterics: namely, the excitability of the hysteric, on the one hand, and the incongruence and inadequacy of this excitability with the thought of the other, as well as the absence of a juncture between the two. Having made this observation, Freud appeared to consider that language at once attests to the abyss between the two sides—excitability/ thought—and possible passageways. Your excitation does not correspond to your thought; the proof is you cannot say it. Thrown over this abyss, however, is the bridge of language, for through language the two sides of excitability and thought will try to connect. You cannot say this traumatic excitability, but, more exactly, you say it without knowing it, unconsciously. The other scene of the unconscious will take shape in language, which will become the space of another translinguistic representation. It allows the transfer—Freud called it the "transference", a term he used first to characterize the functioning of the unconscious and then the link to the analyst—from instinctual conflicts to sensible or reasonable behaviours. From then on, the unconscious will provide the model for a transition between excitation stemming from physiological, on the one hand, and conscious thought, on the other.

From the beginning of the Freudian inquiry into hysteria, psychoanalysis offers itself as a theory of what I call the copresence between sexuality and thought within language; it is neither a theory of sexuality in and of itself nor a biologization of the essence of man, as it is often reproached for being. Though Lacan highlighted this essential characteristic, it was already inscribed in the Freudian approach itself ... Freud, in sum, speaks of the way in which the child's thought is constituted in relation to his sexual conflicts. What happens? A range of heterogeneous elements is offered to the *infans*, a diversity of representations is put in place, particularly through the Oedipus; all of this ends in genitality as well as the active exercise of the symbolic function, that is, the mental capacity to speak, to reason, to be creative in language. (Kristeva, 2000, pp. 81–5)

2. I noticed during this stage of analysis how far the act of recounting gave the patient a power of domination over her colleagues and over myself, allowing her to hold them, and me, under her influence. (I shall return to this point on the sadomasochistic aspect of the act of narration in more detail when I discuss narration in Proust.) Narration, for my patient, was a way of taking revenge on the traumatic consequences of separation, whether phobic or autistic, but it was also a means of elaborating on them.

References

Aulagnier, P. (2001). *The Violence of Interpretation: From Pictogram to Statement*. A. Sheridan, translator. Hove: Routledge.
Cellérier, G., & Ducret, J.J. (1992). Le constructivisme génétique aujourd'hui [Genetic constructivism today]. In: B. Inhelder & G.

Cellérier (Eds.), *Le cheminement des découvertes de l'enfant* [Progress in child discoveries] (pp. 217–306). Lausanne: Delachaux et Niestlé.

Freud, S. (1905). Fragment of an analysis of a case of hysteria. *Standard Edition 7* (pp. 7–122).

Freud, S. (1925). Negation. *Standard Edition 19* (pp. 235–9).

Heidegger, M. (1968). Qu'est ce que la métaphysique? [1929]. In: *Questions I.* H. Corbin, translator. Paris: Gallimard. [(1977). What is metaphysics? [1929]. In: *Basic Writings*, D. Farrell Krell, translator/editor, pp. 95–116. New York, NY: Harper & Row.]

Klein, M. (1930). The importance of symbol-formation in the development of the ego. *International Journal Psychoanalysis, 11*: 24–39.

Kristeva, J. (1970). *Le texte du roman, une structure discursive transformationelle* [The text of the novel, a transformational discursive structure]. The Hague: Mouton.

Kristeva, J. (1989). *Black Sun: Depression and Melancholia.* L.S. Roudiez, translator. New York: Columbia University Press.

Kristeva, J. (1996a). La fille au sanglot. Du temps hystérique [The sobbing girl. Of hysterical times]. *L'Infini 54*: 41–2.

Kristeva, J. (1996b). *Time and Sense: Proust and the Experience of Literature.* R. Guberman, translator. New York: Columbia University Press.

Kristeva, J. (2000). *The Sense and Non-sense of Revolt: The Powers and Limits of Psychoanalysis.* J. Herman, translator. New York: Columbia University Press.

Mandler, J.M. (1983). Representation. In: L. Carmichael & P.H. Mussen (Eds.), *Handbook of Child Psychology, Vol. 3: Cognitive Development* (pp. 420–94). New York: Wiley.

Nelson, K., & Greundel, J.M. (1981). Generalised event representation: basic building blocks of cognitive development. In: A.L. Brown & M.E. Lamb (Eds.), *Advances in Development Psychology, Vol. 1* (pp. 131–58). Hillsdale, NJ: Lawrence Erlbaum.

Segal, H. (1957). Notes on symbol formation. *International Journal Psychoanalysis, 38*: 391–7.

Stern, D.N. (1993). The pre-narrative envelope. *Journal of Child Analysis, 14*: 13–65.

Todorov, T. (1988). *Literature and its Theorists: A Personal View of Twentieth-century Criticism.* C. Porter, translator. London: Routledge.

CHAPTER FIVE

"It seemed to have to do with something else . . .":

Henry James's *What Maisie Knew* and Bion's theory of thinking

Sasha Brookes

This article argues that what Maisie knew, as conveyed to readers of James's novel, can fruitfully be considered and interpreted in terms of Bion's theory of thinking, and especially his concepts of K and –K and the container/ contained relationship. It is shown that James describes a containing relationship that Maisie, the child protagonist, has with her nurse, and the gradual growth of such a relationship in Maisie's own psyche, leading to her capacity to learn from experience. James's text is shown to contain striking instances of the creation and the destruction of meaning (K and –K) by the adults close to Maisie. It is argued that Maisie's own choice to make links and to desire knowledge is made through her complex experience of the Oedipal situation, which gives her opportunities to see herself in "the third position" (Britton, 1998). Maisie's eventual decision about her life, made by herself in the absence of any adequate parent, is based on the unconscious knowledge that destruction of meaning poisons the mind, and she must do her best to avoid it.

Reproduced, with permission, from *International Journal of Psychoanalysis, 83*: 419–31 (2002). © Institute of Psychoanalysis, London.

Earth, Water, Fire and Air
Met together in a garden fair,
Put in a basket bound with skin,
If you answer this riddle you'll never begin
(Robin Williamson)

As Henry James developed as a novelist, his attention became more and more engaged with the minds of his characters, and with the nature of their thinking and the "knowledge" it was based upon. He became more and more interested in how his people variously know and do not know themselves, each other, and the experiences with which their creator presented them. *What Maisie Knew* was published in 1897 at the beginning of the "third period" of his work, in which he was the most preoccupied with the life or death of minds either nourished by or starved of knowledge of themselves and of the world outside them.

In 1896 he wrote in his journal: "It is now indeed that I may do the work of my life . . . I have only to face my problems . . ." These problems were not to be named. "But all that is of the ineffable", he wrote next. The "problems" which, when faced, would yield "the work of his life" are only to be known, either by author or reader, by a process of imaginative acquaintance with "the work" itself.

The title *What Maisie Knew* places knowing as a process squarely before the mind's eye of the reader and also conjures up "the ineffable" by means of the empty, unspecified "what" that challenges the reader's attention and directs it towards something which cannot be named in advance or in the abstract. The story of what Maisie knew is the story of Maisie's problems and how she faced them—of the growing relationship between herself and her external realities; and the closely related growth of her internal world of thoughts and feelings: her knowledge.

What Maisie Knew was being conceived at the same historical moment—at the approach of the twentieth century—as *The Interpretation of Dreams*. Here Freud, in making his understanding of the strange tragedy of Oedipus central to psychoanalysis, did name the problem that must be faced on the road to knowledge. His reading of Sophocles's drama depended upon his most radical postulate: the existence of a dynamic unconscious aspect of the mind. He argued that the tragedy draws everyone deeply into its far-fetched plot because:

there must be a voice within us ready to recognise the compelling
force of destiny in the *Oedipus* . . . his destiny moves us only because
it might have been ours—because the oracle laid the same curse upon
us before our birth as upon him. (Freud, 1900, p. 262)

With the new advantage of psychoanalytic knowledge, Freud
showed that we can become conscious of and stand outside our
identification with Oedipus. We can seek an answer to the principal
riddle of our lives, finding our guesses confirmed by stray facts and
memories of our histories which now make sense to us. This kind
of understanding deeply impressed Little Hans (Freud, 1909a) and
proves its usefulness every day in psychotherapy or in self-analysis,
the source from which Freud derived it. Dora, however, would have
none of it (Freud, 1905a).

The emotional effect of the Oedipal tragedy on its audience was
used by Freud to support his hypotheses, first, that we have deep
feelings of which we are unconscious and, second, that these same
deep feelings give us a sense of recognition of the truth of psychoanalytic insight. This kind of knowledge, which we draw from our
unconscious processes of mind, presents itself in feeling and not in
words. Freud evidently thought it carries its own conviction and is
to be trusted. He was presumably referring to it when he later said
that a man who doubts his own love may, or indeed must, doubt
every lesser thing (Freud, 1909b).

With hindsight, it now seems that Freud was speaking of two
different kinds of knowing, and did not pause in his argument to
make an explicit distinction between them. Winter (1999, p. 45)
quotes the historian of education Fritz Ringer, who noted that the
German academic tradition of Freud's time distinguished between
interpretative understanding, *verstehen*, and another kind of understanding, *erleben*, which is not under conscious control, and involves
the reader in reproducing within him/herself "the inner states which
gave rise to the text". Both are needed, and continual interaction is
needed between them, in order to understand experience, whether
of art or life. "If you [only] answer this riddle, you'll never begin."

At the beginning of a new millennium, and after many years of
learning about phenomena we know we will never measure
or predict, we now recognize without alarm that Freud's view of
knowledge, both hermeneutic and deductive, is self-enclosed. It

addresses the problem of human thought and does not reach outside its own subject-matter: our minds and their way of discovering their unconscious knowledge through the telling of a story: from *erleben* to *verstehen*.

In this paper I intend to draw on a work of art contemporary with the birth of psychoanalysis, and created without access to psycho-analytic thought, to support Freud's contention that the Oedipal situation is the problem that must be faced on the road to knowledge —the ineffable problem which James did not try to articulate, but which he set himself to express and explore in his novel. I also wish to suggest that present-day psychoanalytic theory allows us to add significantly to the understanding of humanity Freud gained from his particular guess at the Sphinx's riddle. Since he wrote, with the help of his discoveries, other thinkers have been concentrating on what we take with us, inside ourselves, when we go to meet the Sphinx. Henry James's story of Maisie's journey towards knowing foreshadows, in my view, the post-Kleinian model of the mind developed by Bion and his successors. Like Sophocles's play, James's novel holds more meaning within it than its creator was aware of or could have been aware of at the time of its writing.

In particular, James continually presents his characters with the choice Wilfred Bion tells us people are constantly facing: the choice between suffering and evading, knowing and not knowing about our experience of life (Bion, 1967). Both Freud and Klein recognized that human children confronted with the riddle of life have a powerful wish to know the facts and find an answer (Freud, 1905b; Klein, 1928). Both also described some of the ingenious ways we find to ignore the facts and falsify the answer. Bion (1967) recognized our lifelong struggle between the wish to know and the wish not to.

In this connection, Freud noted some odd deductions made by children from their observations aimed at finding out where babies come from, but did not recognize the extent of defensive refusal to know in early sexual theories. Chasseguet-Smirgel (1985), referring to McDougall (1986), points out that Little Hans's theory of his mother's widdler protected him from knowledge of the Oedipus situation as Klein defined it. He "defend[ed] himself against reality by repudiating it . . ." as Klein observes in another context. She continues, speaking of development in general: "the criterion of all later capacity for adaptation to reality, is the degree in which [children] are able to tolerate the deprivations that result from the Oedipus situation" (Klein, 1926, p. 128).

Had Hans acknowledged his mother's female genitals, he would have confronted himself with the knowledge that his parents' genitals were complementary, and hence with the primal scene (Britton, 1998). He suppressed the facts that would have brought home the painful truth to him; and in consequence found himself in outer reality imprisoned in the house by a phobia, and in an inner unknown state of fear and guilt about his Oedipal wishes. Knowing the truth about his parents' relationship and his exclusion from it was painful, and involved giving up the phantasy of overcoming his father and taking his place. But it allowed Hans to know himself as a child conceived by a mother and father together, and from this standpoint of reality to continue his exploration of both his inner and his outer worlds.

Britton (1998) has stated unequivocally what is implied by the end of Hans's story. It is only from the "third position" in the Oedipal triangle, which Hans was able to occupy at the end of his "analysis", that we are able to begin knowing. Gathering both kinds of knowledge—objective knowledge of reality, which differs from cherished phantasies, and also empathic knowledge of experience, which requires a capacity to recognize the separateness of loved and desired others—depends on the capacity to take the third position. The process of development confronts everyone with the difference between phantasy and reality and with the separateness of others. But there are tremendous differences between, for example, the characters in *What Maisie Knew* in the degree to which they can embrace this knowledge, make it part of themselves, and build on it. Many of them find it unbearable and unthinkable and turn away from it. The differences between James's characters can be better understood, in my view, by considering which of them is able to take the third position.

Maisie is the one who has the capacity and makes the choice to know "most" as James says. What does she learn and where does it leave her? And where did she get her capacity to know, which her parents seem to lack completely? I shall draw together Bion's empathic and empirical understanding, and James's intuitive and expressive creation of sixty years earlier, to try to show how they "give a sense of truth" by "combining different . . . views of the same object" (Britton, 1998, p. 34): in this case, different views of the process of knowing or not knowing one's experience.

The reader of *What Maisie Knew* shares with Maisie her emergence into consciousness. As far as I am aware, this is unique in James's fiction. He wrote about other children, and occasionally looked back at the childhood of characters we read about as adults, but only in Maisie's case did he evoke the first awakening shock when something longed for is missing. For Maisie, it is fat. Her calves were too thin, as her father's friends told her; they pinched her legs "until she shrieked—her shriek was much admired—and reproached them with being toothpicks" (James, 1966, p. 22).

We find Maisie with her nurse in Kensington Gardens, trying to get to grips with this. James never specifies her age nor tells his readers how much time is passing in the course of the story, but here she sounds as if she is four or five. We have been told, in a dry preamble, that her very tall, good-looking, fashionable parents have just divorced with as much publicity as possible, each accusing the other of being the worst, and battling over their child in a passion of hatred, which was actually the only passion of their lives. At first the court inclined to her father, not so much because he was any better than her mother, but because the disgrace of a woman was more appalling. Then it became clear that Beale Farange, Maisie's father, had spent a considerable sum given to him earlier by his wife for Maisie's maintenance on the understanding that he would not take divorce proceedings. He could neither raise this money nor "render the least account" of it, and his lawyers proposed a compromise that gave custody of the child to each parent in turn. Maisie is at her father's when we meet her, looked after by Moddle, whose only demand was that Maisie not play too far, and who was always on the bench when Maisie returned to it. Maisie has just left behind the time when she had only that desire to meet. James gives a minute account of her first collision with ineluctable reality, which corresponds exactly to the paradigm proposed by Bion in his paper "A theory of thinking" (1962a).

Bion's hypothesis is that the process of thinking comes into being, given good enough conditions, in order to deal with thoughts. Thoughts arise only from an absence of what is desired: when the breast is present there need be no thought. But a hungry baby is filled with the thought that she is dying and cries to rid herself of unthinkable fear and horror.

Sometimes, in good conditions, a mother has an unconscious capacity to register and recognize her hungry child's experience, and can think about it and name it. Consciously, the mother thinks that the baby is hungry and prepares to feed it, while unconsciously she accepts the ejected thoughts that her infant could not bear, and uses her own thinking capacity (called alpha function by Bion) to give them meaning. When this happens, the baby is able to take back into him/herself a meaningful experience ("the baby sounds upset"). When it fails to happen, because a parent either cannot recognize or cannot tolerate the baby's experience, instead of missing an absent breast the baby feels assaulted by overwhelming emptiness and meaninglessness: an abyss, a void, chaos.

In Bion's view, when a meaningful emotional interchange between the inner worlds of mother and infant accompanies physical feeding, it provides for the growth of a mind just as milk provides for the growth of a body. Following Klein's model (1952) Bion specified clearly the intrapsychic processes involved in the interchange. A baby must project its passionate feelings, having as yet no capacity to tolerate them, and, when things are going well, the projections can be unconsciously known and accepted by the parent. In the best case, the parent has sympathy with what his/her infant is experiencing and is also able to think that it is not the end of the world, though the baby may feel it is. After a sojourn, as Bion says, in the maternal unconscious, the infant can receive his/her feelings back, with the sense that they have been thinkable to the parent, though they were not so to him/herself. From many such experiences by an infant of unconscious "maternal reverie" grows an experience of mind, as a place where feelings can be given meaning by the mental capacity Bion called alpha function.

Precisely this happens between Moddle and Maisie. Maisie looks anxiously at other children's legs and asks Moddle if they too are toothpicks.

> Moddle was terribly truthful; she always said: "Oh my dear, you'll not find such another pair as your own." It seemed to have to do with something else that Moddle often said: "You feel the strain—that's where it is; and you'll feel it still worse, you know". (James, 1966, p. 22)

Maisie delivers her painful bewilderment to her nurse's mind, and Moddle does not deny or palliate Maisie's experience. She accepts the truth of it, and goes on to give it meaning by linking it with the events of Maisie's life. Maisie feels the strain of her broken home and warring parents and it shows in her legs; and as she grows older and knows more of her difficulties, she will feel them more acutely. Maisie takes in from Moddle a dim but real sense that her toothpick legs can be accepted; and more, that their meaning can be thought about. At this stage of her life, no one else connected with her is able to know or think about her feelings at all. Henry James provides Maisie, in her relationship with Moddle, with the experience of maternal reverie, within which she can start to grow her own mind.

He tells us that at the Kensington Gardens time Maisie had many experiences that she was unable to think about, and:

> it was only after some time that she was able to attach . . . the meaning for which these things had waited . . . she found in her mind a collection of images and echoes to which meanings were attachable— images and echoes kept for her in the childish dusk, the dim closet, the high drawers, like games she wasn't yet big enough to play. The great strain meanwhile was that of carrying by the right end the things her father said about her mother—things mostly indeed that Moddle, on a glimpse of them, as if they had been complicated toys or difficult books, took out of her hands and put away in the closet. (p. 23)

Moddle seems in this way to have shown Maisie that there were things which a child of her age couldn't and shouldn't think about yet, and Maisie, who couldn't but experience them, kept them in her mental closet. When the time came for Maisie to go to her mother's house:

> The ingenious Moddle had . . . written on a paper in very big easy words ever so many pleasures she would enjoy at the other house. These promises ranged from "a mother's fond love" to "a nice poached egg for your tea" . . . so that it was a real support to Maisie, at the supreme hour, to feel how . . . the paper was thrust away in her pocket and there clenched in her fist. (p. 23)

The relationship between Moddle and Maisie has a more profound meaning and even more resonance and beauty when it is seen in the light of Bion's concept of the "container/contained" relationship, one of his most important contributions to psychoanalytic theory (Bion, 1967). The container/contained relationship happens when one puts unthinkable experience in the closet of a thinking mind, which gives back the sense that somewhere the experience *is* thinkable: the mind's alpha function has "attached" meaning to it. James also used the metaphor of a container in his description of the mental cupboard in which Moddle put the experiences Maisie could not make any sense of. When the time came for them to separate, Moddle created a symbolic container in the unknown "other house" for Maisie to keep in her mind; she undertook that it would offer holding and nourishment to the lonely and frightened child, and, in the piece of paper, provided a physical token of her own function of containment for Maisie to take with her. Maisie's father, however, gave her a message to take to her mother that must have been a very great strain to carry by the right end: that her mother was "a nasty horrid pig".

It is quite difficult even for an adult reader distant by more than a century from this message to think about it, but consideration suggests that its form is more appalling than its content. Its language makes clear that instead of parents Maisie had two infuriated children of her own age who evidently had no closets to put their fury in and no one to help them create any. The two opposite experiences, of containment and the absence of it, seem at this point in the story to come to Maisie with equal intensity. Moddle happened to be there when Maisie's father gave Maisie his message, and was shocked out of her accustomed position of social inferiority and silence, into saying directly: "You ought to be perfectly ashamed of yourself!" Maisie remembered her "sudden disrespect and crimson face" more vividly at the time than the words of Beale's message, although when her mother later asked her for them she was able faithfully to repeat them. Moddle's outrage on her behalf, however, was kept by Maisie in her closet, and must have contributed to her later revelation: that "everything was bad because she had been employed to make it so."

By the time she went to the other house, Maisie had evidently taken in and made part of herself Moddle's belief in a container: a place where thoughts (originally arising from the absence or loss of something) could be kept, in the hope that thinking and linking ("it seemed to have to do with something else . . .") would give the experience meaning. She had also participated many times in the very opposite process: the destruction of meaning through links being broken. James presents a clear instance of this opposite process in relation to Maisie's legs, which had also given rise to her first experience of thinking. It is no accident that her father's friends attacked her in the place where she felt the strain—where her suffering was manifest. Unable to bear her vulnerability, they pinched her calves until she shrieked and admired her vocalizations as a diverting performance.

James presents the creation and the destruction of emotional meaning close together in relation to the same legs, and again the profundity of his vision is made more evident by seeing it in relation to Bion's concepts of K and $-K$ (1967). K signifies the desire for knowledge; knowledge which Bion believed must continually be created in every mind, by linking feeling with thinking and the inner world with the outer. In reading Maisie's story we discover some of the rewards of this process of knowledge creation but, as Moddle knew, it involves meeting painful truth and recalcitrant reality. When this feels intolerable, the alternative is to destroy meaning by destroying the links between inner emotional reality and outer reality, as do the "gentlemen" who divert themselves by making Maisie shriek. The consequences of much destruction of meaning by $-K$ also become clear in the progress of James's narrative.

Maisie's revelation—"that everything was bad because she had been employed to make it so"—came to her through her first encounter with romance. Her new governess, Miss Overmore, "by a mere roll of those fine eyes which Maisie already admired", conveyed to Maisie that there was an alternative to endless tit-for-tat; and this somehow caused a tremendous reverberation in the container, the closet of memory instituted by Moddle.

> It was literally a moral revolution and accomplished in the depths of her nature. The stiff dolls on the dusky shelves began to move their arms and legs; old forms and phases began to have a sense that frightened her. She had a new feeling, a feeling of danger; on which a new remedy rose to meet it, the idea of an inner self or, in other words, of concealment. (p. 25)

Maisie's admiration for Miss Overmore's fine eyes seems to have brought her to an encounter with the Oedipal situation, and this encounter breathed life into Maisie's potential for thinking and learning from experience. Her mother had told Maisie to tell her father that he "lies and knows he lies". Maisie, in the established mode of family communication, had vivaciously asked Miss Overmore: "*Does* he know he lies?" The governess conveyed to Maisie an unspoken message: "how can I say Yes after your papa has been so kind to me . . . ?" (p. 27). Just as Miss Overmore, though employed by Maisie's mother Ida Farange, declined to insult Beale, Maisie saw she could stop taking her parents' messages. "Her parted lips locked themselves with the determination to be employed no longer. She would . . . repeat nothing . . ." Maisie's revelation was of a couple with a relationship of kindness, which she saw shining in contrast to the couple whose retaliatory messages of hate she had been carrying. This vision led to "a moral revolution . . . accomplished in the depths of her nature." How can it have done so?

Maisie was able to commit experience too difficult for her to Moddle's maternal reverie, whence it was returned as thinkable. Together they created mental space for the storage of experience too hard for the child to think about, and found ways to build "a guard within" Maisie to help her at times of crisis (Rilke, 1987). They shared the belief that experience can be faced and considered; in Bion's terms they had a "container/contained" relationship. The "moral revolution" accomplished in the depths of Maisie's nature can be seen as the container/contained relationship coming to life inside herself—in her inner world, where she conceives of herself storing or concealing in her closet harmful messages so that they do no further harm. By this silence she determines to protect her vision of a couple with a relationship of kindness; a vision that sustains her even through being dashed by Ida from the top of the stairs almost to the bottom because she will no longer be a go-between. It is illuminating to consider further the sources and implications of the revolution in Maisie's internal world, in the light of psychoanalytic theory in general, and in particular Bion's theory of the development of thinking.

There is a striking difference in Maisie's position in relation to the two couples in her life at this moment. She is now perhaps eight or nine. She has been employed by the retaliatory couple as a medium to link them together with insults and outrages, and up till now there has been no reason to feel herself separate from them and their relationship. They do not conceive of her as a separate person, although they conceived her. She sees the "kind" couple, however, in a relationship that excludes her; at this point they do not seem to need her to link them together. Maisie thus finds herself in the third position.

There must be a crucial distinction, which James's language here helps to clarify, between the third position and the ignominious and agonizing position of Oedipal defeat. Evidently this defeat cannot be bypassed by anyone, and perhaps experiencing it was what made four-year-old Maisie's feelings about her legs so poignant. But she does not remain confined in the Oedipal triangle where the only possibilities are defeat and triumph, which must alternate, and where blindness is chosen rather than seeing and knowing. In her moral revolution "she had a new feeling: a feeling of danger . . ." born of the realization that she was being used by her parents to hurt each other. Then "a new remedy rose to meet it, the idea of an inner self . . ." It seems that Maisie was enabled to bear the moment of frightening vision because in extremity she found her "inner self" rose to meet her; she was not simply cast into the outer darkness of the excluded (or exploited) third. Readers may be reminded of Moddle's paper of consolations, which Maisie had thrust into her pocket and there clenched in her fist, giving her something unseen, inside, to help her; a symbol of the "guard within".

Maisie's mind-changing vision appeared in her inner world to herself alone, and only after making clear with what a "prodigious spirit" she interpreted and understood it does James show her trying to fit it to the real relations of her visionary "kind" couple in the outer world. There, things were more complicated, and an adult reader can have an advantage over Maisie, who wonderingly remembered Beale's words to the "almost too pretty" young governess: "I've only to look at you to see that you're a person I can appeal to for help to save my daughter." Adult readers see Beale's predatory pounce out of the groves of Kensington Gardens and hear his words as wolfishly unctuous and false. His character for his daughter, however, was still too difficult a book for her age: she kept it to read later. Reading James's novel "later" in the light of Bion's theory of functions (Bion, 1967), it is possible to compare Maisie's relations to her parental couple and to the new couple formed by her father and her governess, and to see that her function was essentially the same for both couples.

Bion's model of the mind (1962b; 1967) gives the need for meaning equal weight as a dynamic mental force with the forces of love and hate. He tried to avoid coining omniscient-sounding abstract nouns to denote mental processes which are unconscious and fundamentally mysterious to us, and instead used letters of the alphabet as signifiers. One effect of this choice is to present with striking clarity his view that each mental force can at any given time be working either creatively (signified as +) or destructively (−). Everyone, for instance, is always engaged either in creating or in destroying meaning; and the distastefully moralistic and hypocritical flavour of Beale's opening line convinces us immediately of his bad faith, that is, $-K$.

It also well illustrates Bion's theory that the dynamics L, H, and K are always performing a relating function (Bion, 1967). In one sentence, Beale stages a paranoid–schizoid alliance with Miss Overmore, in which they appear idealized as goodie rescuers opposed to the wicked Ida. No thinking or understanding will take place in this black-and-white drama. They need something to bring them together, however, in the absence of L, H or K, and Beale instantaneously recruits Maisie to serve as a pretext. Readers are already well aware of her function for Beale and Ida, of linking them together in an addictive and destructive relationship, which, I think, gives us a suggestive glimpse of $-L$ (Bion, 1967). Now Maisie is to be employed as a link again: at first sight it seems her function for the new couple might be different and perhaps better.

James dearly loved to contemplate the overdetermined entanglements of human affairs, presumably valuing awareness of the complexity of experience as Keats did, in writing of Negative Capability, and as Bion did in writing of learning from experience. Maisie's linking function for the second couple emerges from the detail of the narrative as both better and no better, from the point of view of her own welfare, than her function for the first.

As far as she can, Miss Overmore loves Maisie and appreciates what she later called her "plain, dull charm of character": her persevering struggle to know her experience and learn from it. As Miss Overmore's relationship with Maisie develops, however, it raises for the reader the question of what it is for the adults in the story to be parental: what it is to know the child who does so much knowing. Maisie's natural parents are quite incapable of knowing about anyone else: they are trapped in their narcissistic echo-chambers. But that by no means makes them insignificant for Maisie. James makes knowing them and accepting them her deepest and hardest developmental task. Miss Overmore can occasionally know and love Maisie, but she is not able to think about anything from Maisie's point of view or give up any pursuit of her own for Maisie's benefit.

When Miss Overmore appeared at Maisie's father's house, James makes clear that, though delighted to see her, she had not come because of Maisie. She had come, a poor girl with beauty and high spirits, to take her chance with Beale, as an alternative to the social extinction of being a governess. By the time that Beale unceremoniously married her and she became "Mrs Beale", the plot had also thickened at the other house, and Ida had found Mrs Wix as a cheap governess for Maisie. Mrs Wix had had little education and, with her one dress, her thick glasses, and her greasy button of hair, seemed grotesquely unattractive. Beauty is important and skin-deep in Maisie's story: her parents, Mrs Beale, and Sir Claude are all lovely to look at. Mrs Wix, however:

> touched the little girl in a spot that had never even yet been reached ... What Maisie felt was that she had been, with passion and anguish, a mother ... this was something Miss Overmore was not, something (strangely, confusingly) that mamma was even less. (p. 30)

Mrs Wix's passion and anguish partly relate to the death of her own child, but, as she will show, she is richly capable of feeling for Maisie. Being a mother, for James, is evidently not simply a matter of biological parenthood, but has to do with Bion's K: with knowing empathically and "containing" the feelings of a child. Mrs Beale later remarked that Mrs Wix was "as ignorant as a fish" of conventional learning; but Mrs Wix had not only "moral sense" but could also think realistically about basic truths, like generational difference, which were denied by Maisie's other "parents".

Ida next married Sir Claude, "ever so much younger" than herself, with whom, as Maisie learned from Mrs Wix, she was deeply in love. Soon Mrs Wix and Maisie were also in love with the charming Sir Claude, "a family man" who loved Maisie and presently arrived at Beale's to see her, and, inevitably, to be charmed by Mrs Beale. Maisie, as she says, had now "brought together" a third couple. Sir Claude is yet a brighter figure of romance for her than Mrs Beale, and he is also able, in a big-brotherly style, to be a parent to Maisie. Maisie knows this third couple are her dearest and best hope, though she also knows that MrsWix is always there intensely waiting.

Every encounter between Maisie and her natural parents in the course of the narrative consists of the opposite of their knowing her— of their trying either to drag something out of her or to push something into her. When there is no psychic container, feelings must be ejected; and other people are dragged in to fill up the empty spaces. James makes it plain that Beale and Ida connected themselves to others by means of projective identification (Klein, 1946), and he vividly shows us what are the consequences: both come to feel progressively more empty and impoverished. They experience this concretely as material poverty; Beale is last seen as the paid companion of a rich "countess" whose whiskery hideousness frightens Maisie, and Ida, in finally resigning as Maisie's mother, struggles to pay Maisie off with a ten-pound note and can't quite bring herself to give it.

Maisie accepts some of their projections. "Better to reign in Hell than serve in Heaven" might have been their joint motto, and when they cannot make others be what they want they angrily spoil every relationship, becoming more despairing and destructive as the story goes on. This deterioration shows itself to Maisie in various ways; for instance Ida's make-up becomes ever thicker and more dramatic as, presumably, she feels emotionally more unreal: "her huge painted eyes . . . were like Japanese lanterns swung under festal arches." Both parents severally break their ties with Maisie, putting it to her that they are being rejected and deserted by their child. Maisie accepts this from them both, partly because she knows them and what they would be bound to say, and partly because there is an element of truth in it. She knows that Beale and Ida cannot be parents to her and she must cling to the third couple she has linked together, the couple she loves best and with whom she has most chance of a relationship. This couple are betraying her natural parents, but this cannot be any concern of Maisie's. The betrayal seems inevitable, however, in the context of a post-Kleinian reading of James: since Beale and Ida are unable to occupy the third position, they must recurrently move from Oedipal triumph via betrayal to Oedipal defeat.

Unlike Beale and Ida, Sir Claude and Mrs Beale do not only use Maisie to embody aspects of their inner worlds. But Mrs Beale is unable to keep Maisie in mind; James poignantly demonstrates this through Maisie's shocking lack of routine education. Miss Overmore began as her governess but, as soon as she took up with Maisie's papa, had no more time to teach her. Mrs Wix tried, though handicapped by her own little learning, and with constant lapses into romancing about Sir Claude and Henrietta Matilda, her lost daughter who had been run over by a hansom-cab. For long stretches of time at her father's, however, Maisie was completely lonely and neglected, although she had somehow managed to learn the piano and a little French. Once, as part of a projected regime of taking her to lectures in "Glower Street", which had the advantage of being free, Mrs Beale came rushing in just in time to be late for one, which in any case was unintelligible.

Sir Claude had more capacity to think about and remember his stepdaughter, though his tender name for her, "Maisie-boy", shows he did not think of her as a daughter or, evidently, of himself as a father. He erratically and impractically provided for Maisie and Mrs Wix, whose meals at Ida's had become scanty and unpredictable "jam-suppers", so that they were glad of his gift of an enormous iced cake. Maisie's families were now falling apart: her step-parents had an adulterous relationship and her natural parents were growing more and more absent and scandalous. Finally, there was a crisis, and Maisie found herself with the housemaid who had been her only resource in Mrs Beale's absence, fleeing to France with Sir Claude.

In Boulogne, entrancing in its foreignness: its seascapes and golden Virgin, coffee and buttered rolls, Maisie came to make another link in her mind equal in importance to her earlier moral revolution. James articulates it simply. "What helped the child was that she knew what she wanted. All her learning and learning had made her at last learn that . . ." (p. 244). The flight to France had been the project of a fourth couple, also linked together by Maisie: Sir Claude and Mrs Wix. Mrs Wix had inspired Sir Claude to take Maisie (and herself as female attendant and governess) away from Beale and Ida, who had now effectively abandoned her, and to try to make a decent life for them all. Although this would fulfil part of Mrs Wix's fond dream, there is also a sacrifice to be made by her: she cannot have Sir Claude as partner, and instead will be a motherly servant to him and Maisie. In the scene at Boulogne, however, the cast of four—Sir Claude and Mrs Beale (who soon appears), Maisie and Mrs Wix—reveal and discover vital aspects of their inner selves.

Mrs Beale has always known what she wants, and now it is a "family" in the south of France, where living is cheap and she, Maisie, and Sir Claude can be together in a way that will nominally save appearances. If Mrs Wix will come too, so much the better; and Mrs Beale potently "makes love" to her and tries to seduce her out of her "moral sense". A psychoanalytic reading gives a deeper meaning than the conventional to this attribute of Mrs Wix's. She insists that an unmarried couple cannot be Maisie's parents, but her honesty and conviction seem to reach beyond this legal impediment, which the couple are sure they can remove in time.

Readers of the intense denouement of the narrative share Maisie's feelings in a way that so far they have not. We as readers have previously felt for her as she was pinched and neglected, as she was grabbed to Ida's bosom and squashed against her jewellery, or sent flying out of it again with such force that she had to be caught by bystanders. Now we feel with her as she feels "at the bottom of a hole"; feel her "faintest purest coldest conviction" that her beloved Sir Claude, the parent who loved her best, is lying to her, feel that "little by little it gave her a settled terror". Maisie knew all her fear and grief and held it within herself, and as a result of this "she knew what she wanted".

This form of words is important: it indicates again the internal container/contained relationship. There are two "she's" in the sentence, and though they are both Maisie they are different aspects of her. The one who knows is the guard within, aware of what Maisie wanted as an emotional being and human child, and prepared to stand up for her right to it. This assertion on Maisie's part is not entirely new in the narrative. Before their flight, Maisie and Sir Claude had accidentally encountered Ida and her current lover (in the park again). Ida had sent Maisie to walk with "the Captain" while she and her husband confronted each other. The Captain had completely espoused Ida's cause, and told Maisie emotionally: "your mother's an angel . . . Look here, she's *true!*" Maisie was deeply touched by this invocation of idealized womanhood, and sobbing "oh mother, mother", urged the Captain to say he loved Ida, and asked him not to stop loving her.

By the time Ida came to take her leave of her daughter, the Captain had become to her "the biggest cad in London". Maisie had accepted Ida's story that she was a noble, shattered victim of circumstances, who now must "try South Africa" or expire. But she protested against and resisted Ida's attack on the Captain, and the ideal couple in which she had momentarily been enshrined. Knowing the difference between good and bad must begin in splitting and idealization (Meltzer, 1973), and draw from unconscious origins the inspiration to find truth and beauty in "real life" as Maisie does, with grief and pain, at the end of her story.

What Maisie found she wanted was that she and Sir Claude should fly together. If he would sacrifice Mrs Beale, she would sacrifice Mrs Wix. Sir Claude almost shared her exhilarating, momentary hope that they could escape together to Paris; but he hesitated and they missed the train. With her back to him to protect him from her feelings, Maisie swallowed her tears of disappointment, clasping the volumes of the *Bibliothèque rose* he had bought her. When she turned back to him, her terror had gone with her tears. She was beginning to know that they could not be a father–daughter couple: Sir Claude would not leave Mrs Beale. Maisie was faced with a grown-up rival who had risked her reputation for Sir Claude: a partner of his own generation who offered a sexual relationship.

There certainly was a way for Maisie to join this couple, and both Sir Claude and Mrs Beale told her directly that she was essential to it. "You've done us the most tremendous good, and you'll do it still and always, don't you see? We can't let you go—you're everything" (p. 229). Maisie could have her old job back, continue her linking function for her parental couple and with it the split experience of powerlessness and omnipotence that had characterized her strange childhood.

Maisie's moment in the third position at the station, however, knowing that she wants the man she loves and is too young to have him, seems to have done for her what it had done for Little Hans at an earlier age. She knows she is still a child. Mrs Wix's "moral sense" that she should not have parents living in sin seems superficial compared to the sense they perhaps shared: that she should not always and forever be "doing the most tremendous good" to her parental couple. She should be having lessons and reading the *Malheurs de Sophie,* and Mrs Wix in her own more obvious way is also refusing to be a party to the sacrifice of Maisie's childhood.

It seems that at this denouement Sir Claude began to understand what Maisie knew. "I haven't known what to call it . . . but . . . it's the most beautiful thing I've ever met—it's . . . sacred" (p. 242). Maisie, in order to be the child she was, must tear herself away from the beloved but delusive adults she had hoped would be her family. As Sir Claude sees, Maisie can be herself—a child: he and Mrs Beale are unable to be what they should at their age: parental adults. Maisie's revelation could prosaically be called being in touch with reality, or learning from experience, but Sir Claude's allusion to the beautiful and the sacred reminds us that the creative life of the mind starts with acknowledgement of reality. Moddle had tenderly acknowledged of Maisie's legs: "Oh my dear, you'll not find such another pair as your own." Sir Claude now lovingly acknowledged that he lacked Maisie's power to know what was good for her. He could only do what Mrs Beale wanted.

Bion's K is not quantifiable: "Memory should not be called knowledge", as Keats wrote in 1818 (Gittings, 1987, p. 66). K is the linking function by means of which the mind ingests experience and is nourished. $-K$ starves or poisons the mind by denying or distorting reality—for instance, the truth of generational difference. Maisie knew that she must not poison her mind by returning to a pseudo-family, where she would take responsibility for the adults instead of their taking it for her.

The novel ends at this moral and emotional height; but it is characteristic of James that he does not lose touch with the vital question of what Maisie and Mrs Wix were going to live on. Readers have long known that "the child was provided for, thanks to a crafty godmother . . . who had left her something in such a manner that the parents could appropriate only the income" (p. 20). Maisie's thanks are also due to her stepfather, the one parent who has at last come to know her, and to a variety of unidealized mothers—Ida, without whom she would not have been born; Moddle, without whom she would have known nothing; her crafty godmother; Miss Overmore with her fine eyes; and Mrs Wix who is able to be true to her principles. At the last, Maisie is neither omnipotent nor helpless, but realistically dependent.

References

Bion, W.R. (1962a). A theory of thinking. In: *Second Thoughts: Selected Papers on Psychoanalysis* (pp. 110–19). London: Heinemann.

Bion, W.R. (1962b). *Learning from Experience.* London: Heinemann.

Bion, W.R. (1967). *Second Thoughts: Selected Papers on Psychoanalysis.* London: Heinemann.

Britton, R. (1998). *Belief and Imagination: Explorations in Psychoanalysis.* London: Routledge.

Chasseguet-Smirgel, J. (1985). *Creativity and Perversion.* London: Free Association Books.

Freud, S. (1900). The interpretation of dreams. *Standard Edition 4.*

Freud, S. (1905a). Fragment of an analysis of a case of hysteria. *Standard Edition 7* (pp. 7–122).

Freud, S. (1905b). Three essays on the theory of sexuality. *Standard Edition 7* (pp. 130–243).

Freud, S. (1909a). Analysis of a phobia in a five-year-old boy. *Standard Edition 10* (pp. 5–149).

Freud, S. (1909b). Notes upon a case of obsessional neurosis. *Standard Edition 10* (pp. 155–318).

Gittings, R. (Ed.) (1987). Letter to Reynolds. In: *John Keats: Selected Letters.* Oxford: Oxford University Press.

James, H. (1966). *What Maisie Knew* [1897]. London: Penguin.

Klein, M. (1926). The psychological principles of early analysis. In: R. Money-Kyrle, B. Joseph, E. O'Shaugnessy, & H. Segal (Eds.), *The Writings of Melanie Klein, Vol 1* (pp. 128–38). London: Hogarth, 1975.

Klein, M. (1928). Early stages of the Oedipus conflict. In: R. Money-Kyrle, B. Joseph, E. O'Shaugnessy, & H. Segal (Eds.), *The Writings of Melanie Klein, Vol 1* (pp. 186–98). London: Hogarth, 1975.

Klein, M. (1946). Notes on some schizoid mechanisms. In: *Envy and Gratitude and Other Works* (pp. 1–24). London: Virago, 1988.

Klein, M. (1952). Some theoretical conclusions regarding the emotional life of the infant. In: *Envy and Gratitude and Other Works, 1946–1963* (pp. 61–93). London: Virago, 1988.

McDougall, J. (1986). *Theatres of the Mind: Illusion and Truth on the Psychoanalytical Stage.* London: Free Association Books.

Meltzer, D. (1973). *Sexual States of Mind.* Strath Tay: Clunie.

Rilke, R.M. (1987). *The Selected Poetry of Rainer Maria Rilke.* S. Mitchell, translator/editor. London: Pan.

Winter, S. (1999). *Freud and the Institution of Psychoanalytic Knowledge.* Stanford, CA: Stanford University Press.

CHAPTER SIX

Some thoughts on the essence of the tragic

K.I. Arvanitakis

An attempt is made to define the essence of the tragic through an examination of Euripides's The Bacchae, *a tragedy that deals with the origins of tragedy itself. The action here culminates in the dismemberment of Pentheus by his mother. It is proposed that the tragic may be related to the earliest phases of differentiation of the subject as a separate entity breaking off from the original mother–infant unit. Tragedy, in this view, could be regarded as the enactment of a primal phantasy of the birth of the "I" as the result of an archaic act of violence. The process of mourning for the loss of the original unity is central to this development. Pentheus's tragic flaw consists in his repudiation of contradictory dualities and his inability to mourn. The integrative function of* logos, *both in tragedy and in the analytic process, is underlined. It is suggested that* logos *aims to generate meaning not by eliminating contradiction but by embodying the foundational human paradox.*

Reproduced, with permission, from *International Journal of Psychoanalysis*, 79: 955–64 (1998). © Institute of Psychoanalysis, London.

The tragic defines our Western culture and informs our vision of reality: it is our cultural *a priori*. An attempt will be made here to define the essence of what we call "the tragic" as it was first expressed in that unique creation of the fifth century BC Greek tragedy, and to view it in the light of our conceptualization of the earliest phases of psychic development.

Aristotle's treatise on poetry (Butcher, 1951) traces the origins of tragedy to the Dionysiac satyr chorus and the associated dithyramb hymns in honour of Dionysos. This is also Herodotus's view (1981, 5.67). Although questioned by some (e.g. Else, 1967), Aristotle's testimony has shaped all subsequent thinking on the matter. It has been the inspiration for Nietzsche's passionate argument in *The Birth of Tragedy* (1954) and the stimulus for an anthropological treatment of the question by the so-called "Cambridge Ritualists" at the beginning of the century, who based their views on anthropological evidence available to them at the time (Harrison, 1912; Murray, 1918). They believed Dionysos to be a Year Spirit and held that tragedy arose out of a vegetation ritual celebrating the rebirth of nature.

The direct association of Dionysos with the early development of tragedy is now generally accepted. Accordingly, I propose to base my enquiry into the tragic on an examination of this deity.

By his very nature Dionysos is the most obscure and multi-faceted god of the Greek pantheon: a veritable "dark continent". Following Freud's advice (1926, p. 212), then, with regard to the exploration of dark continents, we may turn to the poets for guidance (1933, p. 135). Only one of the surviving tragedies has Dionysos as its subject and this is *The Bacchae* by Euripides, written in 406 BC. The *Pentheus*, *Bassaridae*, and the *Lykurgos* trilogy by Aeschylus, also dealing with Dionysos, are not extant. Thus Euripides—assisted by Aristotle—will be our principal guide in getting a glimpse into the nature of the masked god.

Segal writes: "*The Bacchae* is a play about primordial beginnings . . . because its divinity [i.e. Dionysos] is so closely linked to the origin and form of tragedy itself, an interpretation of *The Bacchae* becomes a reflection . . . on the nature of classical tragedy, and indeed of the tragic in general" (1982, p. 4); and elsewhere: "Euripides uses the figure of Dionysos as a god of the tragic mask to reflect on the paradoxical nature of tragedy itself" (p. 216).

The plot of *The Bacchae*, in summary, is as follows (Schlesinger, 1963): Dionysos, disguised as a traveller, comes to his homeland Thebes after spreading his rites over Asia. Thebes will be made the first site of Bacchic[1] worship in Greece because his mortal mother's sisters, princesses of Thebes, have denied his divine birth. He has therefore driven all the women of Thebes out into the wilds in Bacchic revelry. Pentheus, king of Thebes and grandson of the founder Kadmos, refuses to worship Dionysos. Dionysos summons the chorus of Asiatic women who follow him devoutly. They appear, singing the story of the god's miraculous double birth (from his mother's womb and later from his father Zeus's thigh), and invite the Thebans to take part in the joyous miracles of Bacchic revelry in the wilds.

Tiresias then comes, accompanied by Kadmos, the two old men now worshipping Dionysos. Pentheus arrives, who, suspecting the women of lust for which the novel rites are a mere excuse, has ordered the arrest of all those he could lay his hands on and is looking for their charlatan leader. He is disgusted to see Tiresias and Kadmos in Bacchic garb; had it not been for his respect for old age he would have them arrested too. Tiresias, however, retorts that Dionysos exists as a force of nature, but Pentheus furiously orders that Tiresias's seat of prophecy be destroyed and that the insidious stranger be sought out and arrested. The chorus calls for punishment of the folly of Pentheus and sings of far-famed places in which the Bacchic rites are celebrated. A servant of Pentheus now enters bringing the stranger as a prisoner but reporting that the arrested women have been miraculously freed and have joined the revels in the mountains. The stranger refuses to reveal the secrets of his rites and shows no fear, saying that Dionysos will free him when he asks. He remains calm as he is taken in when suddenly the palace begins to shake and fire breaks out as the chorus sings its awe of the god's power. Dionysos appears (still in his human disguise) telling of the madness that fell upon Pentheus, which made him bind a bull believing it to be the stranger, and plunge his sword into the air, seeing phantoms.

A messenger comes from Mount Kithaeron reporting that he has seen the Bacchae peacefully sleeping with no sign of the misconduct that Pentheus had assumed. They woke up and rejoiced in harmonious fellowship with animate and inanimate nature, while springs of milk were flowing around. But when the men tried to round them up they viciously swept down on grazing herds tearing the beasts to pieces with their bare hands and sacking the villages on the slopes of the mountain. Enraged, Pentheus calls on the citizen army to rout the Bacchae, paying no attention to the stranger's warnings. Then begins the famous *stichomythia*[2] between the stranger and Pentheus, who now wishes to be disguised as a woman (Bacche) in order to watch the Bacchae in their secret places. While Dionysos helps him dress up, Pentheus, now seeing double, anxiously anticipates sharing in the Bacchic ecstasies. Dionysos covertly prophesies his fate as he leads him away. The chorus sings of savage retaliation against those who disrespect the Supreme Law. Next, a messenger arrives, reporting the death of Pentheus torn to pieces by his mother. Agave enters carrying her son's head, believing it to be the head of a lion she hunted down. Kadmos follows with bearers of the fragments of Pentheus's body, before Agave realizes what she has done. Dionysos finally appears as a god, banishing Agave and Kadmos to exile and announcing Kadmos's and his wife's transformation into serpents until their eventual return to the Land of Blessed. The tragedy ends with the chorus singing: "Manifold are the forms of gods, and manifold the things unhoped-for, which they accomplish."

Dionysos

"This mad insolence (*hybrisma*): an incalculable reproach to the Greeks" (Kirk, 1970,[3] l. 779) is how Pentheus refers to Dionysos and his followers. Rohde, at the end of the last century, basing himself on Herodotus, believed Dionysos to be indeed an element foreign to Greek culture, hardly present in Homer, invading Greece's Apollonian soil from the north. This Thracian cult was amalgamated with Apollonian religion, thereby becoming "hellenized and humanized" according to Rohde (1898). Thus, at Apollo's temple at Delphi (4 BC) the east pediment represented Apollo and the Muses while the west pediment showed Dionysos. It was believed that when Apollo migrated to the land of the Hyperboreans in the winter months it would be Dionysos who would reign until his return. The view of a late appearance of Dionysos in Greece, however, appears inaccurate in the light of recent findings. Excavations at Aghia Irene in the island of Keos have brought to light a fifteenth-century BC sanctuary of Dionysos, and evidence from Linear B tablets from Pylos suggest that worship of Dionysos was already established in Mycenean times. It gained prominence towards the end of the sixth century BC, its mystical character appealing to the masses, who had found nothing comparable in the Olympians. The tyrant Peisistratos knew well how to exploit this need and founded the Great Dionysia festival. That powerful Dionysiac forces are present in the individual from the very beginning is, of course, a matter well known to psychoanalysis and so the deity's early presence in Greek culture would appear to be a parallel phenomenon on the cultural level.

Who is this Dionysos then, this strange "stranger", this unwelcome barbarian now uncannily returning to his native land? He is the god of the abolition of rigid boundaries. He is the *ek-static*[4] unity of contradictory realities. He is also the embodiment of primeval cruelty.

Boundaries are abolished, distinctions loosened. Dionysos was called Lysios (the "loosener"), because he represented divine madness, non-differentiation, sacred *enthousiasmos*, confusion. When Pentheus asks who this god is, the answer he receives is "Whosoever he wishes to be!" (l. 477). He is the god of multiple fluid transformations. Anaxagoras, the fifth-century philosopher, held that before Reason or Mind (*Nous*) made its appearance "everything was mixed with everything else" (Kirk et al., 1971, fr. 512). Dionysos stood for such a pre-rational state in which there is no distinction between reality and illusion, subject and object, part and whole.

The *Di*-onysos of the *di*-thyramb is the embodiment of duality, of the "tragic dissonance" (Nietzsche, 1954, p. 1085) of human nature. A human god of two births, he is the masked *ek-static* double of himself, appearing to the Thebans in his disguise, while his "twin"[5] Pentheus in turn disguises himself as a *Bacche*.

Dionysos is the vegetation god of sweet tendrils, of ivy-staves dripping honey, of idyllic innocence and serene rapture (l. 683–711), a god "most gentle" to wretched human beings, soothing life's sorrows with his healing vine (l. 772). But, at the same time, he is the chthonic ruthless sovereign of the darkest forces of savagery: the "most dreadful god" (l. 861). The beautiful effeminate stranger arriving at the City Gates (l. 453–9) soon reveals the explosive unspeakable horror of his primeval cruelty. The two scenes of dismemberment (*sparagmos*) in *The Bacchae* are two of the most potent passages spoken in Greek literature:

> ... They [the Bacchae] attacked the grazing heifers
> with hand that bore no steel.
> And one you could have seen holding asunder in her hands
> a tight-uddered, young, bellowing heifer;
> while others were tearing full-grown cows to pieces.
> You could have seen ribs, or a cloven hoof,
> being hurled to and fro; and these hung
> dripping under the fir trees, all mixed with blood.
> Bulls that were arrogant before, with rage in their horns,
> stumbled to the ground,
> borne down by the countless hands of girls.
> The garments of flesh were drawn apart more quickly
> than you could close the lids over your royal eyes.
> (l. 735–47)

And Agave,

> ... discharging foam from her mouth
> and rolling her eyes all around, her mind not as it should be,
> ... was possessed by the Bacchic god.
> Grasping his [Pentheus's] left arm below the elbow
> and setting her foot against the unhappy man's ribs,
> she tore his shoulder out, not by her normal strength,
> but the god gave a special ease to her hands.
> Ino was wrecking the other side of him,
> breaking his flesh, and Autonoe and the whole mob
> of bacchants laid hold on him; all gave voice at once—
> he moaning with what breath was left in him,
> they screaming in triumph. One was carrying a forearm,
> another a foot with the boot still on; the ribs were being
> laid bare by the tearing; and each of the women,
> with hands all bloody, was playing ball with Pentheus' flesh.
> The body lies scattered, part under blind rocks,
> part among the deep-wooded foliage of the forest,
> no easy search; and the poor head,
> which his mother just then seized in her hands,
> she fixed on the point of her thyrsus ...
> (l. 1122–3, 1125–42)

The tearing apart of the human body is a constant theme in myths related to Dionysos, who was, accordingly, called *anthroporraistes* ("he-who-tears-humans-apart"). Dionysos himself as a child was torn to pieces by the Titans at the command of Hera, the Mother Goddess. *Mothers* who follow Dionysos (Leukippe, the women of Argos, Procne, the daughters of Proitos, the daughter of Pandion, and others) tear their own children apart as they are seized by Dionysian frenzy.

Aristotle defines *œnigma* as an impossible link (*Poetics*, 1458a26), the mixing of immiscibles, the conjunction of opposites. Dionysos is patently an enigmatic god. The god of contradictory yet interchangeable realities is Supreme Law (*nomos*) and Nature's wisdom (*sophia*): such was Euripides's claim in *The Bacchae* (l. 991–4; 395–9). Reality is enigmatic because of its admixture with illusion. The masked god, the prototypical actor, positions himself ambiguously at the border between fantasy and reality, sanity and madness. He doubles himself to be the Other and is a figure of composite identity, always more than what or who he appears to be.

Pentheus, the spectator of secret rites, like the spectator of *The Bacchae*, is irresistibly drawn to witness sights that are "best not seen" (l. 912). The stress on the visual is unparalleled in Greek drama. But what is revealed in the end is the spectacle on the other side of the mask and this is a scene of unnameable dread. The enigmatic conjunction of the opposites reappears as the tragic disjunction of the identical (dismemberment). The "play", in the sense of a child's play (cf. l. 867), ends but the order of the Polis has been irreversibly disrupted. Small wonder that poetry was allowed no place in Plato's ideal State. Tragedy undermines ordered reality by unmasking its polysemic and contradictory character. The *theoria*[6] of *theatron* is a meta-theory (i.e. a theory of spectating) of chaos and of supreme order.

Aristotle's belief—it is worth noting—was that tragedy was born when a member (*exarchon*) of the choral fusional mass broke off and started acting independently and speaking in his own voice, thereby becoming the first actor. The Dionysian theme of the break-up (*sparagmos*) of an original unity is echoed in Aristotle's historical account of the emergence of tragedy. The actor, through the process of identification (*mimesis*), will now assume the identities of various personages, again echoing the ecstatic transformations of the followers of Dionysos. Theory here recapitulates myth. In the evolution of theatre, as in human psychological evolution, verbal language became dominant following differentiation and replaced body language (the dance of the chorus). A second actor was soon added, initiating a dialogue with the first, and then a third. All the personages were now in place for the culmination of the human drama.

The three "principal elements" of tragedy, according to Aristotle, are Recognition (*anagnorisis*) of "who is who" (*Poetics*, l. 1448b16), the accompanying Reversal of the situation (*peripeteia*), and Pathos, which Aristotle defines as a "destructive and painful act" (l. 1452b11). The protagonist, carrier of a Fault (*hamartia*),[7] is inexorably compelled to a progression from a confusing ambiguity of doubles, through *metaphora* ("the art of discerning similarities", l. 1459a8), to the recognition of true identities ("who is who") and the necessary suffering of *pathos* that this entails.

It can now be seen that among the extant Greek plays, Euripides's *Bacchae* is indeed unique because here tragedy is reflecting on its own origins and essential nature. Its plot (*mythos*) is the myth of its own obscure beginnings. The chorus occupies once again the centre of action. *The Bacchae* is a poem about *poiesis*, the *poiesis* of the new order that was emerging in fifth-century Athens. It is, in this sense, a meta-tragedy.

Aristotle considered Euripides to be—although not without shortcomings—"the most tragic of poets" (*Poetics*, l. 1453a29). Most tragic because, both by temperament but also owing to the times in which he lived, he was fated to experience most acutely the profound tensions of a world in transition. A solitary, austere intellectual, known and often ridiculed for his attention to contradiction and paradox,[8] he occupied, more than any other poet of the classical period, a liminal position between the secure world of the old theocracy with its mystical allure and the strains of the new rationality of the *polis*, making man the creator of his own destiny. At the end of his life, torn between rational Athens and the wild forests of Macedonia, it was in Macedonia that he created *The Bacchae*, in which "he reveals, so far as such a thing can be revealed, the secret religion of poetry" (Murray, 1918, p. 96). In his liminal and hence fundamentally Dionysian position Euripides can be said to be indeed always modern (de Romilly, 1986).

The logos of the myth and the myth of logos

At the centre of the orchestral circle of ancient theatre stands the altar of sacrifice (*thymele*) of the animal god: at the core of the play there is an act of sacred violence (Burkert, 1966). The One ruptures to become Two. It is the centre that holds the periphery, as it were, and creates the circle. Without the central act the undifferentiated choral mass would have no boundaries and would spread out to engulf everything in chaos. The central *pathos* of the orchestral circle is therefore, in so far as it creates order and introduces differentiation, a formative *pathos*, a generative violence. It is generative because it gives rise to the individual as a separate, distinct subject, as a *dividuum*, a divided entity fated by necessity to mourn interminably its narcissistic wholeness. It is this process that Pentheus repudiated and that we find at the root of tragedy. It would appear that the Dionysiac sacrifice and ritual enacts a universal primal phantasy of the birth of the individual as the result of an archaic act of violence that brings about the rupture of an original unity (Arvanitakis, 1998). Euripides's *Bacchae* returns to this founding ritual, re-enacting a primeval dynamic between *chaos* and *cosmos*.

By pointing to the Dionysiac origin of tragedy Aristotle puts the emphasis on the pathos of the fragmentation (*sparagmos*) of a primal unit as the defining characteristic of the tragic. The end of tragedy as of all art, he maintains, is *logos alethes*, true logos (1982, l. 1140a11, 21). *Logos* in this context signifies the capacity to distinguish and to integrate differences. The central mutative act in the progression from the *mythos* of an original unity to the *logos* of differentiation is a formative violence that, fundamentally, operates in the service of the life instincts (Bergeret, 1980; Girard, 1972). Following the rupture of the original Whole there is duality with consequent conflict and the appearance of language to mediate in a divided universe. Pentheus's tragic flaw was the prototypical *hamartia* of disavowing contradictory duality and insisting on a unitary state of absolutes. This represents an attempt to bypass the differentiating violence and thereby avoid individuation and separateness. The "mournful"[9] Pentheus refuses to acknowledge and mourn his incompleteness. Thus Dionysos to Pentheus: "You know not your life, nor your actions. You know not who you are" (l. 506).

For Leclaire (1975) the phantasy "A child is being killed" is the most primal and most horrifying of all phantasies and expresses the struggle to eliminate the representation of the omnipotent narcissistic body. The phantasy of infanticide seems to us to be indissolubly linked with the birth scene as a manifestation of the fact that conception is dual: in order for the *infans* to develop a psyche it must be given a death as well as a birth by the conceiving matrix (the parental unconscious)—a death in the sense of an act of separation, of disjunction from the maternal ground.

The primal violence seals the division, as it were, and permits the recognition of "who is who". Via this process (wo)man is born as a divided consciousness capable of, or rather condemned to self-reflection; condemned to be a dislocated subject, to recognize the Other in the self and the self in the Other; to construct meaning that is for ever double; to be a desiring subject and a subject only in so far as he/she is the object of the desire of the Other; to acquire *sapience*, in the evolution towards humanization, which consists in the consciousness of death at the core of being.

We may, thus, conclude that the essence of the tragic is the primordial violence of differentiation, the necessary *pathos* that operates a cleavage in the original mother–infant oneness, thereby creating duality and leading to the birth of the subject as a separate being capable of self-consciousness. Located at the root of the individual the tragic can be said to coincide with the evolutionary origins of *homo sapiens* (*homo* becoming *sapiens* at the moment of rupture). On the ontogenetic scale, it would represent and enact the gestalt of mnemic traces *cum* associated phantasies relating to that crucial generative moment in psychic development when the distinction "me"–"not me" first arises (Winnicott, 1971). On stage, it can be regarded as the enactment of a primal phantasy of origins. That it made its appearance as an art form at a transitional period in Western culture, and in a region geographically situated between East and West, comes as no surprise. Fifth-century Athens was navigating between religious myth and philosophical logic, between theocracy and democracy. With the emergence of the *polis*, the individual as a part of a larger Whole needed to be defined, and his relationship to other individuals depended on his capacity to identify with them projectively. Tragedy arose as a cultural institution that promoted the mapping out of boundaries and relational interfaces between the One and the Many.

And yet tragedy has been considered as dangerous and subversive (Plato, *Republic* Bk. 10, 1. 595a–608c, in Burnet, 1973). It would seem that this was due less to its unmasking of the archaic violence and more to the fundamental ambiguity of existence that it exposes. Vernant and Vidal-Naquet (1972) are correct, I believe, in holding that Plato's banishment of poetry from his *polis* was the expression of the intolerance of the philosopher's logic for the tragic contradiction that allows both members of the duality to be valid. Tragic logic is a logic of ambiguity and makes no clear and irreversible distinction between true and false, right and wrong, subject and object. This radical ambivalence of human consciousness forms the core of Hegel's theory of tragedy. Hegel asserted that in tragedy the Spirit (*der Geist*) is "torn asunder into its two extreme powers" (1969, p. 738) and that "the agent finds himself thereby in the opposition of knowing and not knowing" (p. 739). What is tragic is that both sides are equally valid, neither being absolute since each is a part of a bisected Whole. Thus error (*hamartia*) is inescapable. The tragic conflict is between good and good, and the exclusive affirmation of either side entails wrong-doing.[10]

Now Hegel believed that, in the end, this opposition is reconciled by the synthetic action of the Spirit asserting its absoluteness. The affirmative power of the Spirit, even in its profoundest divisions, and its capacity to heal the tragic gap was for him the deepest truth (Bradley, 1962). In this view tragedy, far from being disruptive, can be seen to have an essentially therapeutic and pedagogical character. This was clear to Pericles, who introduced the *theorikon* subsidy allowing all citizens free entrance to the theatre. The function of tragedy is to reenact the primal violence in order to imbue it with *logos* and by so doing transform it into a life force. This is what Aristotle had in mind when he declared poetry to be indissolubly linked with *logos alethes*. The root *leg*—of *logos*—indicates "to gather" or "to bring together", an action that is contrary to splitting. *Logos* in its synthetic integrative power transcends irreconcilable oppositions (a narcissistic dynamic) and brings opposites into relation with each other (object relation). The principal function of tragedy is, accordingly, to restore and integrate memory: the memory of the forgotten past of non-differentiation and of the generative violence that followed. It is here that we see most clearly the tragic character of psychoanalysis or the essentially psychoanalytic character of tragedy. In its aim to recapture and articulate primal phantasies[11] psychoanalysis, like tragedy, is a confrontation with time. But the retracing of time necessarily entails mourning for lost objects, for lost worlds. Mourning is central to tragedy as it is central to psycho-analysis. Pentheus, "the mourner", would not mourn. He insisted on "forgetting" that which cannot be forgotten, and so it returns to destroy him. Freud described this process at length (e.g. 1911, p. 12ff). The law of nature (Kirk, 1970, 1. 1349) triumphed in its final epiphany as the hunter became the hunted. Unable to be "divinely mad" (see Plato, *Phaedros*, 1. 244a7, in Burnet, 1973), i.e. to allow a Dionysian play in the Winnicottian intermediary area where paradox makes separation possible, Pentheus was struck with pathological madness, a violent restitution of reason.[12] What is experienced as tragic—and what Pentheus had refused—is that the outcome of the break-up of the original unity means that reality, goodness, justice, truth, beauty, and even the "I" are not inalterable absolutes but are multiform. This makes human choice on an either/or basis impossible. It is at this point that Dionysos's paradoxical wisdom (1. 203, 1. 395) intervenes to make life possible and to maintain sanity: permeable boundaries are formed that allow for fluid transitions and transformations among entities that are only parts of a unit.

Winnicott elaborated admirably on the vital importance of the space of play for psychic growth and health. Rigid boundaries and the inability to tolerate contradiction preclude a solid sense of personal identity and the possibility of creative object relations. An inflexible self remains vulnerable to violent transformations and to true madness, which was the fate of Pentheus. Unable to deal with painful depressive anxieties, he retreated to a paranoid fusion with his mother (becoming a *Bacche* himself) and was subjected to a brutal separation–dismemberment—he who would not re-member—robbed forever of an emerging organizing *logos*. The play begins with a *mnema* (1.6), a memorial to the dead mother, and ends with the non-*mnema* of the murdered son. Pentheus has no *mnema* because his tomb is his mother's body and his mourning (*penthos*) is interminable. The memory of the subject is constructed on the memory of a pre-historic rupture. Pentheus, disavowing his past and his present state of incompletion, was a man without memory, a body severed (*choris*, 1. 1137) from collective *logos*.

A fragment of Herakleitos the "obscure" states: *ethos anthropo daimon* (Kirk et al., 1971, fr. 250). The syntactical symmetry of this aphorism creates an enigmatic ambiguity: "man's character is his daemon" or "man's daemon is his character". The ambiguity sharpens if we substitute *logos* for *ethos*: *logos anthropo daimon*. This would posit *logos* as a formative human principle, a primary drive. *Logos* gathers the fragments of memory and constructs meaning. But the meaning that *logos* constructs is not logical as *logos* is more than the rational principle. Alkmaion of Kroton (Kirk et al., 1971, fr. 284) held that human beings differ from other animals in being capable of bringing together and placing side by side in thought (*xynienai*) opposing and contradictory elements. The aim of *logos* is not to eliminate contradiction but to construct a meaning that embodies it and expresses the fundamental human paradox.

There is a poignant moment in Aristophanes's *Acharneis* (1982, l. 395–9), in which Dikaiopolis comes to visit Euripides and, finding the latter's servant outside the house, asks if his master is in. The servant's reply is: "He is in and not in, if you know what I mean". "How's that?" enquires the baffled Dikaiopolis. "Well," the servant replies, "while his mind is outside gathering flowers of little songs, he is inside writing a tragedy." Tragedy cannot be written otherwise. Another of Herakleitos's aphorisms speaks of opposites being taken apart and then brought together again "in a tense yet harmonious to-and-fro, like that of the lyre and the bow" (Kirk et al., 1971, fr. 212). This balanced precariousness of existence is the essence of tragedy.

Notes

1. Dionysos was also known as Bacchos.
2. *Stichomythia* in classical drama is an animated dialogue between two characters consisting of rapidly alternating brief statements of their opposing views.
3. All line numbers quoted in the remainder of this paper are taken from this edition.
4. *ek-static*: standing outside oneself; hence, a manner of doubling.
5. Pentheus is, of course, Dionysos's cousin, but in the play dynamic he is Dionysos's double (see Winnington-Ingram, 1948).

6. From *theorein*: to spectate.
7. A term derived from archery and meaning "missing the mark".
8. See, e.g. Aristophanes's *Acharneis*, l. 396–9 (1982) and *Frogs*, l. 1082 (1979).
9. *penthein*: to mourn.
10. Cf. Girard's view that tragedy is an opposition of symmetrical elements (1972, p. 213ff).
11. This is not intended to suggest that the "past unconscious" is retrievable *per se* in a strict archaeological sense (see Sandler & Sandler, 1987).
12. Note the tragic irony in Dionysos's words to Pentheus: "Before you were out of your mind. Now [that you are seeing double] you are as you must be" (l. 947–8).

References

Aristophanes (1979). The frogs. In: *Aristophanes, Vol 2: The Peace, The Birds, The Frogs*. B.B. Rogers, translator. Cambridge, MA: Harvard University Press.

Aristophanes (1982). The Acharnians. In: *Aristophanes, Vol 1: The Acharnians, The Clouds, The Knights, The Wasps*. B.B. Rogers, translator. Cambridge, MA: Harvard University Press.

Aristotle (1982). *The Nichomachean Ethics*. H. Rackam, translator. Cambridge, MA: Harvard University Press.

Arvanitakis, K.I. (1998). A theory of theater: Theater as theory. *Psychoanalytic Contemporary Thought 21*: 33–60.

Bergeret, J. (1980). La violence fondamentale. Paper given to the Canadian Psychoanalytic Society. [Bergeret, J. (1984). *La violence fondamentale, l'inépuisable Oedipe* [Fundamental violence, the inexhaustible Oedipus]. Paris: Dunod.]

Bradley, A.C. (1962). Hegel's theory of tragedy. In: A. Paolucci & H. Paolucci (Eds.), *Hegel on Tragedy* (pp. 367–88). New York: Harper & Row.

Burkert, W. (1966). Greek tragedy and sacrificial ritual. *Greek Roman Byzantine Studies 7*: 87–121.

Burnet, J. (Ed.) (1973). *Platonis Opera, Vols 1–5*. Oxford: Oxford University Press.

Butcher, S.H. (Ed.) (1951). *Aristotle's Theory of Poetry and Fine Art*, 4th edition. New York: Dover.

Else, G.F. (1967). *The Origins and Early Forms of Tragedy*. Cambridge, MA: Harvard University Press.

Freud, S. (1911). Notes on an autobiographical account of a case of paranoia. *Standard Edition 12* (pp. 9–82).

Freud, S. (1926). The question of lay analysis. *Standard Edition 20* (pp. 183–250).

Freud, S. (1933). New introductory lectures on psycho-analysis. *Standard Edition 22* (pp. 5–182).

Girard, R. (1972). *La violence et le sacré*. Paris: Grasset. [(1979). *Violence and the Sacred*. P. Gregory, translator. Baltimore, MA: Johns Hopkins University Press.

Harrison, J.E. (1912). *Themis*. Cambridge, UK: Cambridge University Press.

Hegel, G.W.F. (1969). *The Phenomenology of Mind*. J.B. Baillie, translator. New York: Harper & Row.

Herodotus (1981). *Historiae*. A.D. Godley, translator. Cambridge, MA: Harvard University Press.

Kirk, G.S. (Ed.) (1970). *The Bacchae* by Euripides. G.S. Kirk, translator. Englewood Cliffs: Prentice-Hall.

Kirk, G.S., Raven, J.E., Schofield, M. (1971). *The Presocratic Philosophers*, 1st edition. Cambridge, UK: Cambridge University Press.

Leclaire, S. (1975). *On tue un enfant: Un essai sur le narcissisme primaire et la pulsion de mort*. Paris: Seuil. [(1998). *A child is Being Killed: An Essay on Primary Narcissism and the Death Drive*. M.C. Hays, translator. Stanford, CA: Stanford University Press.]

Murray, G. (1918). *Euripides and his Age*. London: Oxford University Press.

Nietzsche, F. (1954). *The Philosophy of Nietzsche*. New York: Random House.

Rohde, E. (1898). *Psyche: Seelencult und Unsterblichkeitsglaube der Griechen* [Psyche: The cult of souls and belief in immortality among the Greeks]. Darmstadt: WBG.

Romilly, J. de (1986). *La modernité d'Euripide* [The modernity of Euripides]. Paris: Presses Universitaires France.

Sandler, J. & Sandler, A.M. (1987). The past unconscious, the present unconscious and the vicissitudes of guilt. *International Journal of Psychoanalysis, 68*: 331–41.

Schlesinger, A.C. (1963). *Boundaries of Dionysus: Athenian Foundations for the Theory of Tragedy*. Cambridge, MA: Harvard University Press.

Segal, C. (1982). *Dionysiac Poetics and Euripides' Bacchae*. Princeton, NJ: Princeton University Press.

Vernant, J.P., & Vidal-Naquet, J. (1972). *Mythe et tragédie en Grèce ancienne*. Paris: Maspero. [(1990). *Myth and Tragedy in Ancient Greece*. J. Lloyd, translator. New York, NY: Zone.]

Winnicott, D.W. (1971). *Playing and Reality*. London: Tavistock.

Winnington-Ingram, R.P. (1948). *Euripides and Dionysus*. Cambridge, UK: Cambridge University Press.

CHAPTER SEVEN

Negation in Borges's "The secret miracle":

writing the Shoah

Beatriz Priel

The author presents a psychoanalytic reading of Borges's "The secret miracle" (1943), a short story about the Shoah, for which Freud's concept of negation (Verneinen) and recent psychoanalytic approaches to symbolization and the functions of fiction form the theoretical background. She argues that the effects of negation, present in literary fiction, become forcefully magnified in the fiction of the Shoah, because of its specific inversion of the relations between life and art. This magnification increases the perplexing effect that is characteristic of Borges's heterotopies. The story is read as a metaphor of transformative processes that closely follow Freud's dual conceptualization of negation as a defence and as allowing the repressed a way into consciousness. This study illuminates the conservation of the relations between external and internal realities as a basic difference between negation and related concepts such as disavowal (Verleugnung), and repression, in relation to creative imagination. The author relates the story's perplexing effect to its subversion of fundamental axioms such as temporality, questioning the existence of sense itself and suggests that the

Reproduced, with permission, from *International Journal of Psychoanalysis, 82*: 785–94 (2001). © Institute of Psychoanalysis, London.

malaise the story produces may stem from the way in which its narrative structure negates time, the fabric from which narratives—and life—are woven.

> At times in the evening a face
> Looks at us out of the depths of a mirror.
> Art should be like that mirror
> Which reveals to us our own face
> *Arte Poetica* (Borges, 1960a)

In an unforgettable poem that Borges named "The other tiger" (1960b) the narrator is searching for a fierce tiger. He first finds a tiger in the library, but that tiger consists of "symbols and shadows, a series of literary tropes and memories of the encyclopedia" (p. 824). This is not the dangerous animal he is seeking. Next, there is the terrible tiger that inhabits Sumatra or Bengal but "already the fact of naming it and of conjuring up its circumstances turns it into a fiction of art and not a living creature like those that stalk the earth" (pp. 824–5). Then we are told about the third tiger:

> We shall search for a third tiger now
> But like the others, this one too, will be a form
> of my dream, a system of human words
> and not the flesh and bone tiger
> that, beyond mythologies
> paces the earth. I know these things quite well, yet something
> keeps driving me into this vague,
> senseless, and ancient adventure, and I persevere
> in searching through the twilight hours
> for the other tiger, the one that is not in the verse.
> (Borges, 1960b, p. 825)

This essay discusses the incompleteness, imperfection, and inevitability of literary representations of the Shoah. Moreover, the mere possibility of literature, or art in general, in the context of the Shoah has been forcefully questioned, as in Adorno's often-quoted dictum that "to write poetry after Auschwitz is barbaric" (1962, p. 312). The question of a fictional literature on the Shoah created strong emotional reactions, especially during the first years after the end

of World War II, as if the facts resisted a displacement and transformation through art (Langer, 1990). Fiction might even appear
obsolete, as language itself seemed to have been irreversibly affected,
when everyday words acquired horrendous meanings: *gas, train,
selection, shower, smoke, soap.* Adorno later qualified his statement that
to write poetry after Auschwitz is barbaric, affirming that "literature
must resist this verdict" and added: "It is now virtually in art alone
that suffering can find its own voice, consolation, without being
immediately betrayed by it" (1962, p. 313). Literature, and art in
general, is seen here as a powerful voice, but as a conceivable
deceiver too. And yet, art has not kept silent.

Psychoanalysis has explored the relations between art and the
trauma of the Shoah mainly from its primary therapeutic perspective,
studying, for instance, processes of creation among survivors of the
Shoah and their offspring (Laub & Podell, 1995). The present study,
however, assumes a psychoanalytic perspective on an art object
itself—Borges's story "The secret miracle" (*El milagro secreto*, Borges,
1944a)—and on the reader's response to it. "The secret miracle" is
one of those fantastic stories to which Foucault has referred as
Borges's "heterotopies", i.e. those narratives that subvert language,
questioning myth and destroying conventions (Foucault, 1966). These
are stories that disconcert the reader, creating a perplexity and
"malaise" that is the very opposite of the comfort and consolation
produced by utopic narratives.

In what follows, I assume that the malaise that accompanies the
reading of Borges's heterotopies in general, and "The secret miracle"
in particular, is the reader's acute awareness of the antithetical and
paradoxical functions of negation (*Verneinen*). Moreover, negation is
also the main theme in "The secret miracle", a story that dramatizes
processes of defence and creativity *vis-à-vis* catastrophic trauma.
The reading process effects an awareness of transformative processes
that closely follow the conceptualization of negation as both a
rejection and an acknowledgement of basic aspects of psychic reality
(Freud, 1925).

Freud ascribed to negation a double function: a restrictive
and evasive function on one hand—negation as defence—and, on
the other, a creative, innovative function—negation as enriching
thinking: "The content of a repressed image or idea can make its way
into consciousness, on condition that it is *negated*. Negation is a way

of taking cognizance of what is repressed" (1925, p. 235). Negation points to that which is repressed, as in Freud's comment that when the patient says, "Now you will think I mean to say something insulting, but really I've no such intention", we realize "that this is a rejection, by projection, of an idea that has just come up" (1925, p. 235). Repression persists, however: the repressed is only intellectually, but not affectively, accepted.

The thesis of Freud's paper on negation is, however, that the dialectics of affirmation and negation inherent to *Verneinung* offer a basis for a theory of judgement. The Freudian analysis of the function of judgement is based on the fundamental distinction between external and internal (Freud, 1925). These realms, as Freud wrote, are assumed to be undifferentiated at the beginning; their differentiation follows two sorts of decision. The first is related to the possession of attributes, according to which what is bad is ejected and what is good is introjected. The second is a judgement of existence, in which the question of reality versus nonreality, or outside versus inside, is posed (Hyppolite, 1975). The loss of the satisfying object ("objects shall have been lost which once brought real satisfaction", p. 238) being the precondition for reality-testing. Freud concludes that the performance of the function of judgement, i.e. the act of differentiating between the subjective and the objective, is made possible by the creation of the symbol of negation.

Towards the end of his work on negation, Freud considers negation to be a process, both affirming and negating the fusion of erotic (affirmation, introjection) and destructive (negation, expulsion) instinctual tendencies. To sum up, Freud developed in "Negation" (1925) a conception of the origins and functions of intellectual judgement and, plausibly, of thinking in general, as based on the transformation of lack or absence, and dependent on the creation of the symbol of negation.

A mechanism close to negation is disavowal, defined as the splitting between two attitudes where "the attitude which fitted in with the wish and the attitude which fitted in with reality exist side by side" (Freud, 1927, p. 156). Two main differences between disavowal and negation, however, emerge. In the first place, disavowal and negation differ as to the relations between the two contradictory elements coexisting in each of them. The two aspects of negation—negation and affirmation—are related to each other by means of the symbol of negation. Moreover, the subject who negates points to, and speaks, to some extent at least, about the repressed. In disavowal, in contrast, two parallel attitudes coexist side by side, and the transformations of perceptual reality made possible by speech are lacking (Basch, 1983). Second, disavowal and negation differ as to the source of their specific contents: Freud tended to reserve the term disavowal for the refusal to perceive a fact imposed by external reality (e.g. sexual differences), while he termed negation the defence against aspects of internal reality, such as wishes, as when the Rat Man rejects the idea of having death wishes towards his father (Freud, 1909).

Moreover, the conservation of a relation with the negated brings the idea of negation close to the concept of repression. Negation may be considered a first stage in the lifting of repressed contents. Laplanche and Pontalis, for instance, underscored that for Freud negation indicates "the moment when an unconscious idea or wish *begins to re-emerge* whether during the course of treatment or outside it" (1973, p. 263; my italics). Also Green has defined negation as an intellectual substitute for repression (1998, p. 660). Thus, it seems plausible that negation, like repression, and unlike disavowal, associates to, or allows for, processes of symbolization. This possibility constitutes the theoretical basis for conceptualizations of fictional literature as akin to processes of negation. The conceptualization of negation as involving *the beginning* of the re-emergence of unconscious ideas may shed light on the difference between the perplexing reading effects produced by many of Borges's texts, and the feelings of uncanniness characteristic of the reading process of texts that, like Hoffmann's *The Sand-man*, dramatize the return of repressed contents (Freud, 1919). The uncanny effect is produced when the distinction between reality and imagination collapses (1919, p. 244). In negation, however, the distinction between the objective and the subjective is kept through the symbol of negation.

Ricoeur (1979) defined fictional discourse as preserving reality through its self-definition as fiction, while at the same time it abolishes the ordinary vision of reality. Fiction thus "redescribes" reality mainly through the use of metaphors that bring together distant semantic fields (Ricoeur, 1979). That might be one of the reasons why Majorca storytellers caution their audience that what they are going to tell "was *and* it was not" ("Aixo era y no era"

[Ricoeur, 1979, p. 151]). Fiction is thus described as dramatizing the basic affirmation and negation inherent to *Verneinung*. The affirmative and negative poles of negation are emphasized in psychoanalytic studies of art and literature, that tend to distinguish between the enriching and the defensive aspects of negation, suggesting different forms, or categories, of fiction. Britton (1999) refers to truth-seeking versus truth-evading fiction; the former is germane to the search in dreams for inner truth, while the latter is more akin to the wish-fulfilling function of day-dreams. These different forms of fiction are also seen as corresponding to the basic differentiation between infantile phantasies that accompany experience, and those conjured up in order to deny actual experience (Britton, 1999). Chasseguet-Smirgel (1995) distinguishes between creative processes that integrate diverse stages of development and the obstacles undergone, and creations that circumvent and disguise stages and obstacles. These conceptualizations of the different categories of fictional discourse are congruent with Green's structuring and destructuring modes of the "work of the negative" (1999) and Segal's basic distinction between symbolization as a process of transformation intended to overcome loss, and symbolic equations as transformations used to deny absence (1991, pp. 168–9).

Moreover, the distinction between art that seeks truth and art that evades it, following Britton's expression, implies also a differentiation between art that deals with and art that does not deal with ugliness, pain and death. An important aspect of this distinction is the complex relation with pleasure–displeasure to be found in serious art, i.e. art that does not avoid nor amend external reality, but that symbolizes important, sometimes very unpleasant and disturbing, aspects of psychic reality. While discussing a painting on the Shoah, Chasseguet-Smirgel (1995) notices that the authentic work of art seldom fascinates and may even repel initially. Its attraction for the beholder, however, is related to the object's match with fundamental inner truth.

Negation, in the original Freudian dialectical sense, is to be found only in truth-searching fiction. While truth-evading fiction is seen as only fulfilling a defensive, escapist function, truth-searching fiction can be seen as fulfilling simultaneously both the defensive and the enriching functions of negation. Truth-searching fiction is a defence, as it avoids a painful aspect of psychic reality, and it is enriching as it creates a space–time in which psychic work can be done, that is, a space–time for symbolization. Truth-searching fictional discourse can therefore be seen as the temporary avoidance of reality while "keeping an eye on it". This possibility is the dialectical opposite to Steiner's "turning the blind eye" to reality (1985). By "keeping an eye on reality", I refer to the awareness of reality's accessibility while temporarily ignoring it that is characteristic of negation. The time implied in the "temporary" avoidance or suspension of reality is the time–place where psychic work can be done. Negation, as the mechanism of keeping an eye on the negated, may define some of the conditions for the creation of meaning.

Assuming that the awareness of the role of negation is a main reading effect in truth-searching fiction, my main thesis is that this effect is magnified forcefully in the fictions of the Shoah, because of the specific inversion of the relations between life and art that characterize this literature. Moreover, fictional literature about the Shoah questions basic definitions of the fantastic as a literary genre. According to Todorov (1973), fantastic stories are those that present us with the world we know, as we know it, except that suddenly something impossible, unthinkable, happens that cannot be explained by the laws of this familiar world. We are then confronted with two main alternatives: we can define the event as not real, as an illusion or as fruit of imagination, leaving untouched the laws of our familiar world. Or we can see the event as possible but controlled by laws unknown to us, that is, as a different reality. We can read it either as an illusion or else as a different kind of reality. The uncertainty between these two exclusive possibilities is the realm of the fantastic in literature (Todorov, 1973).

However, this uncertainty acquires a different meaning when we speak about fantastic Shoah stories. In these stories there is no "uncertainty" since the impossible, the unthinkable, has already happened in reality. Reality, not imagination, has overpowered the familiar. This unique relation between fiction and reality is poignantly described by Aaron Appelfeld, a contemporary creative writer and child survivor:

> When it comes to describing reality, art always demands a certain intensification, for many and various reasons. However, that is not the case with the Holocaust. Everything in it seems as thoroughly

unreal . . . Thence comes the need to bring it down to the human
realm . . . That is not a mechanical problem but an essential one.
When I say "to bring it down" I do not mean to simplify, to attenuate,
or to sweeten the horror, but to make the event speak through the
individual and in his language. (1988, p. 92)

Appelfeld's phrase, "to bring it down to the human realm", suggests
that Shoah fictions involve an inversion of the relation between
the fictional and the real, between art and life. This inversion,
characteristic of literary fictions on the Shoah, may play an important
role in strengthening the reader's awareness of the vicissitudes of
negation, since the usual judgement of reality has been subverted:
external reality has gone beyond the bounds of imagination. The
fundamental testing of reality becomes bewildering when the
answer to questions such as "what is outside and what is inside?"
or "is the object still there?" spin back and forth between affirmation
and negation.

The tension between reality and unreality, and the relations
between fiction and art are the hallmark of Borges's creation. Borges's
texts have been characterized as both fantastic and self-conscious
textuality (e.g. Barrenechea, 1957; Ferrer, 1971) and as related to
historical and political reality (e.g. Aizenberg, 1984; Balderston,
1993). Probably the most suggestive indication of the problematic of
reality and unreality in Borges's texts is Molloy's notion of *vaivén* (a
continuous movement to and fro, like sea waves going away and
coming back) between reality and fantasy (1979, p. 194). In "The
secret miracle" the particularly complex relation between life and art
that appears in Shoah fictions seems to add impetus to the *vaivén*
that characterizes Borges's creation.

"The secret miracle"—The story

"The night of March 14th, 1939, in an apartment on the Zeltnergasse
in Prague . . ." (Borges, 1964, p. 88). This realistic introduction to
"The secret miracle" is followed immediately by the description
of a terrible dream dreamt by Jaromir Hladík, a Jewish poet and
researcher of Jewish literary sources. *There is a game of chess between
rival families that had begun centuries before. Both the pieces and the chess
board had disappeared, and Jaromir Hladík runs through a stormy desert,*

unable to remember the forms nor the laws of chess; the sound of terrible clocks mark the passage of time, and the approaching of the end of the game. When Jaromir Hladík wakes up, and the sounds of the rain and the terrible clocks come to a halt, he can hear a rhythmic sound in unison, interrupted by occasional shouts of command, coming from the Zeltnergasse. It is dawn, 15 March 1939, the exact time when the armoured vanguard of the Third Reich entered Prague.

Hladík is a German-language writer in his forties. He has composed poems that were included in important anthologies and was the translator into German of the *Sefer hayetzira* [Book of creation], a cabbalistic treatise on the creative power of Hebrew words and letters. While rather critical of most of his works, he considers that his best work is a history of man's concepts of time and eternity. He also has an unfinished drama entitled *The Enemies*, written in verse, in order to compel readers not to forget that "unreality is the condition of art" (1944a, p. 510; my translation).

On 19 March, someone denounces Jaromir Hladík, who is arrested the same day, having been accused of having a Jewish mother, who used a Jewish name—Jaroslavsky. Moreover, Hladík's research seems conspicuously Jewish. The German officer in charge decides that Jaromir Hladík should be executed on 29 March, at 9.00 a.m. The officer explains that this postponement should make clear that his administration does not act impulsively or passionately, but slowly and impersonally "after the manner of vegetables and planets" (1964, p. 89).

During the ten days left to him (from 19 March till 29 March) Hladík imagines time and again the details of his own execution, exploring infinite variations and possibilities, wavering between the need to imagine the worst so that it won't happen, and the need never to imagine the worst because then it might happen. However, on the night of 28 March, his last night, Hladík's attention turns to *The Enemies*, his unfinished drama. He had written the first act and conceived the idea of the plot, but two acts are still unwritten. In the darkness of his cell, Hladík prays to God:

> If in any way I do exist, if I am not one of Your repetitions or mistakes, I exist as the author of *The Enemies*. To finish this drama, which can justify me and justify You, I need another year. Grant me these days, You, to whom centuries and time belong (p. 92).

Hladík falls asleep and has a second dream. *Hladík learns from a blind librarian that God is hidden in one of the letters of one of the words of one of the books from the immense Clementinum library. Hladík succeeds, by pure chance, in recognizing this letter, and he then hears God's promise to bestow the time he needs.*

Immediately before the execution, when the German guns are ready to fire, "The physical world comes to a halt" (p. 93): external or clock time suddenly frozen: in a miraculous way, a drop of rain on Hladík's cheek and the shadow of a flying bee stay motionless. While speechless and also motionless, Hladík, to his own surprise, is absolutely free to think: mental time and thinking continued to unfold. "The German lead would kill him at the appointed hour, but in his mind a year would transpire between the firing order and its execution" (p. 93).

Using the only document he has, that is, his memory (p. 93), Hladík finishes the mental composition of the unfinished play. He changes, summarizes, and extends the text, going back to the original version, or deleting symbols that were too obvious. During this process, Hladík is very much aware of his surroundings: he gradually becomes familiar with the yard and with the soldiers. The story even tells that one of the soldiers' faces convinces him to change aspects of the story's main character (p. 94). *The Enemies* evolves in Roemerstadt's library, one afternoon while the clock marks 7.00 p.m. Roemerstadt is repeatedly interrupted by strangers; but the audience, and later on he himself, understand that these are secret enemies who intend to destroy him. The name of Jaroslav Kubin is mentioned; he was once interested in Roemerstadt's fiancée, and is now a madman who believes he is Roemerstadt. Roemerstadt is obliged to kill one of the traitors in the second act. The third act of *The Enemies* is a repetition of the first act, but the play becomes more and more difficult to follow, and less and less coherent as when one of the characters, killed in the second act, reappears on stage. Gradually, the spectator realizes that Roemerstadt and Jaroslav Kubin are one and the same; the clock marks 7.00 p.m. Obviously, the drama has not taken place: it has been Kubin's circular nightmare. The moment Hladík finishes imagining the writing of the play, the flow of time is reassumed in external reality and a discharge is heard. Jaromir Hladík is murdered on 29 March 1939, at 9.02 a.m.

"The secret miracle"—An interpretation

The agonizing paradox of lawlessness and arbitrariness masked as order and lawfulness, or the opposition between brute force and the powers of human mind and intellect, are basic themes in the story. However, this story is also a problematization of the powers of imagination to affect internal reality. The story dramatizes a negation of temporality—the "miracle"—as a psychological process in which negation and the negated are subtly associated, structuring a space for creativity. In what follows, I shall refer to the main contents involved in the story, and point out the dialectics of affirmation and negation inherent to them that might play a role in evoking the reader's perplexity.

The story is seemingly enclosed in a very realistic and accurate spatial and temporal frame. And yet, the limits between reality and fantasy, wakefulness and sleep, are slim and fragile. For instance the story's very realistic initial description of time and place ("The night of March 14th, 1939 in an apartment on the Zeltnergasse in Prague . . .") leads to the immersion in an oneiric atmosphere, against a background of the noise made by threatening clocks and desert rain. This noise comes suddenly to a halt, and is replaced by rhythmic and ordered tones pertaining to the real army actually entering the town. The relations between reality and dream are confusing, and there is a nightmarish atmosphere.

Hladík's dreams bring to the fore pivotal Borgesian themes and symbols, which acquire unexpected meaning in the context of Shoah, such as the game of chess, writing, and time (Rodriguez-Monegal, 1973; Balderston, 1993). Moreover, the sequence of the dreams presented suggests a specific internal process of transformation. In the first dream, the game of chess represents, in Borges's writings, a perpetual struggle between opposite forces: white and black, good and evil, chaos and order. Some critics have also found in Borges's game of chess the need to rationalize these irrational conflicts (Mandlove, 1980). But, beyond that, the chess game provides Borges's main metaphor of the illusion of human freedom, a fateful issue in any meditation on the Shoah. In a poem entitled "Chess", Borges elaborates on the meanings of the game. Referring to the chess pieces, Borges reminds us that they fight their war but

They don't know it is the player's hand
That dominates and guides their destiny.
They do not know an adamantine fate
Controls their will and lays the battle plan.
The player too is captive of caprice
(Borges, 1960c)

In the chess dream of "The secret miracle" the questioning of human freedom and rationality is infinitely magnified and expanded: not only is the idea of freedom to play illusory *per se*, but the rules of the game and its pieces are arbitrarily absent.

The second dream in the story, dreamt by Hladík during his last night, is on the creative power of letters and words. This dream encompasses a basic cabbalistic myth that powerfully affects Borges's conception of creative writing. The cabbalistic idea is that Hebrew letters were the instruments used by God to create the world (Aizenberg, 1984; Sosnowski, 1986), and Borges has seen the paradigmatic possibility of human creativity in the written word (Borges, 1944b). Thus, symbols of meaningfulness and creativity substitute in the second dream for the idea of the basic limitations of human freedom and its subordination to unknown fateful powers. The change seems to have begun with Hladík's prayer and God's answer. This internal scene dramatizes basic aspects of creative processes such as the creative artist's need to be involved in some sort of dialogue with another, beyond the illusion of being separate and in a unique contact with his or her own creativity (Steiner, 1999, p. 709). Moreover, Hladík's prayer, "If in any way I do exist, if I am not one of Your repetitions or mistakes, I exist as the author of *The Enemies*", evokes Rorty's belief (based on Bloom's idea of the anxiety of influence) that the main characteristic of the creative poet is

> the conscious need . . . to demonstrate that he is not a copy or replica as merely a special form of an unconscious need everyone has: the need to come to terms with the blind impress which chance has given him, to make a self for himself by redescribing that impress in terms which are, if only marginally, his own. (1989, p. 43)

Hladík's creative gesture affirms both the imminence of death and the continuity of his existence: he is who he was. The scene of mental creation is depicted against a background of different orders of temporality that affect each other, suggesting a conceptualization of art as reconciliation between different levels of psychic organization, images and words, fantasy and reality, timelessness and time. Moreover, even though according to the story time flows only for Hladík, and stands still in "reality", the text tells us he was executed at 9:02, allowing for two "real" minutes to pass, and creating the last, fleeting ambiguity: did the creative writer's work take place in real or in subjective time? The central metaphor of the story—the coexistence of subjective and external temporalities or realities—seems to provide an affirmative answer to Loewald's question: "Could sublimation be both a mourning of lost original oneness and a celebration of oneness regained?" (1980, p. 81). Borges's intuition of the "aesthetic event" or "aesthetic deed" (*el hecho estético*) clearly points to the universal human experience of lack and absence (the precondition for reality testing in Freud) as both negated and acknowledged in the work of art. In "The wall and the books", after defining music as pure form and therefore the ideal of art, Borges wrote:

> Music, states of happiness, mythology, faces wrought by time, some sundowns and some places, want to tell us something, or have told us something we ought not to have missed, or are about to tell us something: this imminence of revelation that never comes, is, perhaps the aesthetic event. (1952, p. 635)

The aesthetic deed is the awareness of the gap, the lack, that which almost is, and therefore is not.

The paradox of time and timelessness is also represented through the relations between the story and the story in the story, i.e. the relationships between "The secret miracle" and *The Enemies*. The play Hladík writes in his mind is almost a parody of circular time, or timelessness, and the reproduction of the same. His play is not a process but the representation of a static, hallucinatory, world, where basic differentiations have collapsed, as we bear witness to the return of the dead and understand that Roemerstadt is Kubin. While Hladík's *The Enemies* is a clear instance of the disintegrating work of negation (Green, 1998), leading to reiterative symbolic equations (Segal, 1991), Borges's "The secret miracle" dramatizes time and timelessness as the background to self-identity and creativity (Priel, 1997).

Moreover, the vicissitudes of temporality play a main role in the story's perplexing effect on the reader. The oscillations between time and timelessness represent dialectical relations between inner, human linguistic reality and outer, brutal non-linguistic reality ("in the manner of vegetables and planets"). Time in the story is both real and non-real; it is both an affirmation and negation of death. However, the main perplexing impact on the reader stems not only from the vertiginous play with different aspects and orders of time, but from the subtle connections between them, as when a soldier's face "convinces" Hladík to change aspects of Roemerstadt's character . . .

In "The secret miracle" it is the reader's idiomatic plotting of very different ways of being in time and in reality—as reflected in the relations between time and timelessness, reality and dream, story and invented story in the story, creation and annihilation, life and death— that produces the "malaise" that Foucault defined as characteristic of Borges's heterotopies (Foucault, 1966). Moreover, this discomfort and perplexity might also relate to the fact that the play with time questions the most basic principles involved in the creation of meaning and in telling stories (Ricoeur, 1985). In this sense "The secret miracle" does not only denounce a specific political or social system, but questions the possibility of system. The effect of the subversion of fundamental axioms, like temporality, is perplexing because it questions the existence of sense itself. It is an effect that stems from its narrative structure that negates time, the fabric from which narratives, and life, are woven.

This reading of "The secret miracle" underscores a process through which the horrendous reality has been necessarily "brought down" (Appelfeld, 1988) to the human realm, that is, to the individual, the idiomatic, the particular, and the idiosyncratic. Does mental creation, the power of the human intellect, have any reparative effect? A fantastic story has been told. This is a story that says about itself, "I am not the (physical or psychical) reality", while pointing to this reality in a manner that bewilders the reader. "The secret miracle" is an outstanding specimen of Shoah fiction that "does not say the unsayable, but says that it cannot say it" (Lyotard, 1990, p. 47).

References

Adorno, T. (1962). Commitment. In: A. Arato & Gebhardt (Eds.), *The Essential Frankfurt School Reader* (pp. 300–18). New York, NY: Continuum, 1982.

Aizenberg, E. (1984). *The Aleph Weaver: Biblical, Kabbalistic and Judaic Elements in Borges*. Potomac, MD: Scripta Humanistica.

Appelfeld, A. (1988). After the Holocaust. In: B. Lang (Ed.), *Writing and the Holocaust*. J.M. Green, translator (pp. 83–92). New York: Holmes & Meier.

Balderston, D. (1993). Prague, March 1943. Recovering the historicity of *El milagro secreto*. In: *Out of Context: Historical Reference and the Representation of Reality in Borges* (pp. 56–68). Durham, NC: Duke University Press.

Barrenechea, A.M. (1957). *La expresión de la irrealidad en la obra de Jorge Luis Borges* [The expression of unreality in the work of Jorge Luis Borges]. Buenos Aires: Paidós.

Basch, M.F. (1983). The perception of reality and the disavowal of meaning. *Ann Psychoanal 11*: 125–54.

Borges, J.L. (1944a). Artificios: el milagro secreto [Arts: the secret miracle]. In: *Jorge Luis Borges: Obras completas* [Complete works], *Vol. 1* (pp. 508–13). Buenos Aires: Emece, 1974.

Borges, J.L. (1944b). Ficciones: la biblioteca de Babel [Fictions: the library of Babel]. In: *Jorge Luis Borges: Obras completas* [Complete works], *Vol. 1* (pp. 465–71). Buenos Aires: Emece, 1974.

Borges, J.L. (1952). Otras inquisiciones: la muralla y los libros [Other inquisitions: the wall and the books]. In: *Jorge Luis Borges: Obras completas* [Complete works], *Vol. 1* (pp. 633–5). Buenos Aires: Emece, 1974.

Borges, J.L. (1960a). El hacedor: arte poetica [The doer: poetic art]. In: *Jorge Luis Borges: Obras completas* [Complete works], *Vol 1* (p. 843). Buenos Aires: Emece, 1974.

Borges, J.L. (1960b). El hacedor: el otro tigre [The doer: the other tiger]. In: *Jorge Luis Borges: Obras completas* [Complete works], *Vol 1* (pp. 824–5). Buenos Aires: Emece, 1974.

Borges, J.L. (1960c). El hacedor: ajedrez [The doer: chess]. A. Reid, translator. In: *Jorge Luis Borges: Obras completas* [Complete works], *Vol 1* (p. 813). Buenos Aires: Emece, 1974.

Borges, J.L. (1964). The secret miracle [1943]. In: D.A. Yates & J.E. Irby (Eds.), *Labyrinths: Selected Stories and Other Writings*. H. De Onís, translator (pp. 88–94). New York, NY: New Directions.

Britton, R. (1999). *Belief and Imagination: Explorations in Psychoanalysis.* New York: Routledge.

Chasseguet-Smirgel, J. (1995). "Creative writers and day-dreaming": A commentary. In: E. Spector Person, P. Fonagy, & S.A. Figueira (Eds.), *On Freud's: "Creative Writers and Day-dreaming"* (pp. 107–21). New Haven, CT: Yale University Press.

Ferrer, M. (1971). *Borges y la Nada* [Borges and nothingness]. London: Támesis.

Foucault, M. (1966). *Les mots et les choses: une archéologie des sciences humaines.* Paris: Gallimard. [(1970). *The Order of Things: Archaeology of the Human Sciences.* London: Pantheon]

Freud, S. (1909). Notes upon a case of obsessional neurosis. *Standard Edition 10* (pp. 155–318).

Freud, S. (1919). The "uncanny". *Standard Edition 17* (pp. 219–56).

Freud, S. (1925). Negation. *Standard Edition 19* (pp. 235–9).

Freud, S. (1927). Fetishism. *Standard Edition 21* (pp. 152–7).

Green, A. (1998). The primordial mind and the work of the negative. *International Journal of Psychoanalysis, 79*: 649–65.

Green, A. (1999). *The Work of the Negative.* A. Weller, translator. London: Free Association Books.

Hyppolite, J. (1975). A spoken commentary on Freud's *Verneinung*. In: J.A. Miller, (Ed.), *The Seminar of Jacques Lacan, Book I: Freud's Papers on Technique, 1953–4.* J. Forrester, translator (pp. 289–97). Cambridge, UK: Cambridge University Press, 1988.

Langer, L.L. (1990). Fictional facts and factual fictions: history in Holocaust literature. In: *Admitting the Holocaust: Collected Essays* (pp. 75–87). Oxford: Oxford University Press, 1995.

Laplanche, J., & Pontalis, J.B. (1973). *The Language of Psychoanalysis.* D.N. Smith, translator. London: Hogarth.

Laub, D., & Podell, D. (1995). Art and trauma. *International Journal of Psychoanalysis, 76*: 991–1005.

Loewald, H.A. (1980). *Papers on Psychoanalysis.* New Haven, CT: Yale University Press.

Lyotard, J.F. (1990). *Heidegger and "the Jews".* A. Michel & M.S. Roberts, translators. Minneapolis, MN: University of Minnesota Press.

Mandlove, N.B. (1980). Chess and mirrors: form as metaphor in three sonnets. In: H. Bloom (Ed.), *Jorge Luis Borges* (pp. 173–83). New York: Chelsea, 1986.

Molloy, A. (1979). *Las letras de Borges.* Buenos Aires: Sudamericana. [(1994). *Signs of Borges.* O. Montero, translator. Durham, NC: Duke University Press.

Priel, B. (1997). Time and self: on the intersubjective construction of time. *Psychoanalytic Dialogue, 7*: 431–50.

Ricoeur, P. (1979). The function of fiction in shaping reality. In: M.J. Valdés (Ed.), *A Ricoeur Reader: Reflection and Imagination* (pp. 117–35). London: Harvester, 1991.

Ricoeur, P. (1985). *Time and Narrative,* 3 vols. Chicago, IL: University of Chicago Press.

Rodriguez-Monegal, E. (1973). Symbols in Borges's work. In: H. Bloom (Ed.), *Jorge Luis Borges* (pp. 133–48). New York: Chelsea, 1986.

Rorty, R. (1989). *Contingency, Irony, and Solidarity.* Cambridge, UK: Cambridge University Press.

Segal, H. (1991). *Dream Phantasy and Art.* London: Routledge.

Sosnowski, S. (1986). *Borges y la Cabala* [Borges and the cabbal]. Buenos Aires: Pardes.

Steiner, J. (1985). Turning a blind eye: the cover-up for Oedipus. *Int Rev Psychoanal 12*: 161–72.

Steiner, R. (1999). Some notes on the "heroic self" and the meaning and importance of its reparation for the creative process and the creative personality. *International Journal of Psychoanalysis, 80*: 685–718.

Todorov, T. (1973). *The Fantastic: A Structural Approach to a Literary Genre.* R. Howard, translator. Ithaca, NY: Cornell University Press.

CHAPTER EIGHT

Killing the angel in the house:

creativity, femininity, and aggression

Rozsika Parker

The author brings to bear an art historical perspective on the psychoanalytic understanding of creativity as an object relationship, proposing that the creative endeavour is determined by a wider, more complex network of internal and external object relationships than is usually assumed. The workings of tradition, language, contemporary practices, methods, and materials are explored. Creative block is considered in the context of the determining relationships, with particular reference to the role of aggression. The position of the latter within psychoanalytic theories of creativity is surveyed and it is proposed that aggression has a pivotal place not primarily in instituting sublimation, reparation or reaction formation but simply because the processes of creativity demand it. Virginia Woolf's image of Killing the angel in the house *is analysed and used to track the implications of gender, focusing on the concept of the muse. It is pointed out that traditionally, the fear, guilt, and anxiety associated with aggressive creativity has been mediated by the muse, which is compared to the internal good object. Drawing on art history, artists' statements, and clinical*

Reproduced, with permission, from *International Journal of Psychoanalysis*, 79: 757–74 (1998). © Institute of Psychoanalysis, London.

material, the author illustrates the disparate means by which the presence of "muse" can be internalized to infuse the relationships that constitute creativity.

> I discovered that if I were going to review books I should need to do battle with a certain phantom. And the phantom was a woman, and when I came to know her better I called her after the heroine of a famous poem, "The angel in the house".[1] It was she who used to come between me and my paper when I was writing reviews. It was she who bothered me and wasted my time and so tormented me that at last I killed her. (Woolf, 1931, p. 3)

Virginia Woolf is describing the impact on her work of a particular mode of relating that inhibited her creativity. The "angel" was intensely sympathetic, immensely charming, utterly unselfish: "If there was chicken, she took the leg; if there was a draught she sat in it—in short she was so constituted that she never had a mind of her own, but preferred to sympathize always with the minds, and wishes of others" (p. 3).

It needs to be emphasized that Woolf is offering the angel both as a persecuting internal object and as the personification of a mode of relating. In the essay "Professions for women", the angel afflicts the woman writer, impeding her work by inculcating an acute awareness of audience and the imperative to please. Woolf writes:

> Directly . . . I took my pen in my hand to review that novel by a famous man, she slipped behind me and whispered; My dear, you are a young woman. You are reviewing a book that has been written by a man, Be sympathetic; be tender, flatter, deceive; use all the arts and wiles of our sex. Never let anyone know you have a mind of your own. Above all, be pure. (p. 4)

The angel in Woolf's essay represents creative inhibition, functioning both intrapsychically and interpersonally. She forbids spontaneity, independence, aggression, and desire. She personifies a state of mind in which the production of a piece of work is dominated and determined by anxieties relating to its reception. Such anxiety is an inevitable component of creativity. A host of complex, often contradictory internal and external object relationships encourage or impede creative work. When we write, paint, garden or sew we never simply make a thing; rather we enter into a network of relationships with, for example, contemporary practices, with our own creative history, with materials, with colleagues, and, of course, with imaginary audiences and internal figures.

Woolf is suggesting, rightly in my view, that creative block is the product of a specific style of relating (to both internal and external objects), operating as a defence against both the pleasures and the fears associated with creativity. But Woolf also implies that because twentieth-century women are heirs to the nineteenth-century feminine ideal of service and subservience (the angel in the house) they alone suffer from this specific inhibition within the relationships that determine creativity. Here I disagree with Woolf. In my practice as a psychoanalytic psychotherapist I have encountered men wrestling with their own version of the angel. And, indeed, Woolf herself is careful to avoid suggesting that women are innately or uniquely incapacitated. She indicates that femininity is historically determined and hence open to change.

Her lecture, "Professions for women", on her experience of being a professional writer, was delivered in 1931 to a group concerned with the employment of women. She tells them, "You who come from a younger and happier generation may not have heard of her— you may not know what I mean by the Angel in the House" (p. 3). I think, nevertheless, that the angel does have a particular impact on women's work—even today over fifty years after Woolf wrote her essay. For creativity cannot be considered in terms of internal reality alone. The links with external reality and the sociocultural context of the maker need to be constantly borne in mind. Focusing primarily on the visual arts, my previous area of work, I shall argue that women have a specific relationship to art history in terms of institutional access, representations of the Artist, genres, and materials. It seems to me that where the angel is concerned women are now in a place of transition. To my mind feminine identifications do impact on the relations that determine creativity but not in an exclusive, singular way.

Where I part company with Woolf is over her assumption that the angel necessarily has a negative effect on creativity. I think the mode of relating signified by the angel occupies a continuum. At the negative end there is the desire to please, placate, and seduce but at the positive end there is a sense of responsibility, availability, receptivity, and the desire to communicate.

For the angel represents a concern with the impact of a piece of work on the other—a concern that is integral to the creative process. Rather than annihilating the angel, the task of those engaged in creative endeavour is to enable the angel to coexist with the devil— in other words to allow an element of aggression, assertion, and ruthlessness into the relationships that determine creativity without losing the critical awareness of the conditions of reception that is the positive attribute of the angel.

A network of relations

The traditional, popular, Romantic concept of the artist as isolated and innately gifted has tended to conceal the determining relation-ships of creativity. Object-relations theory potentially offers a challenge to the notion of the isolated genius (Klein, 1929; Milner, 1950; Greenacre, 1957; Winnicott, 1971; Kavaler-Adler, 1993; Oremland, 1997). But the problem with a predominantly develop-mental focus is that it tends to position art practice primarily as a successful—or unsuccessful—attempt at self-cure or self-reparation. My focus is not on the curative potential of creative work nor on the pathology suggested by the desire to create but rather on the conditions of relations needed for practice to begin and be sustained. Rather than thinking about the creative enterprise as being towards relations with objects, I am concerned with the way object relations determine creativity. Also, following the insights of art history, I am suggesting that an analytic understanding of creative block needs to take into account the determining impact of numerous, diverse relationships. I want, however, to avoid constructing a hierarchy of creative relationships. It is more useful to think in terms of a network of relationships dominated by specific modes of relating. At one time all relationships in the network can be characterized by the subservience insisted upon by Woolf's angel, in response to incapacitating anxiety. At other times a sense of authentic agency can be acquired in one relationship in the network which in turn can impact on the others.

As I mentioned above, the network of relationships that forms this "environment" most obviously includes relations with an audience of real or imaginary individuals (parents, partners, children, mentors, critics, editors, enemies, lovers, etc.). Such relationships necessarily recreate early parental and sibling relations. Britton, for instance, ascribes an inability to write to "fear of rejection by the primary intended listener" (1994, p. 1214). The act of publication, he suggests, constitutes a three sided relationship fraught with fear of loss and rejection because of

> The conflict between the urge to communicate a novel idea . . . and the conflicting wish to say something to bind the author to his affiliates and ancestors by the utterance, in a shared language, of shared beliefs . . . This involves the author in a triangular situation which becomes an incarnation of the Oedipus situation. (p. 1215)

For Woolf's woman writer the feminine Oedipus complex means that she faces an imaginary father. For her it is not a question of binding the other through shared language and beliefs but of *pleasing*. It is her entire person that is at stake.

A patient of mine, whom I shall call Fay, illustrates the play of Oedipal dynamics in the network of the relations of creativity as well as the significance of the conscious and unconscious meanings of medium. The clinical vignettes provided below are intended as illustrations rather than data. In all cases the requirements of confidentiality have necessitated keeping details of creative work to a minimum, but I believe the dynamics are nevertheless evident. I saw Fay for twice-weekly psychoanalytic psychotherapy for seven years. Initially she sat facing me, but latterly used the couch. When she first came to see me she was working towards an MA and finding difficulty fulfilling the academic requirements. She blamed her father. Every time she embarked on an essay she would once again relive the sense that her father thwarted her ambitions.

Before beginning one essay she had a dream, which she understood as fighting and cutting her way out of her mother's womb. When she woke up she had a sensation of there being blood on her hands and feet—a graphic illustration of the aggression she associated with creativity, and with her father, whom she believed had wanted her aborted. For Fay creativity in an academic context signified brutally abandoning a mother for a father who rejected her. But she had one memory from childhood in which the capacity to create was associated with a sense of affectionate partnership. Her mother was a professional dressmaker and taught Fay to sew.

Together they had made some impressive textiles. In adult life Fay continued to sew and felt that here was an acceptable form of creativity that allowed for a sense of a benign link with the people for whom she made the clothes. Nevertheless she spoke somewhat slightingly of her work, for she shared the cultural denigration of sewing, considering it a maternal craft rather than an art form.

After she had been with me for five years, she discovered that I wrote. She was envious and surprised that I could thus "risk attack". However, she also felt—in a way rightly—that in a sense there had been a partnership between us in the writing of my recent book. We had recreated the partnership that she had felt with her mother when they had sewed together.

Two years later, to her surprise, she was able to cope with a final dissertation. She said to me, "I feel I can give myself the time to do it and I'll re-work it if necessary." She was able to experience an internal creative partnership evidenced in that she was *giving herself* the time. Subsequently, she demonstrated both a sense of creative partnership with me and a necessary sense of separateness and independence from me. She came in and told me that she had decided to write a book, "Not the sort of book you would read—an erotic novel—a bodice-ripper." She was going to write the book with her best friend who now lived abroad. They would collaborate via fax.

The erotic novel is a form that in the last twenty years has become an available, accepted vehicle for women's creativity in a way that was unthinkable in Virginia Woolf's day. The angel instructed the woman writer above all to be pure. Nevertheless, Fay importantly experienced the decision to write an erotic novel as an act of defiance against me and my style of book—she could permit herself to move beyond the sphere of what she considered maternal feminine creativity. I was the creative partner whose presence rendered safe the "show of force" associated with creativity, yet she could risk separating from me and displeasing me. She could bring the angel into relationship with the devil—thanks in part to the availability today of the erotic novel as a medium for women.

The plan to collaborate with her friend was the materialization of an old dream of collaboration with a loved, though envied, older sister. The determining relations of creativity evoke not only the parental constellations that Britton describes but also sets in motion sibling dynamics. The sibling/colleague/peer relationship encompasses influence and inspiration as well as envy and competition. An angelic way of relating importantly allows for influence to be acknowledged and used—but jealousy and competitiveness are anathema to the angel.

Less obvious than relationships with an audience or colleagues in the face of a polished end-product are the series of relationships that shaped it, with the drafts, the sketches, the scraped-down oil paint, or with the unpicked stitches. These relationships can be characterized by elation, satisfaction, dread, disappointment, a sense of loss or plenitude, enrichment or abandonment. Key in these is the relationship between artist and tradition (Winnicott, 1971). Identification, separation, emulation, rejection, destruction, and conservation are all dynamics that can come into play with the relationship to tradition. (I am referring to both cultural and personal tradition.) Where the latter is concerned, each book, painting, pot or quilt is linked.

The American sculptor Louise Bourgeois expresses the evolution of her work as a dialogue amongst the pieces, saying of her sculptures, "They are placed in a social situation. They talk to each other" (Bourgeois, 1996). The relationships within an artist's oeuvre are not only between individual objects, as Louise Bourgeois describes, but also with the maker's past endeavours and future aspirations, as well as striking up an ever-changing relationship with the artist in the present. The relationship with a particular piece of work changes, often dramatically, over the course of production— the two-way relationship is obviously very different with a finished or unfinished work. Christopher Bollas's theory of the "evocative object" usefully illuminates the relationship between individual and art work. He writes:

> To my mind, the choice of form is a kind of psychic route, as each subject, possessing many different forms for the collecting of experience, renders himself in a different medium, so that playing with the forms means simultaneously being played by them. The choice of representational form is an important unconscious decision about the structuring of lived experience . . . (1992, p. 41)

The art object is the recipient of the maker's projections but also, in Bollas's words, "brings about an inner profile of psychic experience specific to its character" (p. 33). Hence a garden, a pot, a painting or a pudding carry meanings of their own that marry with and inform the maker's projections. A patient of mine described her feelings in relation to a finished book as follows: "I am feeling less precious about it. So what if it doesn't please everyone. It is my view. I've worked hard to have the right to speak it." Holding her book in her hand and recalling the history of her relationship with it, transformed her representation of herself in the world, cutting the angel down to size and imbuing her with a sense of strengthened identity, satisfaction, and internal goodness.

Other critical relationships exist with professional structures, places of work, materials, techniques, current artistic ideals, dominant styles, language, and genres. The relationship with the medium is of prime importance and can transform an artist's attitude towards her work, reducing anxiety. The artist Rachel Whiteread, who won the Turner Prize for her piece "House", considered that learning to cast constituted a turning point for her. She says, "It was just incredibly liberating—that you could make an impression in sand and pour molten metal into it and then you had an object. I liked the simplicity and the directness of it ... you're changing something that exists" (Barber, 1996). And, of course, *she* was herself changed by it—"liberated".

Inevitable tension

The fundamental aspect of the network of relationships determining creativity that conjure up the angel—for good or ill—is that it is beset by rival claims or impulses (Leader, 1990). Marion Milner's work demonstrates the extent to which creativity depends upon the ability to bear the ebb and flow between conscious and unconscious processes, and the capacity to sustain the conflict between individuation and involvement, emergence and embeddedness. She locates the tension between separation and union, internal and external reality, self and other at the heart of creativity (Milner, 1950).

I want nevertheless to avoid subscribing to the romantic notion of the suffering artist, which conceals the pleasure in finding a mind of one's own and anticipating the impact of its content on an imaginary audience. At the same time I do think that creative endeavour is unavoidably accompanied by more or less turbulent object relations. Profound feelings of ambivalence are inevitably present in the relationship between object and maker. Painful processes of merging, separation, overwhelming preoccupation, and sickening rejection are fundamental to different moments of all creative endeavours, provoking both exaltation and embarrassment. But where "the angel in the house" is concerned the crucial tension in creativity is between destruction and creation; between aggression and reparation. A patient of mine, an artist I shall call Ella, illustrates specific aspects of this tension.

I saw Ella for twice-weekly psychoanalytic psychotherapy over four years. She came to work in the UK in her mid-twenties, joining a group of artists who worked collectively. At first all went well. Being in the group broke down the sense of isolation she felt as a foreigner and she participated in several successful group shows. The experience of a shared focus and common endeavour mobilized a sense of internal good object for all the group members. But for Ella it did not last. She came to see me when her capacity to work became blocked. She felt unable to make any decisions regarding her work. She could not even decide to purchase materials she needed. She would go to DIY shops and stand paralysed even when she had decided beforehand what she needed to buy. Guilt meant that the desire needed to make decisions and the gratification of obtaining what she wanted were beyond her. For the purposes of this paper I shall omit the aetiology of the guilt and focus exclusively on its working in the relationships that determine creativity.

She used her sessions at first as a confessional. She was drawn to group work because being part of a group, supporting and nurturing the other members, exonerated her guilt in relation to self-promotion and exhibition. The group contained her. But after a while, far from permitting competitiveness and ambition, the group increased her guilt. Although her unhappiness was expressed initially as envy of the others, it soon became clear that the real issue was that she secretly felt superior to them. Hence, in order to avoid envy and implement a separation, she handicapped and paralysed herself with indecisiveness. I was the impersonal diary to which she confessed her secret strengths and aggressions and desires. Had I initially been more than a diary I suspect she would have been unable to own aggression, ambition, and desire.

The first major change in the relationships that constituted her creative work was with the material she used. She permitted herself to work with material that simply gave her pleasure, and similarly pleased others. Her first solo show was well received, ratifying her self-esteem. The relationships with the art work and the audience enabled her to experience herself even if fleetingly as fundamentally benign.

So far she had denied any relationship with myself. However, her recent success coupled with her awareness that our work had played a part in her developing capacity to express desire and employ aggression, allowed her to "risk" addressing her feelings for me. She said, "I can only envisage myself as strong, creative, and able to work when I am with you. But I also feel that I have to be with you for you to feel strong and creative." In order to maintain her sense of adulthood and agency and separateness she had to "mother" me whom she needed to "mother" her. Her comment illustrates the fine balance that she had to maintain in the relationships that determined her creativity. She needed both to be supported and to support. If she felt she was failing to support the other, her sense of agency evaporated and she feared merging. Whereas, if she felt she was failing to receive encouragement and belief, she experienced her work as disallowed. Many times she would exclaim that she could pursue her art if only she could be entirely alone, and yet the prospect of isolation was terrifying.

If she experienced our relationship as in any way unbalanced, she began to fear my destructive envy of her work. She would describe the work in detail while constantly telling me that she knew it bored me. Initially, I assumed she was seeking reassurance. Consciously she did want me to know and understand her work, but it became clear that she could only tell me about it if she thought it bored me, otherwise she feared that I would become destructive, envious, and competitive. In the countertransference I was indeed aware of the impulse to exhibit my knowledge of art competitively—and I feared the destructive consequences.

Ella, fearing her destructiveness and her aggression, needed a justified target. She would project her aggression sometimes into a critic and sometimes into a curator. She routinely became angry with the people who organized her shows. The rage would subside and reconciliation would take place as work for the show reached completion. The work itself allowed aggression for it was motivated by, and conveyed, a sociopolitical critique, embedded in beauty and humour.

Her creative block did return when she started a new relationship. Her dreams delineated her lover as small and weak while she was wild and aggressive. She repeatedly told me that she experienced absorption in work as dangerous disloyalty and even infidelity. Unless she was fully attentive to her lover he would leave her.

She stopped working at her art and threw herself into highly creative cooking, which she enjoyed, although with me she talked constantly about her inability to work. She abandoned her large-scale installations and covertly began to do charcoal drawings that did not "count". She never mentioned the drawing to me. In an important respect she was not deliberately hiding the work from me. Consciously she considered she was not working because of the medium she was employing. According to the hierarchy of materials, which, as a professional, she accepted, they truly did not count as art. In some ways the charcoal drawings could be likened to a sketchbook or to a diary—that art form that is considered not art but outpourings; the secrecy rendering the "show of force" safe. It was only when a gallery offered her an exhibition of the drawings that they became "art" and she considered them worthy of mention.

Ella required a context sufficiently reliable and resilient to contain her fears in relation to aggression both as a "show of force" (Greenacre, 1957, p. 62), and in terms of Winnicott's concept of destruction. His theories—in particular his theory of use of an object—are important for an appreciation of the relationship between creativity and femininity in that they deepen our understanding of the role of destruction—so problematic for the angel—in creativity. He believed that the roots of creativity could be traced to an earlier stage of development than that posited by Klein's view of creativity as an act of reparation (Winnicott, 1951), but as both he and Klein emphasized from their significantly different perspectives, creation and destruction sit side by side. It is their constant coexistence that I think produces the persecutory fantasies that accompany creative endeavour. Winnicott considered that destruction was the crucial element in the tension between external and internal reality, writing of "the destructive drive that creates the quality of externality" (1971, p. 110). He was concerned with creative living, while Adrian

Stokes applied the destruction/creation dichotomy directly to the experience of painting. He expresses the role of aggression as follows: "A painter to be so, must be capable of perpetrating defacement in order to add, create, transform, restore, the attack is defacement nonetheless" (Stokes, 1965, cited in Leader, 1990, p. 111).

Most theories of creativity suggest that aggression is needed for the dynamics it sets in train. In my view, aggression is needed not to provide the motivation for reparation, sublimation or reaction formation but quite simply because the processes of creative work *demand it.* Psychological research into the processes of creativity indicate that the necessary capacities for creative work include divergent thinking, transformative abilities, access to affect-laden thought, openness to affect states, passionate involvement, and independence of judgement (Walker Russ, 1993). All require the ability to mobilize and tolerate a degree of aggression as assertion necessary to the process of creativity, providing the ability to pick up the tools or open the computer.

Bollas writes that, "Instinctual urges and libido are an important part of the erotics of self, but we would now have to see the instincts as part of the drive to create" (1995, p. 43). By suggesting a drive to create he offers a way of looking at creativity that allows aggression to have a direct role in art practice rather than being the force that art practice sublimates or exonerates, at the same time he foregrounds the role of relationship between internal objects in creativity, writing of an "endopsychic partnership" and concluding that "Creativity in unconscious work responds to any audience delegated by the self" (p. 155).

Returning to Woolf's angel with the centrality of aggression for creativity in mind, it is clear that the mode of relating advocated and represented by the angel functions as a defence against—almost a taboo—against aggression. Woolf is suggesting that the fundamental issue for women concerning creativity is the taboo on aggression associated with the construction of femininity. Amongst psycho-analytic writers on aggression and creativity the consensus seems to be that feminine identification expressed as receptivity, concern, mirroring, giving, and avoidance of conflict drastically inhibits creative expression. The father has been cited as the daughter's saviour, intervening between the child and her identification with the maternal ideal. Identification, internalization, and incorporation of the father have been considered as the key to a girl's capacity to move beyond a merged relationship with her mother, abandoning a unitary identification with maternal femininity. Nevertheless, at the same time, fear of injuring the father, fear of joining the mother in castration of the father, have been offered as a key explanation for creative inhibition in women (Riviere, 1929).

If we look at the history of women artists it is certainly true that since the Renaissance the majority were the daughters of fathers who have been artists. Fathers were vitally important, not only from the perspective of internal reality, but also in terms of external reality; they were often the only source of training available to women excluded from institutional teaching. Today, however, things have radically changed. Like Rachel Whiteread, more women artists are the daughters of mothers who were artists (Apostolos-Cappadona & Ebersole, 1995).

Bringing theory up to date, Andrew Samuels suggests that parents of either sex are able to mediate aggression as part of a relationship, rather than something to be eliminated. He has coined the term "The good-enough father of whatever sex" (1995). Similarly, Jessica Benjamin describes how women in the analytic situation look for women analysts "who embody the subject of desire with whom to identify, and with whom oedipal competition and phallic aggression can be integrated" (1996, p. 61).

However, as Woolf's essay indicates, a facilitating other is not necessarily all that is needed to break creative block. Of fundamental importance, as I have said, is women's relationship to materials and genres. It was in the context of working as a critic that Woolf suffered the inhibition of the angel—the admonition to please and placate. Woolf's novel writing, backed up by a female tradition in fiction, was left relatively undisturbed. Moreover, literary criticism constellates competition, attack and envy as well as the desire to please and placate. It requires taking a stand. Aggression is foregrounded in reviewing while in fiction it is safely mitigated by the form of the novel. Woolf's answer to the angel was to mobilize forbidden aggression and to kill her:

> I turned upon her and caught her by the throat, I did my best to kill her. My excuse, if I were to be had up in a court of law, would be that I acted in self-defence. Had I not killed her she would have killed me, She would have plucked the heart out of my writing. (1931, p. 4)

Killing the angel is a risky solution. A patient of mine, discussing the stuck state of her writing said, "I feel that I am fighting myself." The aggression that could have fed her writing, that often enabled her to be constructively critical of her work, had turned against it. In other words, killing the angel can be tantamount to depression and self-destruction. And to kill off the angel is also to deny the very real contribution the angelic attitude can make to the relations that determine creativity. For example, without the beneficial influence of the angel, reviewing can degenerate into an exercise in grandiose aggression. The angel can infuse a necessary degree of fairness, thoroughness, and responsibility into the process.

Passion and integration

Woolf conceived of the angel in 1931 and expressed the profound hope that changes in the conditions of creativity for women would shortly banish her. I have suggested that she failed to grasp the necessary and positive attributes of the angel. I want now briefly to summarize the way changes in psychoanalytic theorizing of creativity, contrary to Woolf's expectations, have progressively provided more space for the angel.

As the position of women artists has changed, with the ever increasing presence of women in professional art practice, so psychoanalytic theorizing of art practice has begun to give a place to the attributes of femininity represented by the angel. It is a salutary reminder of the historical specificity and the mutability of both psychoanalytic theory and the attributes of gender.

Freud's theory of sublimation, of course, foregrounds aggression and eroticism. He commented:

> Art brings about a reconciliation between two principles (pleasure and reality) in a peculiar way. An artist is originally a man who turns away from reality because he cannot come to terms with the renunciation of instinctual satisfaction which it at first demands, and who allows his erotic and ambitious wishes full play in the life of phantasy. (1911, p. 224)

Joyce McDougall has elaborated the theory of sublimation, suggesting that the shame and anxiety that so often accompany creativity result from the "libidinal foundation" of all creative expression (McDougall, 1995, p. 59). My view has some similarity to McDougall's. She argues that while profound libidinal and narcissistic drives are "the primal source of the overwhelming urge to create" anger, rage, and even violence are of "equally vital importance to creative expression" (p. 68). However, McDougall writes that the creative worker "seeks to produce pleasure and excitement and interest, thus invading and affecting his partner—the public." She likens the artist to the "sexual innovator" inasmuch as both "wish to impose upon the other his invention, hoping to inspire the public with his personal vision and to pervade it with his illusion of reality" (p. 54).

An understanding of creativity based on the concept of sublimation produces a phallic representation of creativity that renders the angel not only redundant but a serious liability. Theories of sublimation fundamentally exclude femininity from art practice. Art and women in the guise of "the angel in the house" (the domestic feminine ideal that evolved during the nineteenth century) are simultaneously positioned as civilizing forces. Both "shift libidinal impulses into another key" (Waddell, unpublished). In other words, if we look at art as a means of "coping with" aggression, then being the angel is for women an alternative to making art. It suggests that women are and always have been condemned to being the model, never the artist, which is clearly not the case. If, however, we think of aggression as an aspect of art-making it becomes possible to see that women's relationship to creativity can be transformed if they can own and employ aggressivity—if the place of aggression changes in the relationships that construct creativity.

"Stubborn" is how Rachel Whiteread characterizes her mode of relating, while a patient of mine, reflecting on her own work, evocatively defined two different modes of aggression. She said, "There is aggression that burns a hole and aggression that allows for reciprocity." She is distinguishing between aggression as annihilation and aggression in the sense of Winnicott's "destruction".

Turning to ego-psychology, we find a representation of creativity that does offer a possibly productive place to the angel. With the rise of ego-psychology, specifically with the work of Ernst Kris, the elaboration of artistic form was considered a relatively autonomous function of the ego, controlling the primary process. Kris's intention was to "develop the conception of art as a process of communication" (quoted in Spitz, 1985, p. 16). His ideas highlight the role of audience both internal and external. Moreover, his emphasis on the continual interplay between creation and criticism, regression and control, suggests that the angel can signify either the productive role of the observing ego or the stultifying impact of the punitive superego.

Melanie Klein's theory of creativity as reparation of the object gives, of course, full scope to angelic proclivities. In her paper "Infantile anxiety situations reflected in a work of art and the creative impulse", Klein writes, "It is obvious that the desire to make reparation, to make good the injury psychologically done to the mother and also to restore herself was at the bottom of the compelling urge to paint" (1929, p. 235). In other words art practice is fuelled both by reparative and destructive impulses; both by angelic and devilish motivations. Meltzer suggests that they alternate: "in the creative process itself, phases of attack and phases of reparation exist in some sort of rhythmical relationship" (Meltzer & Harris Williams, 1988, p. 299).

To my mind, if either dominate, creative block ensues. This suggests that the resolution to creative block is balance; with creation balancing destruction, the angel balancing the devil. Yet the concept of balance is both dull and insecure. Meltzer's concept of "passion" usefully offers an alternative to balance where breaking creative block is concerned. He writes that, "The most adequate description of 'passion' would seem to be that our emotions are engaged in such a way that love, hate and the yearning for understanding are all set in motion . . . It is the consortium that is essential" (Meltzer & Harris Williams, 1988, p. 143). Passion, he suggests, is not a matter of intensity, but rather of integration of the three impulses when faced with the impact of objects, and of ourselves. The author Eavan Boland, describing her writing, evokes the ebb and flow of angel and devil, creation and destruction:

> I had a soft and angry way of writing a poem, I would take a copy book and a biro, set it down on a table and make a jug of milky coffee. I would sit there, as if beside someone with a fever, waiting for the lines, the figures, the forms to take shape. I wrote it down and crossed it out; I read it out loud and wrote it again, I made it better. I made it worse. (1996, p. 89)

Boland makes herself a jug of milky coffee. Food, drink, cigarettes, even writing in bed, are often employed to counteract the persecutory anxiety induced by creativity. Consideration of the unconscious meaning of the experience of creativity indicates that its roots lie in early mothering. Both Bion (1962) and Winnicott (1951; 1964) from their different perspectives have described how the infant's creative gesture is made possible by the facilitating environment, the loving, reliable, resilient, appropriately reticent mother, able to mediate the infant's omnipotence in the face of the fearful juxtaposition of creation and destruction. My concern is how the network of relationships that determine adult creativity can permit and provoke the necessary passion, and provide the safety needed for creative work.

The following vignette is drawn from a patient in three-times-weekly psychoanalytic psychotherapy, using the couch, over five years. Martha, as I shall call her, was from a family that maintained highly permeable boundaries. She was contracted to write a novel. Her publisher wanted to see the first chapter in the autumn and the second summer break of our work together was looming. Martha was in despair. She felt I was abandoning her in her hour of greatest need and to compound matters, her boyfriend was due to leave the country on the same day as we were to end for the break. She felt herself to be injured and incapacitated and wept throughout our last session.

At the first session after the break she told me that her chapter was complete and she had sent it off to her editor. She said, "I woke up the day after we finished feeling absolutely furious with you and Ben for leaving me. I stormed round the house shouting at you both and suddenly found myself at the computer and able to write." My defection had both mobilized the devil and created safe boundaries, which at a deep level reassured the angel.

As so often when creative block lifts, it is experienced as a sudden, inexplicable, inspired liberation. But, of course, behind the breaking of Martha's block lay months of living with her novel, much work in psychotherapy, and the form of the book itself. She felt quite uneasy writing journal articles. She experienced papers as dangerously without boundaries while a book was her own, safe, contained, couple relationship—and for the present, secret project—although work on her book was all too easily experienced as an attack on those she loved whom she felt she was deserting and neglecting. When her sister became ill and demanded constant nursing she expressed relief at the cast-iron excuse it provided to abandon her writing: "It's so lonely being able to get on with your own thing."

In fact she rarely felt "lonely" at the computer. She had a powerful sense of writing as communion with a loving, encouraging other. Although, inevitably, she was at times overtaken by states of mind in which her sense of creativity as the nexus of loving relationship disintegrated. Instead, writing became fraught with fear of disappointing the expectations of a loving, idealized other. And rather than writing signifying presence and plenitude, it suggested absence and void. This dynamic was precipitated when she experienced her capacity to hate as unmitigated by her capacity to love. Over a long period, a particular set of external circumstances inflated her experience of hating and engendered self-hatred. She began to denigrate her manuscript. She would write all morning, re-read it during the afternoon and by the evening pronounce it worthless.

Although we both understood what had precipitated this state of affairs, my interpretations and comments were experienced as empty maternal reassurance and comfort. Nothing changed. In despair she gave the manuscript to a loved and admired male colleague to read. Witnessing his enthusiasm for the work and receiving his encouragement erased the hatred and self-hatred that had infused her relationship with the novel. She could once more appreciate the value of what she had done.

Disparate muses

Traditionally, the fear, guilt and anxiety associated with aggressive creativity has been mediated by the concept of the Muse who inspires, protects, reassures, and, in a way, takes responsibility for the ambivalence generated by creative work. In the context of psychoanalysis, we could say that the Muse is equivalent to the sense of internal good object. Margot Waddell, discussing the dynamics that contribute to the establishment of the internal good object, defines introjective identification as a process through which the capacity develops (over time) "to take in and then draw on supportive and loving experience which safeguard, protect and inspire." She emphasizes that central to the process is the "experience of being loved and loving, and the deepening expectation of similar feelings to and from others" (Waddell, unpublished). For creativity to flourish, the experience of love is needed to balance hate, mitigating both persecutory anxiety (I'll be attacked for this) and depressive anxiety (this is too attacking). To my mind, the capacity to infuse a sense of muse into the network of relations that constitute creativity is a prerequisite of art practice. My concern is with the conscious and unconscious strategies employed by the adult artist to attain the experience of muse.

Since the Renaissance the representation of this internal good object has transmuted from goddess and allegorical figure to love object—flesh and blood Woman, the object of the male artist's desire. This has set up specific tensions for women artists. Self-portraits by women artists reveal ways in which they struggled with the constraints of being both the inspiring woman and the inspired artist. They tried to resolve the contradiction, either by downplaying or by "angelically" magnifying their femininity in the manner of the French nineteenth-century artist Elizabeth Vigee-Lebrun.

The late nineteenth-century Russian artist Marie Bashkirtseff declared in 1881, "I have nothing of the woman about me but the envelope" (1985, p. 290). She nevertheless highlighted the femininity of the "envelope" by dressing entirely in white to emphasise purity and inspiration, and concealing the intense ambition and application she confessed to her diary. But presenting herself as Muse meant she was unable to internalize a sense of muse: "All that I say does not touch my inner self. I have none. I live only externally" (p. 17). Unable to establish an internal experience of muse, Bashkirtseff sought one male mentor after another. Muses inspire while mentors instruct. Muses are accomplices, mentors are models who all too easily become the repository of the punitive superego. An external mentor could do nothing to heal Bashkirtseff's narcissism. The diary in which she owned her rage and revealed her narcissism and splitting has earned her immortality, but her painting is largely unknown. The conflation of woman and Muse has indeed meant that women's person and presence during their lifetime were accorded as much importance as their products to the extent that on their death, more often than not, their work dropped from sight (Parker & Pollock, 1981).

Virginia Woolf suggests that feminine identifications do, all too easily, condemn women to being always the Muse and never the maker. She demonstrates that the step from muse to maker can profoundly threaten a woman's sense of internal good object. For, as discussed above, it is a step that demands agency and aggression that can feel profoundly at odds with the service and sacrifice associated with the maternal feminine ideal and the female Muse. But in disparate ways women artists, of course, do manage to internalize and infuse the presence of muse into the relationships that constitute creativity—a sense of internal good object to protect both self and Other from the fears of the creative process.

One route is the establishment and maintenance of either heterosexual or homosexual creative partnerships (Chadwick & de Courtivron, 1993). As Zerbe has pointed out, a partner, preferably one engaged in creative activities, "helps creative individuals overcome despair, frustration, anxiety and loneliness." She discusses the role of "secret sharer" in the lives of women artists: a self-object that provides self-enhancing, or life-sustaining supplies, concluding that, "Love can be a reaffirming thread that provides possible transcendence over hostility and alienation" (1992, p. 277).

Zerbe is describing a relationship that enhances—perhaps establishes—the sense of internal good object. In adulthood, being in love—and the experience of erotic transference—for men and women alike can have a powerfully beneficial impact on creativity. The relationships determining the work become, so to speak, imbued with an optimistic benevolence. The sense of the self as hating and hated is mitigated, making the mobilization of aggression less fearful, while the necessary, often frightening, isolated way of working demanded by different creative practices, rather than introducing the spectre of emptiness, is permeated with a containing presence.

The beneficial effect of a "facilitating relationship" can continue long after the contact has ended. Developmentally, absence is, of course, the initial prerequisite for symbolization. Where the adult artist is concerned, absence of a desired other can provoke the need to reinstate their presence through a creative project. The art work is experienced as if made expressly for the imagined pleasure of the absent other—or quite simply to please or propitiate the dead.

However, feminine identifications, carrying the imperative of service and selflessness, mean that being in love also ushers in *fear of loss*. The aggression—the "show of force" demanded by creative endeavour—becomes muted. Far from mobilizing the sense of internal good object, the resulting conflict threatens its existence. Creative work is experienced as a dangerous act of separation from the loved one, guaranteed to arouse envy and rejection.

Not only love but also hate in the context of a sense of justified aggression can produce the passion needed to mobilize angel and devil. The artist Bridget Riley ascribes the development of Op Art to an experience of separation and rejection. The man with whom she was having a relationship decided to end the affair. Looking back Riley says:

> I was angry and hurt. I thought: "I'm not going to discuss anything with you, I can't communicate verbally with you, so what's the point in trying? But I'll paint you a message so loud and clear you'll know exactly how I feel." It was then that I started my black and whites. (quoted in Bracewell, 1997, p. 18)

The energetic aggression Riley believes fuelled the emergence of her Op Art can, of course, be projected outside the relationship with the art object. The creative act is then experienced as if accomplished at the behest of an aggressive other—an importunate editor imposing an inflexible deadline or a curator with a tight timetable. Relations with what could be termed a "negative muse" can be productive. Above I described a patient of mine, Ella, who needed to encounter a belligerent other in order to employ her own aggression and to feel her work was wanted. But the "negative muse" can all too easily arouse incapacitating anxiety.

The passion, purpose, and inspiration needed to mobilize simultaneously angel and devil can, of course, spring from sources other than human relationships in the network of relations that determine creativity. Artistic medium, art theory, an art movement, or political movement can all provide permission, passion, and containment. Take, for example, women's relationship with the form and language of twentieth-century art. The presence of women has, in part, been facilitated by the dominance of particular forms and languages which, in turn, their presence promotes. For instance, the expansion of media and technique has meant that women can employ—to subversive intent—textile art with which they tradition-ally have had a relationship. In Tracey Emin's work entitled

"Everyone I ever slept with from 1963 to 1995", the viewer crawls into a tent lined with bits of material embroidered with a hundred names including Emin's grandmother and teddy bear. The piece provides a witty, aggressive critique of embroidery's historical association with domesticity, passivity, love, reticence, and obedience.

With postmodernism, for the first time in the history of the avant garde, there exists a significant body of important, innovative work by women, both in the visual arts and literature. Aspects of avant-garde practice both address the angel's fears in relation to her concern with the impact of her work, and focus her strivings. For example, there is a tendency to treat the work of art less as an object and more as a process that creates the subject. Writing on the recent international exhibition of women's art at London's Whitechapel Gallery, Griselda Pollock observes that the, "Art is not static and fetishized but above all dynamic: constitutive, rather than consti-tuted" (quoted in de Zegher, 1996, p. 23). In other words, feminist theory has highlighted creativity as a social practice, emphasizing the reparatory aspect of art, hence ameliorating angelic guilt.

Forms of reparation

Thinking about the angel in conjunction with the history of women in art elucidates the relationship between reparation of the object and self-reparation. Janine Chasseguet-Smirgel, like Adrian Stokes before her, has elaborated a distinction between the two forms of reparation. She feels that reparation of the object fails fully to explain why creation so often brings about guilt feelings. She suggests there are two radically opposed categories of creativity that often coexist within the separate creative activities of an individual. Differentiating the categories, she designates reparation of the self as "sublimation" and reparation of the object as "reaction formation". Where the former is concerned she suggests that profound guilt is evoked because to "build oneself requires the destruction of the object in the unconscious . . . Just as the child nourishes himself on his mother, the creator is vampire to his object." Hence, in her view, there are two sorts of creativity "one which enriches and fills up the ego (and which can generate guilt) and the other, which indeed repairs the object" (1984, p. 401).

Kavaler-Adler, however, argues that if creativity is motivated by the urge to repair the internal parental object that has been damaged by one's own aggression, then this is indirectly an attempt to repair the self because self-reparation depends on having a whole and healthy internal object within the internal world (Kavaler-Adler, 1993).

I would think that guilt is inevitably present in the reparation of the object because love and hate are never fully integrated, and the desire to destroy sits side by side with the desire to create. Chasseguet-Smirgel ends her paper exploring self-reparation with the observation that "Further research on factors which inhibit creativity in women might elaborate the notions set forth here" (1984, p. 402). I agree with Chasseguet-Smirgel that the construction of femininity has particular implications for a theory of creativity based on the desire for self-reparation.

For women, self-reparation has been lived as self-improvement for the sake of the other—the angel's desire to please. Hence self-reparation through enhanced self-esteem has been achieved under the guise of reparation of the object. For example, historically women's creativity has flourished in the applied arts. Embroidery is a good example of an art form that covertly permits self-reparation while overtly serving home and family (Parker, 1984). It was termed "work" performed for love not money and its practice importantly signalled the class position of the family.

Women today still contend with the anxieties attendant on self-reparation; similar dynamics underlie different strategies. While embroiderers of the past asserted a defensive, loving amateurism, artists today assert a defensive, uncompromising, almost impersonal professionalism in their relations with audience, art world, and art work. Rachel Whiteread declares, "My job is making the work. I don't see myself as having to stand there and justify it or pander to people" (quoted in Barber, 1996, p. 7).

The history of women suggests that both reparation of the object and reparation of the self are intertwined and, potentially equally, enhance self-esteem and contribute to ego strength.

Creative block, of course, is not determined by gender. But in attempting to gain an understanding of the experience of creativity for individual women, as I mentioned above, it is helpful to be aware of the specificity of women's relationship to art history and how this can impact on their sense of internal good object. The writing of art history, from the mid-nineteenth century onwards, corralled women's work into a separate sphere and characterized it as essentially, inevitably, feminine, while at the same time representations of the artist emphasized the necessity of androgyny (Parker & Pollock, 1981). The woman artist, however, was not accorded androgyny. Femininity in a male artist was viewed as synonymous with sensitivity. Femininity in a woman was evidence of inevitable "weakness" while the presence of supposedly masculine traits was deemed unnatural. Women artists nevertheless consistently found ways of negotiating the psychological and institutional constraints set upon their practice. They were, however, "hidden from history" to the extent that by the 1960s the belief that women were innately incapacitated and incapable of producing great art still held sway. Within psychoanalysis, Phyllis Greenacre could claim that women inevitably and inherently "fear the bisexual elements that they would need to tolerate as creative individuals" (quoted in Kavaler-Adler, 1993, p. 59).

Such generalizations have been challenged within both art history and psychoanalysis by feminist theorists who have deconstructed homogeneous representations of femininity. As Jessica Benjamin puts it, " 'Woman' is not a unitary identity . . ." (1996, p. 11). She has foregrounded the multiplicity and ambiguity of gender identifications. While feminist art historians, critics, curators, and teachers, revealing the heterogeneous work of women artists of the past, argue for the many points of differences between and among women artists.

The work of such contemporary feminist theorists opposing the homogenization of women's work contrasts sharply with Virginia Woolf's endeavour, which was to highlight the specificity of women's experience. Her major feminist essays, "A room of one's own", "Three guineas" and "Professions for women" revealed, in order to remove, the impediments shared by creative women. In my view both perspectives are necessary if feminism is to provide the passion and assurance needed to break creative block. Historically, each wave of feminism has indeed ushered in an expansion of women's creativity. Woolf's own work is a case in point. For while the angel instructed women "never to let anybody guess you have a mind of your own", feminism insists on the specific interest of women's minds; providing the courage to be displeasing and encouraging the self-assertion that the angelic attitude fears and refuses. In other words, feminism, for many women, has provided the capacity to integrate the angel and the devil; to bring them into creative partnership, to use, not lose, the productive aspects of femininity while abandoning subservience and excessive compliance. Women artists, in their struggle to integrate competition, ambition and aggression with a consciousness of the conditions of reception, have, to my mind, developed a rich range of psychological strategies and strategic practices in working with the relationships that can impede or facilitate their work.

Yet the unconscious is notoriously refractory. As Virginia Woolf warned, the angel is always "creeping back even when we believe we have dispatched her." I have been arguing, however, that the presence of the angel is not an impediment if she is accompanied by the devil. The analytic relationship potentially plays a crucial role in enabling them to come into communion. Although when working with creative block, the meaning of all the relationships in the network I have described, besides the analytic relationship, need to be carefully considered. The analyst or therapist is not the Muse, merely one of the key relationships that enables the establishment of the Muse—the internal good object—to take place.

I was made powerfully aware of this in my work with a patient for whom the aggression so needed for creativity, and so feared, in passive form stymied the work. Carol, as I shall call her, dropped out of one course after another because she could not complete assignments. Extremely able, she aroused high expectations in her teachers. The expectations were, of course, in part projected expectations she had of herself. A painful conflict was set up between her experience of expectation as coercion she was compelled to disappoint, and her high expectations of herself promoting the desire to succeed and fear of failure. Invariably she fell ill and was unable to complete the course. Karen Horney has described the dynamic of this creative block in her paper "Neurotic disturbances in work". The unconscious opposition to the sense of coercion, Horney suggests, finally renders the individual "listless and inert" (Horney, 1950, p. 325). All too easily I found myself nurturing "encouraging" expectations of Carol, which she was compelled to disappoint. The environment of the therapy was experienced as impossible expectation and interpretation was felt to be coercion.

Beneath the dynamics prompted by expectation, the dread of loss, and sense of loss lay at the heart of Carol's creative block. The process of creation constantly juggles loss, separation and destruction (Segal, 1986). Even while in the unconscious it may signify restoration and at a conscious level the creation of something new, art-making sets in train a sequence of losses. The initial excitement of conception is lost in the translation to concrete form. Completion of a picture, the handing in of a manuscript, the final polishing of a piece of jewellery, similarly signify a loss. Even payment can fail to provide recompense or reassurance, and can be experienced as loss. Virginia Woolf describes how she immediately spent her first earnings on something unnecessary that she could love: "I have to admit that instead of spending that sum upon bread and butter, rent, shoes and stockings, or butchers bills, I went out and bought a cat—a beautiful cat, a Persian cat . . ." The cat constituted an object intended to compensate for the loss of an object intended to combat object loss.

Loss of control at the moment of parting with a piece of work is perhaps the most fearful experience of loss engendered by creativity. Once sold, published or exhibited the meaning of the work becomes constituted by the other. Woolf's angel wanted to control the essentially uncontrollable—the reception of the review. Nevertheless, as I emphasized at the outset of this paper, a consciousness of reception is an inevitable and important aspect of creativity.

Virginia Woolf, ending her address to her audience of professional women, declared:

> You have won rooms of your own in the house hitherto exclusively owned by men . . . the room is your own but it is still bare. It has to be furnished; it has to be decorated; it has to be shared. How are you going to furnish it, how are you going to decorate it? With whom are you going to share it, and upon what *terms*?

The very concept of "terms" is alien to the compliant angel in the house, while for the romantic representation of the artist the concept of "share" is alien. By highlighting the way creative work involves an engagement with a spectrum of internal and external object relations and looking at the terms of those relations I have been attempting to address Woolf's questions.

Virginia Woolf concluded, "Outwardly, what is simpler than to write books? Outwardly, what obstacles are there for a woman rather than for a man? Inwardly, I think, the case is very different; she has still many ghosts to fight . . ." In my view it can be precisely the fighting of ghosts—the wrestling with the angel and the getting acquainted with the devil—the struggle with the balance of creation and destruction, love and hate, that adds depth to artists' work and breadth in the search for solutions in form.

Note

1. A nineteenth-century poem on married love by Coventry Patmore.

References

Apostolos-Cappadona, D., & Ebersole, L. (Eds.) (1995). *Women, Creativity and the Arts: Critical and Autobiographical Perspectives*. New York: Continuum.

Barber, L. (1996). In a private world of interiors. *Observer Review* [London], 1 September:7.

Bashkirtseff, M. (1985). *The Journal of Marie Bashkirtseff* [1890]. M. Blind, translator. London: Virago.

Benjamin, J. (1996). *Like Subjects, Love Objects: Essays on Recognition and Sexual Difference*. New Haven, CT: Yale University Press.

Bion, W.R. (1962). *Learning from Experience*. London: Heinemann.

Boland, E. (1996). *The Making of a Poem: A Norton Anthology of Poetic Forms*. New York, NY: WW Norton.

Bollas, C. (1992). *Being a Character: Psychoanalysis and Self Experience*. London: Routledge.

Bollas, C. (1995). *Cracking Up: The Work of Unconscious Experience*. London: Routledge.

Bourgeois, L. (1996). Inside the visible: an elliptical traverse of twentieth century art (accompanying video).

Bracewell, M. (1997). A plea for painting. *Guardian Weekend*, 15 March: 14–21.

Britton, R. (1994). Publication anxiety: conflict between communication and affiliation. *International Journal of Psychoanalysis*, 75: 1213–23.

Chadwick, W., & de Courtivron, I. (Eds.) (1993). *Significant Others: Creativity and Intimate Partnership*. London: Thames & Hudson.

Chasseguet-Smirgel, J. (1984). Thoughts on the concept of reparation and the hierarchy of creative acts. *Int Rev Psychoanal 11*: 399–406.
de Zegher, M.C. (Ed.) (1996). *Inside the Visible*. London: Whitechapel Gallery.
Freud, S. (1911). Formulations on the two principles of mental functioning. *Standard Edition 12* (pp. 218–26).
Greenacre, P. (1957). The childhood of the artist. *Psychoanal Study Child 12*: 47–71.
Horney, K. (1950). Neurotic disturbances in work. In: *Neurosis and Human Growth: The Struggle toward Self-realization* (pp. 309–32). New York, NY: WW Norton.
Kavaler-Adler, S. (1993). *The Compulsion to Create: A Psychoanalytic Study of Women Artists*. London: Routledge.
Klein, M. (1929). Infantile anxiety situations reflected in a work on art and in the creative impulse. In: *Contributions to Psychoanalysis, 1921–1945* (pp. 210–8). London: Hogarth, 1975.
Leader, Z. (1990). *Writer's Block*. Baltimore, MD: Johns Hopkins University Press.
McDougall, J. (1995). *The Many Faces of Eros: Psychoanalytic Exploration of Human Sexuality*. London: Free Association Books.
Meltzer, D., & Harris Williams, M. (1988). *The Apprehension of Beauty: The Role of Aesthetic Conflict in Development, Art and Violence*. Strath Tay: Clunie.
Milner, M. (1950). *On Not Being Able to Paint*. London: Heinemann, 1971.
Oremland, J.D. (1997). *The Origins and Psychodynamics of Creativity: A Psychoanalytic Perspective*. Madison, CT: International University Press.
Parker, R. (1984). *The Subversive Stitch: Embroidery and the Making of the Feminine*. London: Women's Press.
Parker, R., & Pollock, G. (1981). *Old Mistresses: Women, Art and Ideology*. London: Pandora.
Riviere, J. (1929). Womanliness as a masquerade. In: A. Hughes (Ed.), *The Inner World and Joan Riviere: Collected Papers, 1920–1958* (pp. 90–101). London: Karnac, 1991.
Samuels, A. (1995). The good-enough father of whatever sex. *Feminism Psychol 5*: 511–30.
Segal, H. (1986). *The Work of Hanna Segal: A Kleinian Approach to Clinical Practice*. London: Free Association Books.
Spitz, E.H. (1985). *Art and Psyche: A Study in Psychoanalysis and Aesthetics*. New Haven, CT: Yale University Press.

Waddell, M. (unpublished).

Walker Russ, S. (1993). *Affect and Creativity: The Role of Affect and Play in the Creative Process*. Mahwah, NJ: Lawrence Erlbaum.

Winnicott, D.W. (1951). Critical notice of "On not being able to paint". In: C. Winnicott, R. Sheperd, & M. Davis (Eds.), *Psychoanalytic Explorations* (pp. 390–2). London: Karnac, 1989.

Winnicott, D.W. (1964). Memories, dreams and reflections [Review]. In: C. Winnicott, R. Sheperd, & M. Davis (Eds.), *Psychoanalytic Explorations* (pp. 482–92). London: Karnac, 1989.

Winnicott, D.W. (1971). *Playing and Reality*. London: Tavistock.

Woolf, V. (1931). *Killing the Angel in the House: Seven Essays*. London: Penguin, 1995.

Zerbe, K.J. (1992). The phoenix rises from Eros, not ashes: creative collaboration in the lives of five impressionist and post-impressionist women artists. *J. Am. Acad. Psychoanal., 20*: 295–315.